Directing for Stage and Screen

D1562641

Directing for Stage and Screen

Marian F. Monta and Jack R. Stanley

First published in 2008 by
PALGRAVE MACMILLAN™
175 Fifth Avenue, New York, N.Y. 10010 and
Houndmills, Basingstoke, Hampshire, England RG21 6XS.
Companies and representatives throughout the world.

PALGRAVE MACMILLAN is the global academic imprint of the Palgrave Macmillan division of St. Martin's Press, LLC and of Palgrave Macmillan Ltd. Macmillan® is a registered trademark in the United States, United Kingdom and other countries. Palgrave is a registered trademark in the European Union and other countries.

ISBN-13: 978-0-230-60136-9 hardcover
ISBN-10: 0-230-60136-7 hardcover
ISBN-13: 978-0-230-60137-6 paperback
ISBN-10: 0-230-60137-5 paperback

Library of Congress Cataloging-in-Publication Data

Monta, Marian Frances.
  Directing for stage and screen / by Marian F. Monta and Jack R. Stanley.
    p. cm.
  Includes bibliographical references and index.
  ISBN 0-230-60136-7−ISBN 0-230-60137-5
  1. Theater−Production and direction. 2. Motion pictures−Production and direction. I. Stanley, Jack R. II. Title.

PN2053.M62 2008
792.02'33−dc22   2007016346

A catalogue record of the book is available from the British Library.

Pictures and images by Tom Grabowski, M.F.A.

Design by Scribe Inc.

First edition: January 2008

10 9 8 7 6 5 4 3 2 1

Printed in the United States of America.

Contents

Illustrations

Figures

Table

1

Introduction

Theatre is theatre—whether it is theatre on a *stage* or on a small screen (TV) or big screen (*film*). If it uses actors to tell a story that someone wrote, it is theatre. This book deals with the elementary techniques of directing theatre for the various media. For too long, practitioners of live theatre have looked on the electronic media as the enemy. We argue it is simply another avenue of delivery.

Traditionally, theatre practitioners tell a story that embodies a theme, using the live stage as the means. So, if they tell the story using television, or film, or video, or yet-undiscovered or perfected means (e.g., holograms), is it so different? It still involves bringing scripts to life with actors for an audience. Live theatre used to tell its stories outdoors in an amphitheatre. At another time, the stories were told in a small indoor theatre, where the audience completely surrounded the actors. Now we have more places and more means for telling the stories. We also have more means of transportation, more means of communication, and so on. Theatre people still do theatre. They just have means to record and deliver the performances to audiences other than live actors in the same physical location as the audience.

Theatre is a way to tell a story by certain means. We call these means the medium. Stage is one medium, film another, TV a third. The medium doesn't always govern the techniques of directors. But, as you will see, the medium certainly impacts methodology. Each medium has different requirements. Each one allows different modes of imaginative expression, and each has it own unique limitations.

This book is based on a number of premises. Let's look at some of them. You don't necessarily have to agree with them. Just think of them as operational definitions that lay the groundwork for this book.

Premises, Premises

Theatre is an art form that involves communicating an idea to other people by means of a scripted production. Feel free to define it any way you want. For our purposes, that is the definition we are using.

A script being produced as a made-for-television movie is directed differently than one that is being shot with four cameras in a studio, live or recorded. The same script, done as a theatrical film, uses different techniques. Productions vary in their directing techniques. We have to use different directorial techniques when mounting a stage play for a large proscenium theatre or a small arena. If we just keep expanding on that premise, we can argue that the story can be told in a variety of media. Each *medium* utilizes the same basic principles, but the application of those principles varies according to the specific needs and restrictions of the medium.

For our purposes, then, we say this book deals with directing theatrical scripts with a beginning, middle, and end, not other theatrical or nontheatrical forms (e.g., sports, "reality" productions). Whether live, taped, or filmed, it's still theatre, just theatre in a different form. Certainly, many other kinds of productions need directors, but this book deals only with directing dramatic scripts.

This book is based on the fact that 95 percent of all jobs available in the theatrical field currently are in the electronic—television and film—industry. Less than 5 percent of them are in live theatre. Since it is the oldest dramatic medium, many people believe that the best basic training for the field is in live theatre, with adaptation so students can work in any medium. This book attempts to provide such a blend of disciplines for directing students. We operate under the premise that if you can direct one kind of scripted material, you can learn to direct others.

This book describes the way things ought to happen. However, frequently other factors intervene. One important factor, which will come up often in this book, is based on the following premise: *The power goes where the money flows.* It is a nasty fact, often ignored in the classroom, but too frequently true. The person with the greatest financial clout over the project gets the most votes and exercises the most power. The checkbook always outranks the organizational chart.

Sometimes, the power is perceived rather than actual. Perception is philosophy. Often, our universe exists the way we perceive it, instead of the other way around. At times, the person who has the most power has been given it because others perceive him or her to have more power. In a classroom, for example, students often perceive the professor to be more powerful than he or she actually is. So the professor has the power because the students believe the professor has it.

For instance, while it is supposed to be true that the director selects the actors for each role, the rule is often broken for financial reasons. A stage director might be told that a certain actor must be used in a particular role because of presumed box office potential or availability. If the director is perceived as having more power, he or she will win the casting battle; if not, the casting will be done by the person perceived as the most powerful in the organization. You often read that a certain famous actor has selected Joe Nameless to direct his next picture. Theoretically, the director selects the actor. But in reality, the actor may have enough power to select the director instead. The importance of this power will be discussed in detail.

Don't Forget to KISS

Most of us have heard that old maxim, "keep it simple, stupid." Directing a production of any sort involves considerable complexity and difficulty. So it is *not* a good idea to make things any more complicated than is absolutely necessary. Many new directors want to "play with all the toys" at their disposal. The final production can get sidetracked if they do. So, we will argue throughout the book that you should make things as simple as the particular project allows.

Before getting into the specifics of directing in the various media, let's talk about a few basic points we think will affect your perception of the material.

Who Owns the Words?

It is important to recognize a significant difference between stage and screen projects. In live *theatre*, if a play or a translation of a play is *copyright-protected, you cannot tamper with the words.* Copyright, under current U.S. law, protects the original creation of scripts for the lifetime of the writer plus seventy years. Cutting a script, taking out language of which you do not approve, or any other "tampering" is forbidden. In order to do a stage script, you have to pay royalties. That includes the obligation to the royalty holder to do the dialogue as written.

Television and Film Work Differently

The writer owns the script he or she has copyrighted. However, *once the script is purchased by the producers*, the writer has no control over the final product, except by specific contract negotiation. A TV or film script is often optioned or controlled until the "first day of principal photography," at which point the full purchase price of the script is due to the writer. After that, the script can be changed in any way the producers see fit. The writer merely cries all the way to the bank.

If you are directing a play version of a stage script written after 1923, you must obtain permission for any changes you make in the dialogue. You are not obligated to follow the stage design or directions if they are printed in the script. They are there to assist you. But the language is the property of the author. Cuts and changes must be approved by the playwright's representative, usually the leasing company.

You are not obligated to follow any blocking instructions, property lists, costume lists, or scene designs included in the script. You won't even find this material in older scripts from centuries past. Modern scripts often have such information to assist the nonprofessional director/producer.

Think of it this way. The script is the writer's baby. In theatre, the producers say, "I love your baby. I will pay you a small fee to keep it for a few days. I won't harm it and won't keep it any longer than I promised." The "parent" is usually thrilled by the fact you love the baby. But don't expect Mom or Dad to visit you and watch the way you play with the baby. The parent-playwright would probably hate the strange way you dress and feed it for those couple of days.

When the writer sells a script to television and film, it works like surrogate parenthood. The writer delivers the baby, takes the money, and disappears from the baby's life. He or she has given up control of the baby from that time on. Singer-actor-producer-director Barbra Streisand[1] once had this retort to novelist Isaac Bashevis Singer,[2] who complained about the difference between the film *Yentl* and the ending to his story, *Yentl, the Yeshiva Boy* (1983): "If you don't want your child molested, don't put it up for sale."

When you buy a film or television script, you can chop it up, rewrite it, keep the title and throw out the script, keep the script and change the title, or anything else. Unless you have a specific arrangement with the writers, it's your script. An example of this is *Pretty Woman*[3] (1990). The film's initial, or working, title was "*$3,000.*" The original story was about a prostitute named Vivian (Julia Roberts) who was addicted to cocaine. At the end, Edward (Richard Gere) leaves her, and she shoots up her drug of choice again, leaving the audience to know this is no Cinderella story with a happy ending. That was the writer's intent. Several drafts and several writers later, the film became a modern-day fairy tale and a worldwide hit.

The legitimate question at this point is, "Was the studio/producer/ director right to make the changes, since those decisions resulted in the box office smash?" It's an ethical question with no firm answer. This is the way film and TV work. All the offended writers can do is insist their names be removed from the credits. Once they take the money, they don't have to take the blame if they hate the final result. You bought their baby, but you didn't buy the parents' name.

The politics of the filmmaker (director) or the studio can also influence significant script changes. When novelist Tom Clancy's[4] third novel was made into a movie,[5] *Clear and Present Danger*[6] (1992), it was altered. The novel was an antidrug story, but it turned into an indictment of a president who oversteps his authority (a thinly disguised Iran-Contra Affair under the Reagan administration[7]).

Whether for stage or screen, beware of using material in a way that violates copyright laws.[8] Students generally have certain privileges in using material for practice projects, but not for personal profit. So, if you are doing a student project and have not gotten special permission to use this material, be careful. The material should be very specifically, fully, and completely labeled as a student project in fulfillment of a course requirement. Usually, when students try to enter such material in contests or have a paid screening of projects based on copyrighted material, problems arise.

Be sure you don't attempt too much of a script. A short scene or two gives you a chance to work on good professional written material to exercise your skills. But don't try to do a long cutting of the work. That is really infringing on your student privilege. Such material cannot be used for public performances, particularly where payment is involved, unless you have secured permission from the copyright holder. This permission usually costs some money. Some holders are very generous in allowing student versions of their work, and some zealously forbid all such use.

Sometimes you may get material off the Internet. Be sure to know what the copyright responsibilities are, and stick to them. Don't use the material just because it looks as if it is free. Search for a statement of your rights to reproduce the material.

At The University of Texas–Pan American, we require all student productions to have, on the paper programs for theatre or in the titles and credits for video and film projects, the following: "produced in partial fulfillment of the course requirements for COMM 4302, Directing II." Students add this line as a continuous crawl at the bottom of the screen or as a single title card in the credits. Stage directing projects must have paper programs that contain the same statement. This material is shown only to other students enrolled in a specific class and not to the general public. Absolutely no money is involved.

Suppose you do some play scenes for a directing class and someone asks you to show those scenes elsewhere. Perhaps a local public library wants to present them. At that point, someone must pay royalties. Even if the library does not plan to charge admission, it is a public showing, and the copyright obligation goes into effect. Select a play that is out of copyright. Do Shakespeare. He's out of copyright. Why do you think everyone else does his works?

Some local libraries actually show old films and announce the showings publicly. However, usually they describe the film without mentioning the actual title. We doubt that this is legal, but at least they are not advertising a particular film, even if it is possible to guess what will be showing.

If you view a tape that is released to a company like Blockbuster or Hollywood Video to help the managers order store copies, you'll see that a crawl is on the screen constantly. It reminds the viewer that this product is not for purchase or rental. Even Blockbuster, with all its clout, has to watch out for intellectual property rights. The manger can invite a few friends over to view the film with him before ordering copies. But he cannot rent out this version, as it is not paid for.

Plays, films, TV episodes, and even "Saturday Night Live," "Mad TV," or other production scripts are intellectual property; therefore, they have property rights. It is stealing to use them without the appropriate permission. Yes, it is tempting. You are, after all, a poor student, and the copyright holder is rich. But how will you feel when you are a rich copyright holder? Stealing is stealing, whether the victim is rich or poor.

Generally, rights are easy to obtain when it is clear they are for classroom or training purposes only. Often, if the student is not going to make money on the work, the holder will allow it to be used free under specified conditions.

Where to Find Material

Look and Read

For your first directing exercises, a few practice scenes are suggested in this book. After that, you are on your own. If you complain that you can't find anything to do, perhaps it is because you haven't looked around enough. How many scripts do you read? Taking classes in dramatic literature and film history are good places to start. See as many plays and films as your budget and time schedule allow. Watch on TV the kind of productions you want to direct. It might be a good time to take some speed-reading lessons. If you want to marry a prince, you have to kiss a lot of frogs. If you want to find a "princely" script to do, you will probably read a lot of "froggy" ones before you find it.

It helps to read and see the best material you can. Time is limited. If you fill your mind with junk, you can't produce anything but junk. You have heard the computer expression, "Garbage in, garbage out." That applies to the output of your mind as well. Read and see the works of people who produce quality material. It will help you reach their level.

We all know we are supposed to play tennis, golf, or even computer games with someone who is a little better then we are so we can improve our game. It's easy to win when you play against weaker players, but you won't learn anything from it.

An old professor told us about a colleague of his who wanted to write great, serious novels. He didn't have the time as an underpaid and overworked English professor. But he wrote a fast and easy "bodice ripper" one year and sold it to a publishing house. This was back in the 1930s. Soon he was churning them out with speed and ease. Many of them sold to Hollywood, and those films were very successful. That created a demand for more of his romantic stories. They were somewhat in the mold of today's Harlequin novels.

Soon he was so rich, he bought his own Greek island, and he set out to write the great tragic novel. To his horror, all he could write was junk. He'd been writing trash for so long, he couldn't write treasure when he finally got the chance. Like any good student, we believe this story. Those bodice rippers are still somewhere on cable and on forgotten shelves of libraries. The writer is long dead, wealthy but presumably unfulfilled.

Love It or Leave It

You will spend a tremendous amount of time working with this script, from first selection to completion. Be sure you like it at the start. By the time you finish, you will have had moments when you detested it. Producer David O. Selznick fought for the rights and went through eleven writers[9] and four directors[10] to bring Margaret Mitchell's novel *Gone with the Wind* (1939) to the screen. When the film was finished, he sent a famous telegram saying, "The damn thing is finally done." You need to remember that initial enthusiasm to carry you through the difficult parts of the process.

Everyone gets bogged down once in a while. But if you start with something you have no enthusiasm for, you will hate it by the time you have it finished or you become so disheartened that you can't summon up the courage and energy to complete it.

All students know the problem of having a deadline and needing to write a paper or read an assigned book they hate. Dragging the eyeballs over the pages feels like carrying a hundred pound sack up a cliff. The same student might sit down and read *The Da Vinci Code*[11] (2003) or another best seller in a weekend. The difference is in the "like" factor.

Keep Re-Reading It

After the initial reading, go back and read the script again. See if it still holds up for you. You will discover a number of factors about the script that you overlooked in the first reading. If your interest is still there, spend time analyzing the script. What do you like about it? What production problems does it present? Can you afford to do the script? Can you think of ways to do it so you can solve the production problems in interesting and acceptable ways?

Two scripts we find attractive are *Angels in America* (play, 1993[12] and TV miniseries, 2003)[13] and *Spiderman II*[14] (2004). Yet one of us has no interest in doing either of them, while the other would take on either project. While both of us thoroughly enjoy and appreciate the productions we have seen and have great admiration and respect for those who brought them to life, deciding to take on either script would be an individual choice. It is kind of like admiring someone else's choice of a mate—good for you, but not for me.

Actually, script selection is a lot like choosing a college roommate. Can you stand to be around that person for a few months or years? The analogy is not a particularly good one, but it is useful. Put your imagination to work. In spite of what appear to be massive challenges, can you approach it differently?

Years ago, Broadway produced *K2*[15] (1993), a fantastic play about a pair of mountain climbers. It had a five-story-high set designed by Ming Cho Lee—Shanghai born, prolific, and celebrated American theatrical set designer and a longtime professor at the Yale School of Drama.[16] The scenery was made of sprayed Styrofoam. One of the characters was injured and could not move off the ledge. The other actor had to climb up and down the set all during the performance, using traditional climbing gear. In spite of that, you can envision a very simple production done with two great actors and a set that was nothing more than a large table, completely blanketed with black drapery. All you need is a cramped acting space, two great actors and a terrific script. As a stage director, that is more than enough.

Film critic Pauline Kael[17] once described movies as "places, chases, and faces." This to some extent explains why even great film scripts with limited locations rarely score well with moviegoers. A couple of exceptions are Alfred Hitchcock's 1944 film *Lifeboat*[18] and Chris Kentis's 2003 picture, *Open Water*.[19] *Lifeboat* is a film about survivors of a torpedoed ship during WWII who find themselves in the same lifeboat with one of the men who had sunk it. *Open Water* is based on a true story of two scuba divers accidentally stranded in shark-infested waters when their tour boat leaves them behind. Media critic Terrence J. Brady's review of the Hitchcock film read in part: "With its confined quarters and drama created without flashback, *Lifeboat* reads more like a stage play than a motion picture. In the capable hands of Hitchcock though, it is hardly a tale of just words."[20]

When audiences sit down with their popcorn and nachos, they're looking to go places and see things they have never seen before. The claustrophobia of a limited set is a turn-off to many, but certainly not all, filmgoers.

When plays are translated to the big screen or the small one, one of the first goals of a director is often to find ways of "opening up" the story, adding locations and breaking up scenes, so they will play out in more that a single set or location.

In the early days of television, live studio drama and soap operas (both shot live—we're talking about the days before videotape) were commonly known as "kitchen sink dramas." The bulk of studio cameras and problems with microphones caused video directors to keep their films restricted to small spaces. In those days, the 1950s, the film industry tried to win back the audiences it had lost to TV by offering movies with spectacular locations.

It doesn't take much thinking to come up with recent examples of TV shows that have had limited locations (generally because of budget limits) but that have done very well. Sitcoms fit this bill very easily: *Married with Children*,[21] *The Drew Carey Show*,[22] and *Seinfield*.[23] But TV dramas like *West Wing*[24] and *Law and Order*[25] also fit within this category.

For filmmakers, dialogue is cheaper to shoot than car crashes and exploding buildings. Dialogue in a limited location describes the modus operandi (method of operation) of many independent films (*Clerks*[26] [1994], *Sex, Lies & Video Tape*[27] [1998], and so on.)

Students, beginning filmmakers, and TV directors need to find a script they can produce that is not under copyright. This is where the wise use of public domain material (material no longer protected by copyright) comes in. The material under public domain generally was written (or translated) before 1923. The exceptions are when the heirs of the original copyright holder renewed the rights. Copyright protection also applies to new translations of old works, so even the version of *Oedipus Rex* by Sophocles that you are considering may be in a translation that is still under copyright.

Once you have found material you want to direct, here are some suggestions for how you might alter seemingly old material and make it accessible to your audience through a fresh point of view. What if . . . :

> . . . you take a script from ancient times and set it in the current day or even the future?
>
> . . . you change the locale of the story from its setting in the script to a totally different culture?
>
> . . . you turn the humans in the script into animals or cartoon characters or vice versa?
>
> . . . you make a comedy into a drama or a drama into a comedy?
>
> . . . you make the script into a musical? A Western? A mystery?

Break It Down and Put It Back Together

You need to know all about the script and how it works. It's like working on your own car. You're the mechanic. If you don't take it apart correctly and know what the parts do, it won't work when you put it together. And that part you have left over—how will the car run without it?

Script Analysis Is a Long Process, But a Necessary One

You need to know why each element is there and what it does. Years ago a colleague directed a stage production of *Kiss Me Kate*[28] (1948). She thought she knew the show cold. One brief musical interlude is absolutely dreadful. It is boring and drags, so naturally she cut it. The show ran smoothly with a nice momentum. Then came the dress rehearsal. The actress playing Kate had no time to change to her wedding dress. She went directly from the courtship scene to the bridal scene. The costume change was mandatory. So that night the director blocked the interlude back in— very poorly, of course, because she was totally unprepared.

The scene was a dud, but it gave the actress a minute and a half to make a costume change. We have always suspected Cole Porter wrote that segment in the dress rehearsal phase of the production for the same reason she had to put it back in—to make time for a costume change. Maybe not. Perhaps they just did a better job with it than she did because they were better prepared.

You need to be as prepared as possible. You need to know how it works or you will break it. Because of the out-of-sequence shooting of most TV and film productions, you as the director need to know the material in your head so well that you can see how each moment of a given scene will impact what comes before and after it.

Classic film director Henry Hathaway[29] believed there were only three or four good scenes in a film and the rest of it was filler. His approach was to focus time and effort on the important scenes and get through the rest as quickly as possible. We see his point, but we disagree.

The Buck Starts Here

In general, the director works with actors. That's who and what a director directs. He or she may have greater or lesser control over other elements of production, but actors are a director's prime responsibility.

In a stage situation, you are the one who decides on the interpretations. You welcome input from anyone (or not), but all directions to the actors come from the director, not from other "helpful" cast members, producers wandering through a rehearsal, or designers who don't know where their creative boundaries end.

In some screen situations, other people may have the right (or assume it) to direct the actors once you have finished directing a scene. On a national network half-hour show, we saw twenty-seven people speak to one actor to give him directions in the course of the week's shoot. That's our body count. That actual number could have been higher. How an actor is supposed to know which direction to follow is beyond us. Using the mantra about money and power, one can only assume that the actor pays the most attention to the person who gets paid the most!

Time and Money

We see another difference in stage and screen work. Generally, a stage director and actors have the "luxury" of working together on a script for a considerable number of days before their work is seen by the public. The production gets built layer by layer, and most of the people involved are there, working together, most of the time. Ideas have time to generate and mature.

That's why actors and directors love to work on the stage. It doesn't pay much, but it is immensely satisfying. You get to rehearse long enough (okay, never long enough, but a lot). You can all work through the entire script until you feel as if you have a grasp of the whole. Then you go out and do it, all of a piece, without a safety net. No one calls "Cut" or does a retake. If something messes up, you get out of it the best way you can. That's what makes it live and exciting.

The frustrating part of screen work is the apparent lack of time. Rehearsal time is a luxury few can afford. The actor with a really large part or a recurring role in television has time to develop a character, if not a specific scene. But these actors are working with people who are on the set for just one episode of a television show or a scene or two in a film. The new actors barely have time to learn where the craft table and the bathrooms are. They also have to learn lines and blocking, both of which are being constantly changed because of demands by the director, producer, lighting crew, director of photography, and strange people in business suits. So, instead of a lot of rehearsals, the actors have a lot of "takes" until it finally comes out as close to right as they can get it in the time they have.

Your job as a director in any medium is to prepare the actor to do his or her best work. You need to know the script better than anyone. You also have to have enough directing and communication skills to work with a wide variety of people. Your job is to help them do their best work. Each director has a different style of working and so does each other theatre artist. Your effectiveness depends on your ability to tap what is best in the people on your project.

Casting

A great deal of your result will lie in effective casting. Even with apparently unlimited budgets, major directors rarely get the person they think is best for every role. So part of good directing is being able to pick the best cast. The rest is being able to bring out the best in the best cast you can get. We will discuss casting in greater detail later in this book.

Where Does All the Time Go?

When we first begin as directors, we think of the distribution of our time as a little preparation, a lot of doing, and a little postproduction. Actually, it works out differently. Each medium has different time demands. The only constant is—you always want more time than you have. Time is money, and there is never enough of either.

For film, assume that your time is distributed in thirds. Your preparation will take about a third of the total time, the production another third, and the postproduction a final third. Television has the same time distribution, but as a director, you often are less involved in the first third and usually have little involvement in the final third. In TV you are usually talking about a week to prepare an episode, a week to shoot it, and a week to get it edited.

Stage work comes closer to half and half. You spend half your time preparing for the production and half the time in rehearsal. Once the show opens, you're done. Take the money and go to Barbados. If it is a hit, come back and bask in the glory. If it is a failure, change your name.

The time the director spends on preparation is the cheapest time spent on the project. No one else is getting paid to do it. The better prepared you are, the more efficient and probably the faster the production phase will go. The production phase is the most expensive phase, since it involves the most people.

Even on an amateur production, time is money and it should not be wasted. You may not finish the rehearsal or the day's shooting if you are unprepared. The production will suffer. Although you are working with an unpaid cast and crew, you owe it to everyone, as the director, to be as well prepared as possible. Then you can use the time you have to improve the production. Nothing is more irritating to everyone else than sitting around idly as the director mulls over a decision that could and should have been made already. Trust us, you will have enough times when circumstances force you to stop and make a decision because things have become undone. Try to cut that time as much as possible.

This book will help you to learn to be a little more organized and a little more efficient. It won't make you a genius. It should help you to do things a little more efficiently so you get more done and better work accomplished in the time you have. The genius part is up to you. We are here to teach you the rules, because rules are generally true. Knowing when to break the rules is the genius part, and we don't think anyone can teach that.

Which Comes First?

What is more important—the words or the pictures? Stage directors generally need to focus more closely on the written words of a script than on the visual aspects of it. Usually, in a stage play, it's the dialogue that carries the production. On screen projects, the visual image generally is somewhat more important than the spoken word.

Think of it this way. Character A is in love with character B but has not declared this love. If it is a stage play, directed for a 1,500-seat proscenium house, having actor A look at actor B in a certain way will not communicate the idea to the audience. Most audience members can't even see their eyes. You depend upon the playwright for a line of dialogue to convey that idea, short of having the character come right out and say it.

If it is a screenplay, the script may indicate: A looks at B undetected. A's eyes clearly speak of a love that has not been declared. On stage, the audience member thirty rows back from the stage may not even be able to see the eyes of actor A. On a film screen, those eyes may be three feet wide. On a television shoot, the director may choose to use an extreme close up on A's face. That way, the eyes are still visible on a thirteen-inch screen at home. Regardless of the medium, the director has to know what choices are available in that medium to convey the information that A loves B.

So the rule seems to be that, if we have to sacrifice one element to another for some reason, each medium has different priorities. On stage, the words come first. On screen, the picture comes first. We mentioned earlier about the role of hearing in the live theatre—theatre and auditorium. Audio means "I hear." An auditorium means "a hearing place." Look at the vocabulary of the screen. We call it television (to see far away), video (I see), motion pictures (moving images), and movies (moving pictures).

Of course, we try to get all we can out of each picture and sound. Ideally, we do not have to choose one over the other. But when you must, that's the rule.

Rules Are Only Rules

A rule is something that tends to be true more often than not. Rules can be broken. This book discusses the rules for directing dramatic productions. There are not that many laws about directing. We are looking at the way things are generally done, as experience has shown these ways are usually more efficient and lead to a better production. But there are times when we need to break the rules.

Think of driving autos. If we didn't have rules, we would have more accidents than we do now. So someone invented the idea of "lanes," so we could stay on the same side of the road to go in the same direction. That's why we call them the rules of the road. It's a rule in the United States that we drive on the right. It's a rule in Great Britain that we drive on the left. At times, we have to break the rules and cross into the other lane for safety's sake.

Laws are supposed to be immutable and unchangeable. You can't break the third law of thermodynamics, whatever that is. So this book is full of rules—things that are true at least 51 percent of the time. These rules can be broken. But if you know the rules, you save a lot of time and energy. Then you use your artistry to decide when to break a rule or make a new one.

Don't decide to be an artist before you have become an artisan. Picasso could draw as well as any draftsman. He first learned the rules, then he began to break them and make new rules—new ways for us to see.

In the early days of the industry, film artists started by using the rules of theatre to govern their filmmaking. Then, as they learned the new medium and what it could do, they made new rules and discovered old rules could successfully be broken. Eventually, theatre learned to break old rules by observing some of the rules broken by film.

Let's take the example of time as depicted in theatre. Early plays, with virtually no exceptions, depicted time linearly on stage. Scene one occurs in time before scene two. Scene three takes place after scene two. So when film came along, the same time system was used. Look at old films and you see calendar pages fly by to indicate the passage of time. On stage, the curtain could close or the lights dim, and the audience knew that the next scene took place later. On screen, the pioneers assumed that the audience would not understand that time had passed without a similar device, so they used flying calendar pages or spinning clock hands to show a time lapse between scenes.

Over the years filmmakers discovered something wonderful. Somehow, without these clues, audiences could tell if a scene was taking place before or after the previous scene or even at the same time in another place. The audiences had developed a grammar of film and understood the sense of time. Filmmakers even developed the flashback—a scene where time shifts occur effortlessly. A character can remember a past event while living in a present one.

Finally, in *Death of a Salesman*, a play was written in which time shifted constantly as Willy, the central character, had flashbacks on stage. Flashbacks were common by then in films. Through the use of Jo Mielziner's[30] stage designs, live audiences could keep pace with time shifting effortlessly also.

New rules keep getting made, and old rules keep getting broken. That's a rule.

Conclusion

This overview should give you an idea of the point of view we will use to discuss directing. We want to be open about what we think this book can and will do for you as a director. Between the introduction and the table of contents, you should have a good idea of the material we will cover and our approach to it. We want this book to be practical and not full of fancy theories. We want to help you get started and not intimidate you.

We hope you will learn to learn—to always try to find ways to get better at what you do. With a combined experience of nearly one hundred years of directing, we are still learning things. It is one of the most interesting and exciting parts of our job.

Summary

In this introduction, we have tried to point out several important concepts that underlie the entire book.

This book is based on the concept that theatre is theatre—whether it is live on a stage or delivered in electronic form through film or television.

Each of these media are dramatic forms, and only the medium is different.

This book argues that theatre is an art form that involves communicating an idea to other people by means of a script.

This book deals with directing only scripted materials, not other forms of directing, like live sports or documentaries.

This book presumes that if you can direct in one medium, you can learn to adapt to another.

This book describes the way things ought to happen but acknowledges that, in professional practice, different rules often prevail.

This book stresses the director's responsibility to acknowledge the writer's contribution to the final product.

This book stresses the importance of the relationship between the actor and the director.

This book points out the importance of preparation to give the director more time on the set to spend wisely.

This book discusses casting and how it related to the overall function of the director.

This book stresses the wise and efficient use of time.

This book discusses the differences between and among directing forms in different media.

This book gives the reader a lot of rules—not laws. It will suggest ways that directors can work to achieve good results efficiently. But it will recognize that new artists will always come up with new rules or new ways to use old rules.

Suggested Reading and Viewing

Reading

Stage
Albright, Hardie. *Stage Direction In Transition*. See chapter 1.
Catron, Louis E. *The Director's Vision: Play Direction From Analysis To Production*. See chapter 2.
Dean, Alexander, and Lawrence Carra. *Fundamentals of Play Directing*. See pages 12–20.
Hodge, Francis. *Play Directing, Analysis, Communication and Style*. See chapter 1.
Patterson, Jim. *Stage Directing*. See the prologue.

Screen
Armer, Alan A. *Directing Television And Film*. See chapter 1.
Bare, Richard L. *The Film Director*. See chapter 1.
Lukas, Christopher. *Directing For Film and Television*. See the introduction.

Notes

1. Streisand directed *Timeless: Live in Concert* (2001, video), *The Mirror Has Two Faces* (1996), *The Prince of Tides* (1991), and *Yentl* (1983).
2. Singer is the 1978 Nobel Prize–winning writer of novels and short stories.
3. Directed by Garry Marshall.
4. Clancy is the author of *Without Remorse, Patriot Games, Red Rabbit, The Hunt for Red October, The Cardinal of the Kremlin, Clear and Present Danger, The Sum of All Fears, Debt of Honor, Executive Orders, Rainbow Six, The Bear and the Dragon,* and *The Teeth of the Tiger*.
5. *The Hunt for Red October* (1990), *Patriot Games* (1992), *Clear and Present Danger* (1992).
6. Directed by Phillip Noyce, who also directed *The Quiet American* (2002), *The Bone Collector* (1999), *The Saint* (1997), *Sliver* (1993), *Patriot Games* (1992), *Blind Fury* (1989), and *Dead Calm* (1989).
7. A member of President Reagan's administration secretly sold weapons to Iran from 1980 through 1988 while that nation was engaged in a war with Iraq. Profits were diverted to the Contra rebels fighting to overthrow the leftist Sandinista government of Nicaragua. Both transactions were contrary to acts of Congress, which prohibited the funding of the Contras and the sale of weapons to Iran. In addition, both activities violated United Nations edicts.

8. Current U.S. Copyright Law covers material for the life of the copyright holder plus seventy years. Any unauthorized use of such material beyond one hundred words of the content is a Copyright Law violation.
9. Sidney Howard (credited), Ben Hecht, David O. Selznick, Jo Swerling, John Van Druten, John L. Balderston, F. Scott Fitzgerald, Michael Foster, Oliver H. P. Garrett, Charles MacArthur, Edwin Justin Mayer, and Winston Miller.
10. Directed by Victor Fleming; uncredited directors were George Cukor, Sam Woods, and William Cameron Menzies.
11. Written by Dan Brown.
12. Written by Tony Kushner, original music by Anthony Davis, directed by George C. Wolfe. Performed November 23, 1993, to December 4, 1994, Walter Kerr Theatre, New York.
13. Directed by Mike Nichols.
14. Directed by Sam Raimi.
15. Directed by Terry Schreiber, written by Patrick Meyers. Performed March 30, 1983, to June 11, 1983, Brooks Atkinson Theatre, New York.
16. *Execution of Justice* (1986), *K2* (1983), *The Shadow Box* (1977), *For Colored Girls Who Have Considered Suicide / When the Rainbow Is Enuf* (1976), *All God's Chillun Got Wings* (1975), *Gandhi* (1970), *Little Murders* (1967), and *Mother Courage and Her Children* (1963).
17. Kael was a *New Yorker* magazine movie critic from 1967 to 1991.
18. Directed by Alfred Hitchcock.
19. Directed by Chris Kenis.
20. Terrence J. Brady, "Dial H for Hitchcock," film review, http://www.teako170.com/dial32.html.
21. Fox network, 1987–97.
22. ABC network 1995–2004.
23. CBS network 1990–97.
24. NBC network 1999–2005.
25. NBC network 1990–2005.
26. Directed by Kevin Smith
27. Directed by Steven Soderberg.
28. Book by Bella Spewack and Samuel Spewack, music and lyrics by Cole Porter. Based on *The Taming of the Shrew*.
29. Director of *Hangup* (1974), *Shoot Out* (1971), *Raid on Rommel* (1971), *True Grit* (1969), *Nevada Smith* (1966), *The Sons of Katie Elder* (1965), *North to Alaska* (1960), *From Hell to Texas* (1958), *Prince Valiant* (1954), *Down to the Sea in Ships* (1949), *Nob Hill* (1945), *Wing and a Prayer* (1944), *Sundown* (1941), *The Shepherd of the Hills* (1941), and *The Lives of a Bengal Lancer* (1935).
30. Mielziner's striking designs included *Streetcar Named Desire*, *Death of a Salesman*, *Carousel*, *South Pacific*, and *Guys and Dolls*, among others.

2

Directing and Style

What Is a Director?

What is a director? What is the director's responsibility in the entire production process? If you have already studied theatre history, you know the formal role of the director has changed considerably over the years. According to some books, the job description of the director, as we know it, was invented by the Duke of Saxe Meiningen[1] in the late nineteenth century. Yet as long as there has been theatre, someone had to tell the other people what to do, to some extent. If you have studied film history, you know that film has been around a little over a century, so it is far from being the world's oldest profession.

Generally, in the contemporary world, we can define three different kinds of directors: (1) stage directors, (2) television directors, and (3) film directors. We can give a brief job description of each. First, however, it's important to understand who has the ultimate power in each medium. As a rule, it breaks down this way: the stage is the writer's medium, TV is run by the producers, and film is where the director is in the driver's seat. But remember, there are exceptions to every rule.

Stage Is the Writer's Medium

Directors of plays under copyright are legally bound by the dialogue on the printed page (although not the stage directions). This is not true for directors who are mounting plays in public domain. Cutting the script is, in fact, a common practice for directors who work with Shakespeare and many of the great playwrights of the past. One must grasp the distinction between scripts under copyright and those in public domain, because the stage director is limited by law when dealing with modern, protected material, but totally free when dealing with the older scripts. To be safe, assume that anything written, adapted, or translated after 1923 is still under copyright

Television Is the Producer's Medium

In TV, the producer, who rises primarily out of the ranks of writers, is responsible for creating and guiding series or a single production. The person who has the most artistic control over the show is called the "show runner" and generally serves as the producer. With a very few exceptions (Sidney Sheldon[2] with "I Dream of Jeannie," David E. Kelley[3] with "Ally McBeal," "The Practice," and "Boston Legal," as well as Aaron Sorkin[4] with the first year of "West Wing" and then, with "Studio 60 on the Sunset Strip," and a minuscule list of others), it is impossible for the producer to write all or even most of the episodes of a series, TV's primary production unit. ABC did a two-hour show early in January 2005 on the making of "Dynasty," a top-rated 1980s TV series. If you can get a copy, it is worth watching to see the various power relationships that the show demonstrates.

Networks, studios, production companies, and stars all understand the importance of the script. However, TV evolved more along the line of film than stage when it came to the written word. In both TV and film, the writer actually sells all the rights to his or her script, as opposed to playwrights who only lease the "performance rights." The TV producer is involved with productions from the very beginning all the way to the conclusion of the project. The producer sees that a series remains true to the characters, themes, and styles he or she was commissioned to deliver.

Film Is the Director's Medium

Thanks primarily to a 1954 essay by French film critic, director, and actor François Truffaut,[5] the idea arose that the director is the author or the auteur of the film. American critic Andrew Sarris[6] imported the notion to the United States. Here it was picked up by other historians and critics, much to the delight of those in the directors' chairs. Detractors are quick to ask that if the director is the author of the film, what is the point of a script writer and a script? Regardless of the truth of the matter, the evolution of the film business has placed the director's name above the title and given the director the possessive credit (e.g., "a John

Ford[7] film"). Along with the best parking space on the lot, the director also has the most power in the decision making of the film from day one. All of the above can be demonstrated by this simple test:

- How many stage writers (playwrights) can you name? How many stage producers? How many stage directors?
- How many television writers can you name? How many TV producers? How many TV directors?
- How many film writers can you name? How many film producers? How many film directors?

The whole issue is complicated further by hyphenates: writer–directors, producer–directors, or even actor–directors. The hyphenate muddies the water to the extent that each such person has to sort out and negotiate the amount of power and/or influence he or she commands in whatever type of production is in question. What follows are general guidelines, but a director's experience and track record counts for a tremendous amount. In Hollywood, one hit can make up for three flops. Number four had better be another hit, or that director is going to have a hard time finding work.

Specific Tasks of Directors in Each Medium

Stage Directors

Generally, stage directors have final casting privileges. Their first and principal job is selecting the actors for the parts. Most stage directors will tell you that casting the actors is the most important part of the job description. If they do that well, everything else falls into place with greater ease and artistry.

The stage director is usually the one with the main idea, the concept, the focus and the heart for the production. He or she decides the theme and emphasis the play should present. The designers of a stage production get their main ideas of the play's significance from the director, and their ideas are filtered through the director before being executed. The producer may also be the director and the person responsible for setting the budget and its parameters.

The smaller the venue, the more likely the director wears multiple hats. High school and small community theatre directors may be the director, producer, and designer of the production. The larger the venue, the more likely other people will exercise considerable control or at least input into the directing process.

Television Directors

On most television productions (like situation comedies, hour-long dramas, or soap operas), the directors are usually hired for several shows throughout the season but not for all the episodes. For hour-long soap operas, each director usually does one show a week. Some situation comedies use the same director for a whole season, but more often several directors will be used, each for one episode at a time. Some dramatic series employ an "A" and "B" director. Each alternates between actually directing and preparing for his or her next turn.

Other series may use a "stable" of directors, five or six per season, each of whom take the helm for several episodes. Yet there are exceptions. As mentioned, some series employ the same director for every show for an entire season. In that case, the director is probably fairly young, very energetic, and has no personal life! For a single director to guide every individual show effectively with consistent insight, creativity, drive, and enthusiasm is as emotionally and physically demanding as the stress level of a soldier under fire in combat on a daily basis. There are no purple hearts or veteran's benefits for burned-out directors.

A miniseries generally uses one director for the entire production. Again, there are exceptions to this rule. "Band of Brothers"[8] (2001) used multiple directors on the same miniseries. Some directors specialize in pilots only and rarely direct individual episodes of a program.

Usually, television directors have no input into casting, unless they were hired to direct the pilot of the series. Normally, directors simply play the hand they are dealt in this regard. The series regulars remain the same from episode to episode. Casting directors supply performers for the minor walk-on or day players, but a director might be consulted about a guest star or significant one-time-only character actor.

A TV director can get the first cut of an episode directed. But it is also a common practice for a working director to move on to another series and another show, leaving the editing to the editor and the producer. The director is at least given a courtesy viewing of his or her show. Since the show runner has the most artistic control, the TV director may have somewhat less emotional investment in the product and not see the production until it airs (if even then).

An interesting exception to this practice occurred on the long running Western series on CBS called "Gunsmoke." Director John Rich[9] directed an episode and moved on to another assignment. The series editor cut the program together and Rich was asked to join the producer for a screening. The story didn't make much sense, and the dumbfounded producer thought that the entire production was a total waste. Rich, watching in disbelief at what the editor had done with his work, asked the producer if it would be possible for Rich to recut the footage. The producer, figuring there was nothing to lose but doubting there was much to gain, told Rich, "Yes, John, you go do that."

A week later, viewing the reedited show, the producer was both pleased and impressed with the result. In fact, that particular episode was entered into the television Emmy Awards competition for 1958 and won for Best Editing of a Film for Television. Rich was also hired as one of the series' regular A/B directors.

Film Directors

Film directors have considerable power over a production. They generally have the most artistic control over all the other areas of the production. The director can get contractual power to cast the picture and hire every hand that touches the production, from the cast all the way to the caterer who will provide the food on the set. The film director also gets the first and final edit, although the studio may reserve the right to recut the film yet again. (This explains why "The Director's Cut" has become a popular DVD version of many films.) In return, the director agrees to bring the film in on a strict number of shooting days and under a predetermined budget. When the budget seems to explode (*Jaws* [1975] is a prime example[10]), the director can get more time and money if the studio is happy with the progress of the film.

Frequently, the film is known by the director's name—in the possessive credit above the title—rather than by the leading actor's or the writer's (e.g., Steven Spielberg's *Schindler's List* [1993]). Writers are more likely to get the blame if the film is a failure, even if there have been a number of writers on the project. Directors are more prone to get all the glory if it is a success. Famous actors are apt to get the best financial deal, and they can always blame the failure of the film on one of these other people. Powerful actors can also overrule the director, if the actor is big enough.[11] The higher the salary anyone commands, the more likely that person is to be able to override others in the chain of command.

As much as you can, learn to direct by observing the work of directors. In film, DVDs give every would-be director a way to learn by observing the best. Seeing the films mentioned in this book is an education in itself.

Take advantage of every opportunity to observe a director in action—on the set or in rehearsal.

What Do I Direct?

Ideally, you pick a project that really excites you. Select one that is neither beyond your reach nor so easy it will bore you. Select well-written material that offers you real challenges and has a message you want to share. If you come across a script and think, "I wish I'd written that," you probably have your next project.

In the real world, you often have to direct because you need the work. Once we asked a particular director, who had done some really great stage work, why he had chosen to do a total stinker of a script. It was a stupid potboiler that made you wonder about the mentality of audiences. He replied that his wife, who was much better off financially than he, would support him when he was out of work but refused to pay a penny of his child support payments. So he had taken on this project because he was four months behind in his child support.

Being hungry is a great motivation. At times, a script starts looking really good because the money is great, or because this is the first chance to do a script of this magnitude, or because you're afraid people will assume that you have retired or died because you haven't done anything lately. Comedian George Burns once explained it this way: "If it's a good script, I'll do it. And if it's a bad script, and they pay me enough, I'll do it."

In academic theatre, you have to pick a play to balance the season, fit with the production schedule, stay within your share of the yearly production budget, be able to be cast with the group of actors available, be within the scope of the design and technical staff, not upset the Dean or anyone else in the upper administration, and not embarrass your institution. Considerations of subject matter, language, and nudity vary greatly from campus to campus.

In academia, you may also have to direct because that is one of the "duties assigned by the administration over and above the other items mentioned in this contract." In other words, it's part of the job. Now there's a motivation for you! Which script are you eager to do that fits all the previous parameters and doesn't take up the time you were planning to spend on that theatre journal article you have to complete or that scholarly conference presentation you need to make in order to get tenure?[12] In community and other amateur theatres, the considerations driving the choice of material by the director may be financial first, community acceptance second, and artistic third.

But, leaving such crass considerations aside, try to find work on something that you find attractive and stimulating. In TV and film, the end product is much further away from any original commitment date than is generally the case with stage. Don't pick something because it is in line with some trend or fad that is currently hot. By the time the production is before an audience, the trend could well be over and, with it, any chance of success for your efforts. Try not to pick a project to please another person. Try to select one that will challenge you, interest you, and give you pleasure, because it will surely also give you pain.

What Is the Difference in Stage and Screen Directing?

For the Stage

When you direct for the stage, you have to keep in mind that the audience can see everything on the stage all the time. But everything on that stage is not as important as everything else all the time, so you have to direct the focus of the audience. The principles of stage directing are based on the idea that your job is to decide who or what is the most important element at that moment in time. You do what is needed to get the audience to look where you want them to look, see what you want them to see, and hear what you want them to hear, You need to know directing techniques to get these people to do what you want, yet make sure that everything else is what and where it is supposed to be. No matter how good you are, someone in that theatre is looking someplace other than where you want him or her to look.

For the Screen

On the screen, you have control over what the audience sees and hears. To get them to look where you want them to look, you aim the camera there. To get them to see what you want them to see, you edit out everything else. To get them to hear what you want them to hear, you go back and loop everything you have shot already, if needed, or raise the volume, add sound effects, or introduce music for emphasis. In effect you are saying, "Look at this. Now look at this. Now look at this. Now look at this."

Multicamera

Multicamera television productions, such as sitcoms, as opposed to single camera film-style productions, give the director a variety of choices of views of the exact same material and performance. A typical network show involves four studio cameras. Each camera records independently on its own recorder with a unified time code (hour, minute, second, and frame number). This is true for video or film. Sitcoms, soap operas, game shows, reality shows, and talk shows are filmed or taped using multiple cameras. The only significant difference is the medium The recording stock doesn't matter to the director or the performers, but the style of the entire production will be governed by the multicamera or single camera style of shooting.

Live audiences in the studio experience a multicamera film shoot like a stage play, except for the cameras and microphones intervening between the players and the viewers. There is nothing else for the audience to watch. In video, the director calls the show and the Technical Director switches it to be seen by the studio audience. The audience can watch the players or watch large TV monitors hung strategically over the heads of the audience. This too is recorded and becomes the rough cut of the program.

The director can tweak this version in a final edit or even start all over with the basic shots all there. (This last option rarely happens.) The multicamera-filmed show is edited on video in postproduction. The choice of film versus video may depend on the look the director wants, but usually it is based on the budget the producer provides. Still, the multicamera production is being shot from several angles with the same lights and the same audio—normally two boom microphones just out of the shots, above the actors' heads. The microphones and the cameras are repositioned as needed throughout the production.

For both the single camera film-style video director and the true film director, shooting the script involves individual camera "setups" and what is called "coverage."

Setup

A setup occurs each time the camera is positioned for a shot. The camera, lights, and audio all move and are adjusted for this angle. The whole scene or a single moment of it can be captured from this perspective. The lights and sound changes make a film-style production look and even feel different from a multicamera shoot. It is easier to emphasize a moment and even examine it differently with a different camera setup than merely with a different shot of the same event under the same lighting and sound conditions.

Coverage

Coverage involves the filming of a scene or moment from multiple angles with different setups. Coverage is important. The more coverage of a scene, the more options a director has when editing. Directors who really know what they are doing can give an editor only a few options and thus control how the production will be edited without having to go to the editing room.

John Ford, the famous film director of the 1930s through the 1960s, was known to control the coverage of his pictures to limit any editor's choice of footage for particular moments. Ford knew how he wanted the scene to be cut together, and he also knew that if you give an editor a lot of footage (coverage), the possibilities for different interpretations become endless. So Ford would sit beside the single camera of his productions and put his hand up in front of the lens during the filming of part of a scene that he did not want to be seen from that angle. Then he would remove his hand for the portion he planned for the editor to use. As a result, the editor had to use the shot or shots Ford wanted for this particular part of a scene.

This is a dangerous game. Lack of coverage can get the inexperienced director in trouble at editing time. The director cannot edit around continuity gaffes or a mistake by an actor. But low-budget films generally do not allow for very much coverage, so the director must be well prepared and know exactly what needs to be filmed and what does not. On bigger budget projects, footage is cheap, so plenty of coverage is the rule of the day.

Contrasting Stage and Screen

Stage Directing

Simply put, we can say that stage directing, even on a professional level, usually involves a smaller number of people as well as a smaller bankroll than film. The entire production has to be complete and correct before the first paying customer sees it. So it needs to be rehearsed in its entirety.

Generally, you get to spend a considerable amount of time with the cast. You do not have a lot of other people interfering with the process. You get to try things and work things out in a through line: the beginning, middle, and end of the character's arc, or the arc of the particular scene. By the time the first paying customer sees it, every cast member knows the entire play and has been through numerous run-throughs.

Screen Directing

Screen directing, whether for television or film, is a daily process of assembling a puzzle. You get to spend as little time alone with the cast as the producer can manage. You probably have never worked with most of these people before, and you definitely won't work with everybody every day. Most of the actors won't know, or even get to read, the entire script, which may change considerably from day to day and again in postproduction. So the best the director can do is cast with care (when the director has the option) and do whatever is needed to get the best possible performance out of the actors.

How Does the Eye See in Each Medium?

The human eye is better and more dynamic than any camera. It constantly changes focus, fixing on one part of the entire visual field and then another. Your eye is constantly cutting to close-ups, extreme close-ups, long shots, and so on, faster than you can call the cues in a TV control room or editing suite.

Much to the surprise of many beginning film and TV directors, the ideal is *not* to call attention to any individual shot. The change from one shot to the next, the cut, the dissolve, the wipe, or the fade should be invisible to the audience. If the audience ever stops and says, "Hey, that's a great shot!" then the director has lost the audience and pointed out to them that this is a film or video production. When the audience is completely taken in by the production, they never realize the director's touch. The audience sees what they need to see, when they need to see it, and they see it in such a way as to be swept away by the experience instead of jolted out of it.

On stage, you have to move something to get the eye to focus on it. You have to make it lighter or brighter. You have to make it more visible—taller, say—or frame it in a more obvious position. And you have to do this without moving any of the furniture or set pieces on the stage.

Do It with the Camera

In TV and film, you direct the attention and focus of the audience with the camera. The educated audience eye understands the grammar of the screen. It understands that a close-up means this part is more significant at this moment than the whole. It knows that when the person in the picture is listening and the speaker can't be seen, then the reaction of the listener is more important than the action of the speaker. It knows that when the camera cuts to another person, the first person is still there. It knows that when the picture fades to the next shot, the new image may have no relation to the shot that preceded it.

The More They Pay, the More They Pay Attention

Television makes different demands on the audience, and thus some other rules come into play. Audiences watching television are not as likely to be paying as close attention as audiences watching a film. The presumption is that, when you have paid your ten bucks and filled your arms with overpriced junk food, you will sit and behave and pay attention if it is a film. On the other hand, television has become an electronic baby-sitter and home companion. We often have it on and watch it only when it catches our attention.

For film, you go into a cool, dark room in which you look up at a large, bright image and are surrounded by magnificent sound. The TV often is in a brightly lit room, but it is the same room where the telephone rings, the baby cries, the pets want attention, and sirens go screaming by just outside. Also, most of us look down at our TV (and look down on the medium of TV metaphorically without realizing why). Depending on the size of your screen, the images you see will vary greatly.

The more you pay to see a stage play, the more likely you are to pay close attention. Paying a hundred dollars or more for a seat is a real attention-getting device. But that also means the expectations of the audience are greater. They have gone to a lot more trouble to see this play than that film. So as the director, you have to make it worth the added time and money.

Three Things a Director Does in Any Medium

Clarify

As a stage director, your job is to do the best with what you have to achieve the finest production possible. You prepare the actors so that in their oral and visual presentation, they make the ideas of the script clear. Of course, that means the actors are visible and audible. Once you have worked through the overall production concept, which we will discuss later, most of your directing skills will be put to use to do many of the sorts of things that one can do on screen with editing, camera angles, and looping.

First you have to have a clear idea yourself of the ideas and themes embodied in the script. Then you have to make these clear to everyone else connected to the project, from the lighting designer to the program cover artist. The entire production ought to reflect the same point of view. It is false advertising to promote a show as a sexy bedroom farce when it is a serious philosophical discussion. Perhaps the first kind of promotion sells more tickets, but your audience won't trust you after that.

In film or television, a frustrated director often sees a tender, delicate work billed as an action film. There is nothing the director can do to prevent it. *Collateral* is a good example of this kind of problem. Obviously the promoters did not trust the film as it was done. So the ads and previews made it look like a Jean Claude Van Damme or Arnold Schwarzenegger kick-chop-bang-bang flick. People who wanted action did not get their usual overdose, in spite of the fact that a tremendous number of bullets got fired. (How many bullets does Tom Cruise's gun hold at a clip? He fired a lot more than he reloaded. Maybe he reloaded off camera.) How many people didn't go to see a film they might have appreciated for a different reason?

In fact, audiences, individually and collectively, decide what the production is about. It's one of the basic facts of communication: the receiver determines the value and the content of the message. You can say "good morning" to people, but if they hear, think they hear, or believe they understand you to be saying "go away," then "go away" is the message communicated. Therefore, it's important for the director to be sure of what he or she is trying to communicate.

Listen

Good directing means the production is clear, visually and orally. The audience sees and hears clearly what they should. In many of today's productions for stage, television, and film, directors are so busy playing with the visual elements, they forget that audiences need to hear the dialogue clearly.

In the production, the audience hears the dialogue only once. The director has heard it, in rehearsal or editing, a hundred times. Therefore, many modern productions are marvels of mumbling. Frequently major dialogue points are missed because the audience had only one chance to hear it, and the lines were not clear. As a director, remind yourself to *listen* with a fresh ear to be sure the material is coming across the first time someone hears it.

Stage Listening

Playgoers often complain they didn't hear certain scenes or lines. They assume it was just mumbled dialogue. But the sound problems can be caused by jumbled directing. If the stage director has a distracting stage movement, the audience shifts attention to it and may miss the line.

In the "Matchmaker" song from the 2004 Broadway version of *Fiddler on the Roof*, a cute line of the lyrics doesn't always get a laugh. Three sisters are singing about the problems of getting a husband with the help of a matchmaker. One of the sisters has a line that usually gets a laugh in productions. This director chose to block the two younger sisters running into the scene at that point. That distraction often causes the audience to shift focus just enough to miss the line and therefore the laugh.

Many times stage actors have apologized for dropping a line we hadn't noticed was missing. We knew it was supposed to be there and could have sworn we heard it. Of course, at other times, we are acutely aware of a significant line that was dropped or changed in a production we haven't seen in years. That's why the missed laugh in *Fiddler* was so noticeable. We had seen it on Broadway and film over the decades with three different leads and had produced it at our university two years before we saw that production.

On stage, the director has to focus the attention of the audience by more subtle means. The visual elements must be controlled so they don't detract or distract from key dialogue. The speaking actor must be emphasized at these key points. The actor must have particularly clear speech, because a line of dialogue can't be fixed in the control room later. What the audience hears at that performance is all they get.

In Shakespeare's time, audiences spoke of going to hear a play rather than to see it. Auditorium means "hearing place" in Latin. Although theatre comes from the Greek word for "seeing place," the Greeks used to say, "Let's go hear a play." All the technology in the world won't save a play that can't be heard and understood.

TV Listening

Years ago, the late Princess Diana was being pilloried by late night comedians about the supposed affair with her riding instructor. One night, David Letterman made a joke about it that fell totally flat. The audience just didn't get it. Letterman looked as if he could murder a writer, but that wasn't the problem. His articulation wasn't clear. The audience heard "writing instructor," and the joke made no sense. By the time we figured out what he meant, the monologue was three jokes down the line. So whether it is a line by Neil Simon, a late night one-liner, or a Shakespearian epigram, the audience has to hear it immediately and correctly and not take the time to figure out later what the actor meant to say.

What is the next to the last line of the theme song of "All In the Family"? You have probably heard the song dozens of times. It's "Gee, our old LaSalle ran great," but that is a hard line to decipher for two reasons.

First, they are singing a line with a bunch of "soft" consonants, like "l," "r," and "n"—the only hard one is the t in "great." (They don't sing the d on old—they sing "ole.") Second, what is a LaSalle? The reference to a long-discontinued line of autos makes no sense to most people under sixty and a few who are older.

Film Listening

Several friends watched the DVD of *Mystic River* on an excellent high-end sound system. Certain key dialogue lines were unclear. Even using the rewind button, we could not always decide what the line was supposed to be. We had to employ the subtitle feature. Whose fault was it? The actor's? The director's? The sound editor's? The company that cut the DVD? Somebody got sloppy and spoiled the flow of the narrative.

In spite of that example, filmgoers usually have a special advantage. In all media, the director's job is to hold the audience's attention. Motion picture directors can control attention by close-ups, careful editing, and sound looping to cut out interferences. In a close-up, the audience can also lip-read as well as hear a key line. Unfortunately, it isn't that easy for the TV director for reasons we'll discuss later.

All Media

In film or television work, postproduction often lets sloppy dialogue slip by because familiarity breeds contentment. We have heard it so often, and it is right on the page in front of us, so we mistake seeing the dialogue for hearing it. Stage directors, after sitting through what seems to be innumerable rehearsals, may think they heard entire lines that have been skipped.

Ultimately it is the director's responsibility to see that the actor knows what he or she is saying. The actor is responsible for learning the lines and for knowing what the line means. As a director, you can't learn the lines for the actor, but you need to be sure the actor knows what the lines mean. Some actors may have the mentality of parrots—they can say the words, but they have no idea of what they really mean. In other cases, they misunderstand the ideas or interpret them incorrectly.

The director has to make clear all the elements, both visual and aural, so that the end result is complete and the emphasis, moment to moment, is properly balanced. One aspect of listening is often out of your control on any project. Go to a Broadway musical. Try to listen to the lyrics. The sound is so loud that the lines are lost. I often have to put my fingers in my ears to avoid acute pain. Yet each time I complain to the sound engineer—and I track these people down to complain to them—I am told that management wants it that way. It's audience abuse, and you can't always blame it on the director. I have yet to figure out the rationale for performing a live musical at a decibel level that violates the safety standards of the Occupational Safety and Health Administration.

When the sound is deafening in a movie theatre, blame the management. Seriously, track down the manager and complain. If enough people did it, perhaps the problem would lessen. We can understand why they turn up the volume during previews and commercials—everyone is talking and no one is paying attention. But why do they play the entire film that way in some cinemas? (We always choose our local Carmike over the Cinemark for the sound levels.)

Watch

One of your responsibilities is to see that the final production, in any medium, contains all the dialogue spoken so it can be understood. You have to watch the script as well as listen carefully to do this. You can't learn the lines for the actor, but you can have theAssistant Director (AD) for stage, or script supervisor for screen) keep an eye on the script at each run-through.

We ask the script watcher—usually a prompter, script supervisor, or an AD—to put a slash beside the line the actor missed. If the actor misses a line just once, no problem. That is part of the rehearsal process, and the actor was probably more aware of it than the AD. If the actor misses the same line a second time, the person following the script marks a second slash across the first one, forming an X. At the end of the rehearsal, the prompter lets each actor know which lines had X's. Then the prompter erases that X. If the director is made aware that the actor has had a number of X's on the same line, then it's up to the director to figure out what is giving the actor trouble. Most times, the actor thinks the line has another meaning, and it doesn't make sense to him or her in context.

Naturally, actors need to know the sense and context of the line. It is supposed to be their jobs to do all the research on their characters. They should know what their lines mean, how their characters fit into the script, and all that other good stuff actors are supposed to learn. But you had better know it all. You look like a jerk in rehearsals if someone asks a question and you give the wrong answer.

You can't count on the actor necessarily having done all the homework you have done on the production. You could have been working on the script for months before casting. The actors may have had the scripts a day before the first rehearsal. If you are doing *Hamlet*, be sure you know what a bodkin is. Don't depend on the actor to find out for you. If you don't know what every line of that script means, you are not ready to start rehearsal.

You need to "read" actors as they rehearse. For instance, even if an actor seems to know the lines, you may hear him or her inhale deeply—almost like sucking in air—at certain points. You can bet that the actor is about to dry up and forget a line. Why do actors do that? Many of them have this habit, but we don't know why. When you hear actors inhale like that, you know they are weak on the script at that point.

William Ball wrote a terrific book, *A Sense of Direction*,[13] with a wonderful suggestion in it. It's scary, but it works—in live theatre productions. If any actor gets a crazy idea, like she wants to play her part, that of a forty-eight-year-old woman, pregnant, you don't just say, "no," (that is the hard part.); you say, "try it." In a couple of rehearsals, the actor will (almost always) realize the idea doesn't work and abandon it on her own. Then she will start coming up with some really good stuff that adds wonderfully to her character. Read the book to see how the system works.

Ball's technique may not work in a film or television production for several reasons. First, the actor may not have the script or the part or even the character long enough to get an idea about the character. Then he won't have enough rehearsal time to realize it doesn't work and come up with a better idea. Finally, someone else on the set is sure to immediately tell him it doesn't work and to cut out the crap and get down to business. That actor won't dare to think for himself ever again, but he will never try a foolish notion either.

What Is Style?

We are not discussing the kinds of clothes you wear so that people will know you are the director. We need to look at style as an inescapable element of a director's craft. In the short version, style means way. It's the way something is done. Styles come in four main types. We can speak of personal style, regional style, historical style, and philosophical style. In each case, the way things are done changes under the influence of each of these styles.

Personal Style

Personal style means the way you do things. You already have a style, even if you don't recognize it. When people say, "That's just like you," they are commenting on their view of your style. You probably tend to pick clothes a lot like other clothes you already own—that reflects your style of dress. You have a speaking style, a writing style, and so on.

When you are familiar with a professional person's work, you can recognize his or her style. If you can't tell Beethoven from Mozart, you are not familiar with classical music. If you can tell one hip-hop artist from another within sixteen bars, you have a lot more familiarity with the genre than we do.

Someone's style can be studied through observation, even if it is not obvious immediately. If you really study the medium, you can spot the directorial style of different people. Think of the work of directors you like. You can probably write a few sentences about each one, describing the way he or she does things. Even if you have not watched them directing, you can spot the differences in their productions. If you have seen them at work, you can see the stylistic differences in the way they approach their tasks.

When you tell a classmate how Professor A differs in the classroom from Professor B, you are comparing their styles. When you notice that business school professors tend to dress more formally than political science professors, you are also commenting about style.

Football quarterbacks and coaches have different personal styles, as do baseball pitchers. Cars have style—you are very familiar with them. Cooks have style. You can see the different ways they cook and the differences in the taste of their productions, too! As you grow and develop, your directing style will change. Whether or not you are aware of it, you will develop your own style.

Great artists usually study the styles of others—other practitioners, other periods, other places, and other idea systems. They learn the basics of their craft and then, out of all that knowledge and experience, their own styles emerge, develop, and improve.

Regional Style

Regional styles are most apparent in architecture. You recognize the basic differences in the design of buildings in different regions. Most of the original differences in these designs came out of the actual needs of the geography and climate. Flat roofs work in some climates, while they are less energy efficient and less useful in others. Without getting into a long discussion of the requirements dictated by the climate, these differences exist. Even though modern technology allows us to build almost any building in almost any place, these stylistic differences originated for very practical reasons.

We see those differences in our own professions. We talk about New York actors and LA actors. We see great differences in the films of Russian directors and Italian directors, or Hollywood and Bollywood[14] films. It isn't just language that separates a Canadian film from a Mexican film. These differences are regional. Look at "CSI" (the original set in Las Vegas), "CSI: Miami," and "CSI: New York." You can see differences in everything from the looks of the actors to the look of the settings. They have to have a different look to reflect the different localities in which they take place.

Regional differences exist in many professions. Dentists say they can spot from a new patient's dental work what part of the country the previous dentist was trained. And plastic surgeons say they can tell where film stars had their lifts done by the stylistic structural differences in the results.

Period Style

Period styles are most obvious in furniture, but you can see them in clothing, houses, novels, and films. In the United States, entire neighborhoods were developed in the same time period, and all the houses have a similar period look about them.

An interesting use of period style can be found in the recent film, *The Aviator*[15] (2004). It was shot in the film stock of the period in which the scene is taking place. So a 1927 scene was shot on the kind of film that was used in the 1920s, and so on. Other examples of film with unique looks include *Moby Dick*[16] (1956), which looks very much like a watercolor, *Dick Tracy*[17] (1990), which looks like a Sunday newspaper cartoon, and *Hero*,[18] (2002) which has the appearance of classic Chinese murals.

The writer Ernest Hemingway had a distinct personal style as well as a very twentieth century period style in his writing. As you channel surf, you can spot within minutes what period that old movie is from. Whatever else your future personal style will have, it will have a twenty-first century style about it. You would have to work very hard to have it otherwise.

Philosophical Style

Philosophical style is not a particularly good name for the final style factor we discuss, but we can't come up with a better one. Even our definition could stand improvement. We say philosophical style is the result of all the "isms" you believe in. If you follow Catholicism, romanticism, socialism, negativism—any belief or combination of belief systems you uphold—your work will reflect these beliefs.

Let's take your political "ism." You and a friend with a different political "ism" watch the evening news together. You both hear the same fact—Congress passed a certain bill today. One of you will be pleased and the other disgusted. Our reactions to the same stimuli are filtered through our belief systems. You interpret the world a certain way, and it is reflected in your work.

We two authors have entirely different political leanings. One of us is as far to the Left as the other is to the Right—so we figure that as a team we are in perfect balance! But as directors, our choice of material and method of execution are undoubtedly altered by these perceptions, even if we don't realize it. In writing this book, we discovered, and you can too, which of us wrote which parts. The liberal tends to use active voice more than passive, and the conservative tends to use passive voice more than active. Why are there more active voice sentences than passive? The liberal did the final edit.

Religious beliefs or lack of them certainly influence the artist. So do all the other beliefs a person has. This comes out in the way an artist behaves in every day life as well as in the artist's creations. Many times, the differences we notice in the style of a favorite artist are a reflection of a change of values—artistic or other values.

In painting, we see a vast difference in the works of artists. They come from very similar backgrounds in all the other respects; yet their way of seeing the universe is very different. Look at Van Gogh, Manet, and Monet. Although they would seem to end up with very similar styles, they are so different. An impressionist sees the world with a completely different view than an expressionist, who can't understand the view of a cubist.

Summing Up Style

Theatre follows many of the same trends as painting, only it seems to take longer for the movements to become evident in theatre. Someone theorized that artistic movements always start with the cheapest trends and then move more slowly towards the more expensive ones. An artistic movement like expressionism costs a painter only a few dollars per painting to practice. Then, if the stuff doesn't sell, the investment is not that great. As a movement gains in popularity, it seems to spread to the more expensive arts. A composer will first write small string quartets in an experimental form before writing a symphony. It takes more people to support the symphony—both more performers and a greater audience base. Only when it is more popular with both performers and audiences can it become more widespread.

Theatre movements start in small venues, too, and then spread to larger ones. University theatres can afford financially to do riskier and more experimental works than Broadway. (However, many times university theatres don't do these kinds of works because of community or administrative pressure.)

Small independent filmmakers start artistic developments that take a while to spread to the commercial screen. Large-scale commercial operations of any sort are usually run by business people who worry about the net profit and the stock market impact of their decisions. They rarely take chances on anything that is not already proven.

Directors of film should know the style and simplicity of John Ford. Steven Spielberg once said his three best directing influences were John Ford, John Ford, and John Ford. Still, you would never mistake a Spielberg film for one of Ford's. Spielberg reacted to criticism that he couldn't direct without using a camera crane and made *Schindler's List* (1993) specifically without using a crane.

Some directors are noted for the fact that they move the camera a great deal while others rarely move at all. Look at the work of Orson Wells[19] and his use of both a still camera (*Citizen Kane*, 1941) and the camera in motion (the first five minutes of *Touch of Evil*, 1958).

We need to remind ourselves that there are lots of rules about directing, but no laws. There are rules to tell you when to move the camera or where to place it. But they are only guides—things that generally tend to work well. When you decide to break or change or make up a new rule, those decisions all come from you and out of your style. They reflect how you see the world and how you see the story you are trying to tell. Great directors step back and become unseen, unless someone is studying their work. Your style will become evident to you and your critics the more you work. Most of the audience may not notice, nor should they.

A Hollywood phrase says it very well: "We're not in the motion picture business; we're in the *emotion* picture business." When the director becomes more important than the story, in any medium, the audience suffers, the story suffers, and ultimately, you will suffer.

Suggested Reading and Viewing

Reading

Stage
Albright, Hardie. *Stage Direction in Transition*. See chapter 5.
Catron, Louis E. *The Director's Vision*.

Hodge, Francis. *Play Directing: Analysis, Communication and Style.*
Russell, Douglas A. *Theatrical Style.*
Vaughan, Stuart, *Directing Plays.* See chapter 3.

Screen
Armer, Alan A. *Directing Television And Film.* See chapter 1.
Lukas, Christopher. *Directing for Film and Television.* See chapter 4.
Proferes, Nicholas T. *Film Directing Fundamentals: From Script to Stage.* St.
  Louis: Focal Press, 2001. See chapter 1.

Suggested Viewing
Try watching the DVDs of well-respected films, and make every effort to observe
directors in action.

Notes

1. An affluent aristocrat and chief of a small German principality who studied
   the arts and created his own court theatre group in 1866 (the Meininger
   Players), the duke served as theatrical director and designer of this company
   and developed many of the basic principles of modern acting, stage design,
   and directing.
2. *A Stranger in the Mirror* (1993; TV, novel); "If Tomorrow Comes" (1986; TV
   miniseries, novel); *The Naked Face* (1984, novel); "Master of the Game"
   (1984; TV miniseries, novel); *Rage of Angels* (1983; TV, novel); "Hart to
   Hart" (1979; TV series; creator, writer); "I Dream of Jeannie" (1965; TV
   series; creator, executive producer, producer); *Dream Wife* (1953).
3. "Boston Legal" (2004; TV series; creator, executive producer); "Boston
   Public" (2000; TV series; creator, writer [multiple episodes, executive pro-
   ducer]; *Mystery, Alaska* (1999; TV; writer, producer); "Ally McBeal" (1997;
   TV series; creator, executive producer); "The Practice" (1997; TV series;
   creator, executive producer; "Chicago Hope" (1994; TV series; creator,
   writer); "Picket Fences" (1992; TV series; creator, writer); "Doogie Howser,
   M.D." (1989; TV series; creator, writer).
4. "The West Wing" (1999; TV series; creator, writer, executive producer)
   "Sports Night" (1998; TV series; creator, writer, executive producer); *The
   American President* (1995; writer); *A Few Good Men* (1992; play, screenplay).
5. *Breathless* (1983); *Femme d'à côté, La* (1981; screenplay); *Fahrenheit 451*
   (1966; screenplay, director); *Jules et Jim* (1962; adaptation and dialogue,
   director); *Close Encounters of the Third Kind* (1977, actor).
6. Sarris is generally credited in the United States with popularizing the theory
   and coining the term "auteur theory" in his essay *Notes on the Auteur
   Theory*. He is also the cofounder of the National Society of Film Critics. For
   many years he wrote for *The Village Voice*. His most influential book was
   The American Cinema: Directors and Directions 1929–1968.

7. Ford directed over 145 feature films including *Cheyenne Autumn* (1964); *Donovan's Reef* (1963); *The Man Who Shot Liberty Valance* (1962); *Two Rode Together* (1961); *The Searchers* (1956); *Mister Roberts* (1955); *The Long Gray Line* (1955); *The Quiet Man* (1952); *Rio Grande* (1950); *She Wore a Yellow Ribbon* (1949); *3 Godfathers* (1948); *Fort Apache* (1948); *My Darling Clementine* (1946); *They Were Expendable* (1945); *How Green Was My Valley* (1941); *The Grapes of Wrath* (1940); *Drums Along the Mohawk* (1939); *Young Mr. Lincoln* (1939); *Stagecoach* (1939); *The Informer* (1935); and *The Iron Horse* (1924).

8. *Band of Brothers* (HBO) was directed by Phil Alden Robinson (part 1), Richard Loncraine (part 2), Mikael Solomon (part 3), David Nutter (part 4), Tom Hanks (part 5), David Leland (part 6), David Frankel (parts 7 and 9), and Tony To (part 8).

9. Rich is an award-winning TV director whose series include "The Man in the Family" (1991); "Murphy Brown" (1988); "Newhart" (1982); "Benson" (1979); "Barney Miller" (1975); "The Jeffersons" (1975); "Good Times" (1974); "Maude" (1972); "Sanford and Son" (1972); "All in the Family" (1971); "The Brady Bunch" (1969); "My World and Welcome to It" (1969); "Hogan's Heroes" (1965); "I Spy" (1965); "Run for Your Life" (1965); "Gilligan's Island" (1964); "Gomer Pyle, U.S.M.C." (1964); "The Dick Van Dyke Show" (1961); "The Andy Griffith Show" (1960); "The Twilight Zone" (1959); "Bonanza" (1959); "The Rifleman" (1958); "Gunsmoke" (1955); "I Married Joan" (1952); and "Our Miss Brooks" (1952). Rich is also a TV producer whose credits include "MacGyver" (1985; executive producer); "Benson" (1979; executive producer); and "All in the Family" (1971; producer).

10. The shooting schedule mushroomed from 52 to 155 days.

11. Director Richard Stanley got fired from his dream project, *The Island of Dr. Moreau* (1996), by actor Val Kilmer and was replaced with John Frankenheimer.

12. Tenure is an academic state of almost perpetual employment granted to scholars who have "proven themselves" of value to a college or university through scholarship or creative publication/production, service, and teaching.

13. William Ball, *A Sense of Direction*.

14. "Bollywood" films are films made in India's massive film production business.

15. Directed by Martin Scorsese.

16. Directed by John Huston.

17. Directed by Warren Beatty.

18. Also called *Ying xiong*, directed by Yimou Zhang.

19. Wells was a director, writer, and actor whose directing credits include *Touch of Evil* (1958); *Macbeth* (1948); *The Lady from Shanghai* (1947; uncredited); *The Stranger* (1946); *The Magnificent Ambersons* (1942); and *Citizen Kane* (1941).

3

What About the Script?

The script is your starting point. For our purposes, we regard the director as the person who interprets the script and the writer as the person who composes it. At times, that is the same person. Perhaps the person is called the "writer-director" (the hyphenate). But this chapter deals with the script from the point of view of someone who is not involved in its creation. Someone else wrote the script, and the director decides to execute it.

What is the best way to learn to direct? Work on scripts that have already been produced and are available either online or in book form. You know the material has worked. It has been more or less successful in the past. Now you need to decide if you like it well enough to spend the time needed to carry it out. You may feel you have something to contribute to the process. Your job is not to slavishly imitate a production you saw on stage, TV, or in a film or to copy one you acted in when you were in high school. Your job is to see the script with a fresh pair of eyes and bring it to life—or back to life.

Analysis

You have read the script several times. You have developed your personal reaction to it. You have your own sense and feel of it. You are ready to analyze it.

Analysis is not a dirty word. Many young directors think they should operate strictly out of their gut feelings. They dislike the idea of analysis because they think it has a dry, academic ring to it. They are afraid analysis will "destroy" their love of the script and the process. They think they can operate out of their guts and make all the right decisions by instinct.

Actually, once you have decided you like the script, you need to develop your own perception of it. Perception implies both the strong feeling you have for the script and a basic objective awareness of how the script works. Perception is your total view of the script after you have felt it and then examined it closely.

If your feelings are strong after the first reading and you have analyzed the script thoroughly, you will have a much greater respect for, and understanding of, the script. A script is an artificial object you can disassemble and reassemble as you can any other object made by a human being.

Think of analysis as your *objective support* for your feelings about the script. Directing is not a totally intuitive process. You need to learn the strengths and weaknesses of the material in order to do the best possible job of putting the material on stage or on film. It is safer to learn to analyze realistic scripts rather than those with unusual stylistic elements. Learning to analyze is a process, and it is a bit easier to learn on realistically grounded pieces.

When you are *directing* a script, you should write down your analysis. Then you will be prepared to communicate it effectively to the actors, designers, and others involved in the production. You already know that at least one third of the time spent on a project should be spent in preparation before you ever see an actor, a rehearsal hall, or a studio. This is part of your homework. That means you do it at home, before you come to the workplace, not as you are trying to get the second phase of the process done.

Doing your homework requires writing it down. That way, you won't forget it, and the important ideas won't get lost. Yes, you can change them, but you should not have to keep reinventing them. It becomes easier, not harder, to include the good ideas of others—actors, designers, cinematographers—if you have your homework written and done before you meet with them.

Different people work differently, but the steps in the next section, as originated by stage directors and longtime theatre teachers Stuart Vaughn[1] and Francis Hodge,[2] seem to us as good ways to analyze. Other methods can be found in the readings suggested at the end of this chapter. Any of these methods should do until you are experienced enough to develop your own method of analysis. Then again, why reinvent the wheel?

Before we start on analysis, here's a suggestion. At this point, forget about the screen or stage directions or anything else in parentheses in the script. Use only the *dialogue* as the source of your information. If you're dealing with a stage script, you are working on material that has been produced previously. All the words that are not dialogue are most likely directions for another version of the script. They are the work of the "people behind the curtain" for that specific production. Pay no attention, at this point, to the people behind the curtain. In a screenplay or teleplay, the visuals in the script are important. But when you're starting your analysis, as with a stage play, focus on the dialogue.

Once you have finished your initial analysis, you can do your research. What have other people done with this material or these kinds of material? Is the work historically accurate? Does it have to be? But start with the script first.

Whether you are directing, acting, or designing, you should be able to take a script and do a good analysis of it. You can't do a good job working on a script in any of those capacities without knowing the basic steps of analysis.

If you have taken dramatic literature courses, much of this material is already familiar to you. You have come across most of it, sometimes in different forms. If the material is not familiar, this chapter should give you a variety of tools to analyze a script.

But we first should define our terms before we look any further in script analysis. Don't get put off by all the terms. After all, these are the words you will use, and it is important to know what they mean. These are part of the vocabulary of your profession. Would you trust a mechanic who told you that the thingy disconnected from the doohickey?

Defining the Terms of Dramatic Analysis

Presumptions

Let's start with our basic presumptions.

What is *art*? Your definition affects your judgment and perception. Look at it this way. In previous centuries and in some cultures today, the definition of what constitutes art is clearly spelled out. In the United States today, we tend to say, "If you think it's art, then it's art."

Would you spend $75,000 for a toilet and have it placed in your living room as a work of art? Someone else did. True, we think they are crazy. Yet, some of us saw an art exhibition in a modern art museum in London. One piece was a urinal, mounted sideway. It actually looked rather lovely. We assume the artist was trying to say that sometimes things look different from a different point of view. Sometimes the most ordinary objects have an unexpected beauty. So we can be willing to consider it art, even if we are still unwilling to buy it. At the Guggenheim Museum in Bilbao, Spain, a group of us saw an installation that looked exactly like a gigantic pile of fecal material. Obviously some Guggenheim representative thought it was art and bought it. To us, it was still a pile of s—t.

In our culture, we define the term "art" very freely. We even speak of the culinary arts, the artistry of a sports performance, and so on. It's a free country. The art is expensive, but the country is free. Remember that when we talk about theatre, we are talking about the art of storytelling that employs actors performing a script for an audience—on stage and screen.

Live theatre can be the most ephemeral of the arts because it is live. Ephemeral means momentary, impermanent. No two performances can exactly duplicate each other. Electronic theatre has the advantage of being the same at every showing. Once it is on tape or on film, it remains the same performance each time it is seen. Yet the fact that no two performances of a live production are the same gives the performance an excitement and immediacy that adds to our satisfaction as actors and audience members.

Have you seen *Noises Off*[3] (1992) as a film? It is wildly funny, and the entire cast does a wonderful job. Yet something more exciting happens when we see it reasonably well performed on stage. All that business with the sardines has to be perfect on stage each time. If Carol Burnett[4] or another actor had messed up a take, the director could reshoot the scene. When we see a live performance and it works, it is the difference between homemade cake and a Hostess Twinkie. The cake is ephemeral, too. It won't be quite the same the next time you use the recipe.

Theatre tends to be the most powerful of the arts because it involves more of our senses as audience members. Symphony audiences hear a great variety of sounds, but there really is very little for them to see in comparison to a play or film. That's why symphonies today, in an attempt to increase audiences, are trying to add visual elements to what is basically an auditory medium.

Painting, architecture, and sculpture are essentially visual. When other elements are added, the work is often redefined as performance art. Today's audiences expect a greater degree of stimulation and more of a multisensory experience in their arts as well as their lives. Even some pricier restaurants are becoming theatrical experiences. Theatre uses our eyes and our ears, so it tends to be more involving than some of the other arts. The more of our senses we are using, the more powerfully we are involved.

Theatre is the most objective art because it is peopled with human beings. The level of abstraction that can be reached with live theatre or film is generally less than music or even painting. This is a good thing. It is easier to fathom the meaning of a play or a film than a piece of music.

That gives both music and theatre their special attributes. And that is why we now use so much music in stage and film, to get both the abstraction and the objectivity. Generally, theatrical works tend to be more specific. They use human beings speaking words to get across ideas, so the ideas are more immediate and accessible.

So that brings up our next point. Theatre is the most complex art because it uses many or all the other arts in its creation. Theatre uses music, light, sound, sight, dance, architecture, and many other art forms in a single work of art. When artists use all those elements in another art form, they transform it into theatre. They even give it a different name, like performance art.

What is the difference between theatre and drama? Not a lot. For academic purposes, we say that theatre is on the stage and drama is on the page. Generally, we tend to refer to scripts as drama, such as dramatic literature. We tend to refer to theatre as performance, a script that is staged. Usually these days, the two terms are used interchangeably.

For our purpose, we expand the definition of theatre even more. We call theatrical productions on television and film "theatre," to the horror of some of our colleagues. They call this inclusion blasphemy. Many traditional theatre people think film and television are crass, unworthy, and unartistic. Obviously, we hold a different view.

What is the difference between "theatre" and "theater"? Basically, it is just the spelling. Academics tend to prefer the term "theatre" to refer to the art in general. Actually, "theatre" is supposed to be the French spelling and "theater" the British (and *New York Times*) spelling. Just be consistent. Some people refer to the building as a theater and to the art as the theatre.

Because theatre is so powerful, we tend to be drawn into it and feel the same emotions as the characters. We cry when something bad happens to a character we like. We scream when something very scary or exciting happens, even though, deep down, we know it is not happening to us. That reaction is *empathy*.

"Pathy" is a Greek root meaning emotion. We feel sympathy when we recognize the emotion of a friend who has lost a parent while ours are still alive. We have not experienced the feeling, but we recognize it. We feel empathy when we know what the experience feels like and tend to relive it somewhat when it happens to another. We feel apathy when we lack the emotion.

Aesthetic distance is an awareness that reminds us it is not real, and while watching Shakespeare's *Othello* (1604), we should not warn the wife Desdemona that her husband Othello is about to put her lights out.

Empathy is the sensation we get when someone describes a bad earache and we grimace in remembered pain. Empathy makes scary movies frighten us. Aesthetic distance keeps us from running out of the theatre when we are scared.

Concepts

Dramatic Action

Dramatic action should be a sequence of events organized to accomplish the purpose of the script. The writer has a world of choices to make. A good writer chooses those events that will make the audience know what the writer wants them to know. Dramatic action leaves out all the actions that could have happened, or even did happen, that are not part of the purpose of the script.

Purposeful
Generally, good dramatic action is purposeful—*it* leads to the end the writer wants. It includes those events that advance the story. Just because I had lunch today doesn't mean you have to know about it if it is not part of the story I'm trying to tell.

Complete and Self-Contained
The story is able to stand by itself and not depend upon the audience having to see something else in order to "get it." Most films that are sequels don't depend on your having seen the other part. *Shrek*[5] (2001), *Shrek II*[6] (2004), and Shrek III (2008) are each complete and self-contained. What about *Kill Bill: Vol. 1* (2003) and *Kill Bill: Vol. 2*[7] (2004), or *The Matrix*,[8] or the *Lord of the Rings*[9] trilogies (2001, 2002, 2003)? Soap operas are just the opposite. They are designed to be incomplete so you will continue to watch them.

As important as this characteristic is in some forms of theatre, it may be less important in others. TV series, as writer-producer Aaron Sorkin[10] points out, are about "middles" as opposed to "beginnings" or "ends." Steven Bochco[11] introduced the three-stories-at-a-time concept: one story line beginning, the second in the middle, and number three concluding in each episode.

Varied
While a script does not need to be action-packed, it should have some variety in it to avoid monotony. If you have not seen some of the incredibly boring films of the experimental auteurs,[12] you don't know what

boredom is.[13] On the other hand, if you have ever had a long class with a professor who has no vocal variety, you have a good idea. Nearly everything is more engaging when there is variety, even a fifty-minute lecture.

Engaging and Interesting
If it isn't interesting, why would I watch it? Exactly what is interesting? That's a bit more problematic. We all know what interesting is—we just can't define it. And we discover that what is interesting to me is not always interesting to you. Isn't that interesting!

Probable
It must be able to occur within the logical system created by the writer. The story should be able to happen in the world of the playwright. The world of Star Wars[14](1977) or any of its sequels[15] may contain all sorts of incidents that would be both improbable and impossible in a Civil War film. But in the universe of Star Wars, the improbable is the reality.

Conflict

Conflict refers to the elements in the narrative that arouse and maintain our interest and suspense. The action of a drama is usually arranged in a climactic order, with conflicts occurring all along the story line. Conflict does not necessarily mean physical violence. The character may have a conflict of values with which to contend. The work could be a conflict of ideas between two different people. Political debates are full of conflict, but not violence—we hope! The story of "The Village of the Happy People" has no conflict and is, therefore, boring.

Plot

Plot is the overall structure of a play. It is the *story line*. Plot involves the story events told in sequence and refers to the organization of all the elements into a meaningful pattern. When someone asks you what happens, you summarize the main events of the story. You have given the plot. A plot is a carefully constructed story, like a good joke, which works only if the plot is resolved in a surprising, yet satisfying way.

Traditionally, the script contains all or most of the following ten elements.

Beginning
The audience needs to know the world of the script, so the writer usually sets up the following steps in the beginning of the script: the

exposition, the inciting incident, the point of attack, and the major dramatic question.

Exposition. The exposition sets forth the necessary information. Who are these people? Where and when is the story taking place? This is where many of the given circumstances come out.

Inciting Incident. The inciting incident is an occurrence that sets the main action in motion. Some event starts the story off. It's the first action of the story. A letter arrives. Someone comes in with some bad news.

Point of Attack. The point of attack is the time at which the story is taken up. If you write a script that starts at the beginning of a person's life and ends at his death sixty years later, that is an early point of attack.

Many of Shakespeare's plays have fairly early points of attack. Scholars argue how long a time span *Hamlet* (1602) has. It has to last a number of months. Rosencrantz and Guildenstern must get all the way to England and the news has to come back. *Gone with the Wind*[16] (1939) has a very early point of attack.

If the script starts shortly before it ends, it has a late point of attack. In many Greek plays, the time period in which the play takes place is only a couple of hours. Events that happened before the play starts are mentioned and previous necessary information is brought in, but the play resolves itself in less than two hours of both stage and real time.

In Sophocles' immortal Greek tragedy *Oedipus Rex* (468 BC), for instance, the detective (Oedipus) discovers that a crime has been committed. In an hour and a half, he solves the mystery, discovers the murderer (himself), and metes out the punishment he has promised. The shorter the script, the more likely it is to have a late point of attack.

Citizen Kane[17] (1941) has a late point of attack. The entire film is told in a series of flashbacks, sometimes telling the same events from different points of view. *O Brother, Where Art Thou*[18] (2000) is another example of a story told from a late point of attack. The story is a chase with all the necessary information about the past spelled out as needed through the dialogue. Don't worry too much about point of attack. It is just a phrase meaning "where the story begins."

Major Dramatic Question. The major dramatic question is the thread or spine that holds the events together; it is the focal point, frequently the *controlling idea*, on which an action is centered. It controls the dramatic action. We will discuss more about this later.

Middle

Complication. Complication is any new element that alters the course of the action. A second letter arrives with news that changes things. Something happens to "complicate" the current situation. It does not have to be good or bad. It merely has to complicate matters.

Discovery. Discovery occurs when the script reveals something not previously known by the audience. Not everyone in the script is in on the discovery. We find out when A tells B that C is illegitimate. C might not discover it until later or not at all. In another story, a trace of the victim's blood is found in the truck of the suspect. These are discoveries.

Crisis. Crisis is the turning point of an action. A work can have a number of crises, but usually it has just one climax. Every time the situation gets changed by events or actions, a crisis will occur. Yes, it is a lot like a complication, but we usually think of a crisis as being a more substantial change in the situation.

End

Climax. Climax is the peak of intensity. The climax typically occurs when things reach their most crucial point, usually near the end of the script. In one script, the murderer stands there with the gun, ready to do in the hero. In another script, she walks away to leave him forever as he agonizes whether he should dare to tell her he loves her.

Resolution. Resolution is the final portion of the script, from crisis to final credits or curtain. Denouement is the French word for it. In one script, the murderer is caught just as he is about to kill the last victim and is cuffed, read his rights, and led away by the ever-vigilant policeman. In another, the hero finally comes to his senses, chases after the girl, and proposes.

Obligatory Scene

The obligatory scene is what happens ever after. Once the script has reached and resolved the critical issues, a short scene usually occurs to "wrap up" the story. In our first example, the killer gets led off in handcuffs, and the potential victims smile and hug each other in relief. In the other example, she accepts his proposal, and the music swells as they kiss.

Character

Character can be broken down through these four levels of analysis. This information should be found in the script. Character is revealed through (1) descriptions in stage directions, (2) what the character says, (3) what others say about him, and (4) above all, what he does. Actions speak louder than words, in this case. No matter what others say about the character, we know him by his actions. Other information is provided by the words of the character, though he could be a liar. Other characters can say things about him, but they could be wrong. Tartuffe, the title character in Molière's classic French comedy *Tartuffe*[19] (1664), says he is honorable, but we see by his actions he is not. Orgon, the husband, thinks Tartuffe, the religious leader, is a saint. But we have seen him in action and know he is not. Some modern writers tend to write elaborate character descriptions. These are instructive, but not binding. Remember, you don't have to perform the parentheses, just the dialogue.

The six items that follow list the information that practitioners need to know about the characters. When the information is not present, then the interpreters—designer, *actor*, director—can make it up, but it must not contradict the information in the *dialogue*. (If all the characters in the play call Jack Falstaff[20] "Fat Jack," it is pretty hard to reconcile casting him as a very skinny guy.)

Physical Attributes

Physical attributes are what the character (*not* the actor) looks like. Hamlet is supposed to be Danish, but that doesn't mean he has to be blonde or Danish. Hamlet has very few physical requirements specified in the script. He should be younger than Claudius and Polonius, but there is still a great deal of variety available in the way he can look physically.

Social Status

Economic status, trade, *and* family relationships are examples of social status. How does the character relate to the other characters in terms of social status characteristics? Hamlet is the prince, not the servant.

Psychological Attributes

Habits, attitudes, desires, and motivations are examples of psychological attributes. What is the psychological and emotional makeup of the character? Hamlet's psychological attributes are very complex and drive the story.

Personal Values
These can involve *motives*. What value systems does the character hold? They can be implicit in the script or stated explicitly by the writer. What would drive Hamlet to contemplate murder or suicide? He does both.

Typification
Attributes that make a character like others of his kind are an example of typification. Scripts are done in relatively short periods of time; so the audience needs to be able to grasp all these characters fairly quickly. Having them act or look typical of their group helps the audience members make that identification. A novel can build character over several hundred pages. Scripts are not that long. We tend to think of detectives as being observant. That is typification.

Individuation
Individuation involves *attributes that* make a character differ from others. If all the characters are *too* typical, we say they are stereotypes, so we expect some individual characteristics in the important characters, at least. Monk[21] is an interesting character. Not only is he very observant, like all good detectives, but he has those quirks that make him Monk. You don't confuse him with Colombo,[22] another detective who has his own individual characteristics.

Thought

Thought is another word for *theme*, argument, meaning, or the significance of an action. Theme can be a difficult concept for someone to identify at first. Students, in particular, sometimes find it difficult to distinguish between a theme of a piece and a motif.

Motif

A motif is an idea that appears in a script but is not as fully developed as a *theme*. In another work, that idea could be the theme. If an idea is merely discussed in a script, it is called a motif. That's why we say if you can make a sentence of the idea, it is a theme. If it appears but cannot be put into sentence form, it is probably a motif.

Find the main idea of the script. Put it in a sentence. If you can make a sentence out of it, a generalization, then it is a theme of the work. In *Oedipus Rex*, for instance, you can make up the sentence, "It is better to be physically blind, like Tiresias, a blind prophet, and know the truth, than to be intellectually blind like Oedipus, the king, and have eyes that see." If an idea—not a thing, but a concept—occurs frequently in the script but doesn't seem to develop into a sentence, it is probably a motif.

In *Oedipus Rex*, we can make a theme out of blindness. In Henrik Ibsen's *The Wild Duck*[23] (1885), blindness is significant but may not be a real theme in your mind. In the film *The Sixth Sense*[24] (1999), the twist in the story works when the audience is blind, like some of writer-director M. Night Shyamalan's characters.

You may decide it is just a motif. Blindness, light, and darkness are concepts that are often used in scripts as motifs but not as themes. Someone could argue that every character in *The Wild Duck*[25] (1885) is blind to something. That person would say that the theme is "everyone is blind to some truth or another, even if everyone has physical sight." So, it is possible for different people to interpret the same work different ways and get different themes and motifs from it. That is the basis for different interpretations of the same script.

Remember, a theme is more than a single word. The term "blindness" by itself tells us nothing. Depending on what the script and the production do, the end result could be "Blindness is a good thing" or "Only the deserving get blindness." A better way is to make a sentence out of the theme using the words "leads to." For example, "Moral blindness leads to destruction," or "Curing one's emotional blindness leads to greater awareness and understanding."

Many contemporary directors prefer the term "spine." Theme has a leftover feeling from poor English classes that may leave us feeling trapped. Spine means the same thing—a one-sentence statement of the script's message, what idea it has to convey.

Be careful of going way off the deep end and violating the integrity of the script. If you must, do it to a writer whose work is not copyrighted. Practically everyone has violated poor Shakespeare. Think of those awful movies featuring famous bad actors in "revisionist" Shakespeare. Try to do better than that.

When you select a spine, anything goes, as long as it is not contradicted by anything in the text of the script and every part of the script contributes to the spine. When you have formulated the spine, you should read the script over again. If you find exceptions, parts of the script that don't fit the spine, look for a better, stronger spine.

We say that a good script has *universality*—the quality of a script that allows it to communicate with audiences. It "says something to me." If it were not for universality of theme, no one else but you would get what the writer was trying to communicate.

The material also should have *individuation*—uniqueness. The script has to be something more than a remake of the same old material. Most films with a number behind them are considered weaker than the original. *Rocky*[26] (1976) seems to have a lot to communicate, while *Rocky IV*[27] (1985) and *Rocky V*[28] (1990) seem to be just a bunch of fight scenes. Some recent sequels, like *Shrek II*[29] (2004) and *Spider-Man 2*[30] (2004), are considered even better than the originals—not because more blood was spattered or more bullets were fired, as in so many sequels, but because these sequels had different and even more interesting themes than the first movies.

Dialogue

Dialogue is a term meaning the *words of the characters*. The dialogue lines are the main source of your analytical information. The dialogue spoken by the characters reveals information, reveals character, directs attention, reveals theme and ideas, establishes tone and level of probability, and establishes tempo and rhythm.

Reveals Information

Actually, all the information the audience needs should be in the dialogue, not the stage directions. The rule holds true in plays always and in films most of the time. We once worked on a play in which the playwright had one of the characters open and drink six beers in the course of the show. We pointed out that we had no obligation to put that many beers in the production. The playwright revised the dialogue so A said to B late in the play, "That's the sixth beer you've had since you came in here." Then we had to figure out how to block the play so the actor opened six beers by that point in the script.

Needless to say, the actor didn't drink all that beer; the character did. Each night we had to drain an entire six-pack through a tiny hole in the bottom of each can, and leave the tabs intact so he could pop them. The prop crew cried at the waste of beer, and the audience was very impressed by the actor's apparent liquid capacity. But we didn't change the dialogue.

Reveals Character

You get a pretty good idea about an element of B's character by the six beers.

Directs Attention

Dialogue directs attention to important plot elements. It is very important to the plot that B is a loser and an alcoholic.

Reveals Theme and Ideas

The play was about people who were united in that they were all at the end of the line—in a position where they were down as far as they could go, in one sense or another.

Establishes Tone and Level of Probability
It also establishes tone and level of probability. Clearly, from the one line we quoted, you know the play is probably modern, realistic, and not about rich people. Someone wealthy might drink a more expensive beverage. Brandy, anyone?

Establishes Tempo and Rhythm
In that single line, we can tell the pace is fairly brisk and the characters are not highly verbal. Dialogue tells you if the material moves along at a rapid clip, is slow and leisurely, or picks up pace here and gets a more languid tempo there.

Spectacle

All the visual elements of the completed work are lumped under the word spectacle. It is not a pair of glasses or a wild sight. Spectacle is everything that is seen in the production: the scenery, the setting, the clothing, the lighting, the camera tonalities, the physical appearance of the actors, and the articles that are visible. All of these elements come under the heading of spectacle—from a Latin word for "watch." It is everything you can watch while attending a production. When done properly, spectacle accomplishes the following: it gives information, aids characterization, establishes level of probability, establishes mood and atmosphere, and should be practical, appropriate, and expressive of the production's values.

Gives Information

In *Who's Afraid of Virginia Woolf*, both the play[31] (1966) and the film[32] (1966) begin with Martha repeating a Bette Davis line from her 1949 film

Beyond the Forest[33] (1949): "What a dump." Actually, particularly in the Davis film, it is a pretty classy joint. We know that from the spectacle. The apartment is elegant looking.

Aids Characterization

We know a great deal about what the character is like from the costume. The minute Tom Cruise, as Vincent, is seen in *Collateral*[34] (2004), we can tell by his suit that he is an extremely successful businessman. The business he is in may be a bad one, but he is doing well in the business with a suit that expensive.

Establishes Level of Probability

You know it is fantasy and science fiction the minute the opening credits start to crawl in the *Star Wars*[35] movies (1977–2005). Everything visually reinforces this information.

Establishes Mood and Atmosphere

It was a dark and stormy night. You know because the spectacle shows you. The first line of George M. Cohan's play *Seven Keys to Baldpate*[36] (1913) tells us, "You know, Mother, I think it's colder in here than it is outside."

Should Be Practical, Appropriate, and Expressive of the Production's Values

First, the door needs to work. Visual elements that mess up a production hurt rather than help it. Second, take the wristwatches off the actors in a period play. The visual elements should be appropriate to the rest of the production. They should match in terms of style, time period, and other production values. Third, a sleazy bar should be totally sleazy, not clean and new. The visual elements should support the story and make it easier to grasp rather than send out confusing messages.

Forms

Forms are the general category for something. We can analyze the formal aspects of works. It is the way we classify them. When we speak of a symphony or a concerto in music, we are talking about its form. We call a television show a situation comedy, a detective story, a quiz show, or a reality show. A film might be a western, a chick flick, sci-fi, or a cartoon.

Fixed or Organic

Some forms are *fixed*, meaning there are rather strict rules in their *composition*. Others are *organic*, meaning the structure comes out of the individual piece rather than the piece fitting a known structure. In poetry, everyone knows what a sonnet is—how many lines, what the rhyme scheme is, and so on. Yet many modern poets produce works that defy standard descriptions. The poem might be about a waterfall and the words on the page are set in type to resemble a physical waterfall, for example. A form like that would be organic—coming out of the work itself. It really isn't that important, but you ought to know the material in your own field well enough to know if it is a standard form or format or if it is different in structure from anything that preceded it.

Cars are forms of transportation, as are trucks, RV's, and campers. Cars and trucks were fairly old forms before a new form, the airplane, came along. The first ones were organic. Now they are fixed. We call them passenger jets, fighters, cargo planes, and so on. Tragedy, comedy, comedy of manners, comedy of ideas, and so on are all classifications of plays by their forms. These forms also appear as types of film or television productions. These words are shorthand to communicate to others what the script is.

Style

Style is the term for traits attributable to a mode of expression, a period, a nation, a movement, or a person. Style can mean a characteristic way. For more information, see Chapter 2.

Symbol

A symbol is an object that assumes greater significance because it becomes emotionally or intellectually linked to ideas larger than itself.

Symbols operate to give a great deal of information by imbuing an object with an emotional load greater than the object itself. A *natural symbol*, such as the sun standing for intellectual illumination, operates on assigning properties in a metaphoric way: the brilliant light of the sun is metaphorically applied to intellectual illumination. Think of the way it contrasts with the moon as a metaphor. Natural symbols are objects found in nature that develop a specific value in a particular culture or in a specific work.

An *arbitrary symbol* is an object that has arbitrary, conventional, or traditional associations with an idea, feeling, or abstraction without any natural or inherent similarities. While the sun is a natural symbol for intellectual illumination, a light bulb has become a cultural or arbitrary symbol for an idea. For instance, the cross and the fish are arbitrary symbols for Christianity. Historical association, not inherent properties, makes the connection meaningful. Other examples include the dollar sign and the symbol for the Euro. Flags are good examples of arbitrary symbols.

A simple object in a script gains great power as it develops or is shown to have symbolic value. You already know how much Othello the Moor values that handkerchief, so you know how devastated he is when Iago, his newly appointed ensign, says he found it in the bed of his wife's former lover, Rodrigo. In *Casablanca*[37] (1942), the "letters of transit" take on weight and meaning beyond a passage out of Nazi-held North Africa.

Genre

Genre is a term for classifying works that have similar characteristics. Groups of films or plays that have similar characteristics are said to be in the same genre. Westerns, detective stories, and romances are examples of genres.

Tragedy

Tragedy has been around so long, it has acquired more definitions than Hilton has hotels. So we made up our own: in tragedy, both the *protagonist* and the *audience* become aware of a major philosophical insight. We say that all plays deal with human behavior. Tragedy and drama usually deal with a *major idea* about human beings and the nature of life, the universe, and so on. Don't define it strictly by the body count at the end. *Hamlet*[38] is not a tragedy because eight corpses litter the stage by the final curtain.

An unusual way to think about tragedy is how critic Walter Kerr[39] puts it: "Tragedy has a happy ending." By this he means not necessarily "happy" but somehow satisfying, even cathartic. The main character may die or sacrifice everything and everyone he or she holds dear, but in so doing, this character has somehow brought about justice to his or her world.

Drama

Drama is a much newer term in theatre history, so we have defined it as follows: in drama, *the audience* gains the awareness, but the *protagonist* does not. By our definition, *Oedipus* is a tragedy because at the end of the play, Oedipus "gets it." So we argue that *Death of a Salesman* is a drama because by the end of the play, we "get it," but Willie still doesn't have a clue. Playwright Arthur Miller insists that *Salesman* is a tragedy. Take your choice. Just have a reason for the choice you take.

Comedy

Comedy also has been subject to a number of definitions. People tend to think of comedy only as humor. Sometimes comedies are not meant to be funny, so we have come up with our own definition of comedy: it is a work that demonstrates the relationships of human beings with each other rather than the universe.

We say that tragedy is philosophy and that comedy is sociology. When the script deals with the relationship of a human being to a major philosophical question, it is a tragedy or a drama. The insights of tragedy tend to encompass every culture. Comedy tends to reflect human behavior in all its peculiarities. When it deals with relationships between or among individuals with regard to their behavior toward each other, it's a comedy.

The other half of the Walter Kerr definition is that not only does tragedy have a happy ending, comedy has a "tragic" ending. The thief may get away with the jewel and thumbs his nose at the detectives waiting on shore as his ship sails away. But then, as he moves aside, we see the thief is sailing on the *S.S. Titanic*. He's doomed but he doesn't even know it yet. How often have you seen a comedy that ends with the main character somehow getting the raw end of his conniving in spite of his or her best efforts?

Doing Your Own Analysis

So now you have a basic grasp of the elements of play analysis. Take a script you want to do, and do the analysis on it. What do you know now that you didn't know before? We will describe two methods of analysis we have used. Other books will give you other systems to use. Find one that works for you.

The first one we describe seems to be more popular with our students. The terms used are generally familiar to those who have studied the Stanislavski system of acting.

Short Method of Analysis

Spine

The spine is *a single sentence statement of the message of the script. It is the theme.* If everything in the script doesn't contribute to the spine, you found the wrong spine. Find another.

Once you have found the spine—which may not be the same spine as someone else found for the script—then every choice made for the production must support that spine. So everyone working on the production must know what the spine is.

Superobjective

Each character in the script has a superobjective. It is the *driving motivation* that propels all the actions of the character with regard to the events of the script. Each actor must know his or her own character's superobjective. What is the superobjective of young Hamlet? Or his advisor, old Polonius? Or Peter Parker in *Spider-Man II*[40] (2004)?

Beats

Scripts are divided into acts, the acts into scenes, and the scenes into beats. Each *beat* is a single unit of conflict in the larger structure. A beat is the smallest logical piece of a script you can rehearse.

Intentions

In each beat, each character has something he or she wants to do—either to another character, or to an outside object, or to himself or herself—a result he or she wants to accomplish.

Adjustments

The moment-to-moment efforts of the character to fulfill these intentions are called the adjustments. Director Stuart Vaughan has a great method for preparing a play script. In his prompt book, the text or dialogue is on the right-hand page, and the left-hand page is blank. First he divides the right hand page into beats. Then he divides the left hand page into three vertical columns. He labels the first column, which is the narrowest, INTENTIONS. The second column is the widest. He labels that one ADJUSTMENTS. The third column, the one nearest the dialogue, he labels ACTIVITIES. Then he reads the play carefully, filling in each column.

Let's look at a word that comes up a great deal in the discussion. What is a unit? It's the same as a "beat." What's a beat? That's another word that has been defined to death. It's the smallest unit of conflict in a play. "Unit" is Stanis1avski's word for divisions in dramatic action, the word for delineating all the segments of the plotting, even the very smallest ones.

When you get to blocking, planning the actor and camera moves, you will be told to break the script down into beats—or units. It all seems impossible until you think of it this way. If you are rehearsing and have to stop on any given line of the script, what is the most logical point at which you can restart the rehearsal? That point makes the beginning of a beat or unit. The next one marks the next, and so on. Actors often tell you where the beat is. When you say "Pick it up where we left off," an actor will say, "Can we go back to—?" They instinctively, like homing pigeons, want to go back to the start of the beat.

Why do we use the word "beat"? According to several sources, it started because a Russian director, rehearsing in the United States, was trying to say, "Let's do that bit again." His accent was so strong everyone thought he was saying, "Let's do that beat again." So, to this day, we call it a beat rather than a unit.

Most directors have trouble finding beats at first. Look for some sort of change. It can be a change of subject in the conversation or a change of characters as when a character enters or leaves the scene.

The method just described gives you a considerable amount of information. It will work well for you, even if it may leave out some information you have to supply later.

Next, we will describe a more extensive method of analysis that supplies a tremendous amount of information you will find useful. Because it is more extensive, it requires more time to do it. When you are applying either method, try to develop your answers in detail. Telegraphic-style writing tends to fade with time. "What did I mean by that note?" is a terrible question to need to ask.

You can use either analysis method shown in this chapter or another method you find more useful. The important thing is to do a thorough analysis of the script. Remember that every problem you did not anticipate and every matter you should know about the script but don't will somehow rise and bite you in the back during the production process. So *be prepared*!

Francis Hodge was a noted directing teacher in the twentieth century. His method of analysis consisted of seven steps that one does in a certain order. It is progressive and thorough. The previous one works from the whole down to the parts. This one is more linear in its approach. You start with number one and work your way through number seven.

Some of these topics will be approached more extensively later on in this book, but below are the seven steps, with the first four explained in great detail. The last three are discussed in Chapter 8. Not all of the elements will appear in every script. Your job is to look for them, not always to find them. If it isn't there, mark it N/A.

Whether you use the method that follows, which is exhaustive, or the method discussed earlier, which is more compact, either will give you good results in your analysis. You may use a combination of both, or you may find another method of analysis you prefer. But give each of them a try before you decide.

Long Method of Analysis

Given Circumstances

The term given circumstances covers all the aspects of a script that are part of the writer's setting. It includes all the material in a script that defines or describes the special "world" in which the action takes place. As we mentioned earlier, when you are first studying a script, try to avoid reading stage or camera directions. Read these directions after you have studied the script. By then you will have a strong conception of the inherent setting, and you can separate what the writer considers significant about an environment from another designer's or another director's interpretation of it.

Remember that a published play script contains, for your convenience, all the important information in the stage manager's notebook on opening night. In Rodgers and Hammerstein scripts of musicals, even the light cues are given. You are under no obligation to use them, and they can get in your way if you are planning your own production. Old scripts, such as Molière's, don't have them, so you have to do all your own homework.

When you are doing student projects, you are not going to be able to duplicate the Broadway show, your college production, a famous film, or a commercial television show. So imagine it afresh, and don't think about doing a bad copy of someone else's idea.

Given circumstances are found in the dialogue. Scripts are written about the time in which the writer lived. Shakespeare could set a play in ancient Athens, but it is really the world in which he was living in London during those years. He wasn't concerned about historical authenticity—he wanted the audience of his time to "get" his ideas.

Don't worry about the actual historical setting. Setting is a matter of feeling about objects and places; it is about time and what has happened before the play begins; and it is about the feelings of the characters for the special world of the play.

A famous Latino actor, now deceased, told us he always wanted to do *Death of a Salesman*[41] (1949) by changing the names of most of the characters and keeping the rest of the play the same. He wanted the lead character, Willie Loman, to be Willy Lopez. The wife Linda's name could be the same, as could the two sons Biff and Happy—presumably he would have changed Charlie to Carlito.

Apparently he never got the chance to do it, or he couldn't get permission from Arthur Miller for the change. But does it work if you do it that way? It probably would, because the world of the play is basically unchanged. Just start your analysis by sticking to the dialogue. And don't change the names of the characters without author approval.

Environmental Facts

Scripts almost always specify the place and time of the action as well as give particulars about the environment. Whether the playwright has been historically accurate or not, this is the world of the script.

Numerous films have been made about King Arthur. The environmental facts differ widely, especially in the one released the summer of 2004. Since he probably never existed, it doesn't matter. Above all, do not try to reconstruct your own idea of historical fact surrounding a script. If it is not in the script, it does not exist. A playwright or screenwriter is not writing a history but telling a story. He may not know his history well at all, or he may be deliberately shifting the facts to suit his own purposes. It didn't stop Shakespeare, and it probably didn't stop your writer.

Can you answer in some detail all the following questions about the script you are analyzing?

1. Where is its geographical location, including climate?
2. When does it take place? What year, what time of year, what part of the day?
3. What is the economic structure of this particular universe?
4. What is the political structure, and is it important to the script?
5. What kind of social structure do the characters inhabit?
6. Does the religious environment or attitude matter?

Previous Action

First, distinguish between what an audience actually sees happening immediately in front of it—and what the dialogue or flashbacks tells us happens before the present action begins. Modern scripts generally begin somewhere in the middle or toward the end of the story—a late point of attack. So, naturally, the dialogue must reveal given circumstances that generally have some dialogue that reveals important past action. The present action usually has a base from which to move forward. Sometimes a script does not "have a past" in those terms, but you need to be sure.

The script may take a long time to explain fully the previous action, but it establishes the point where the present action actually begins. A good script deals with the past in dialogue that avoids dull exposition. The characters reveal the "necessary past" through the way they deal with and discuss matters in the present. These previous actions relate directly to the present actions happening in the script.

Attitudes

From the beginning, we need to know the attitudes of the main characters. Usually, as a script progresses, the true nature of a *principal character* does not change, but his or her attitudes do. Other forces and characters exert changes on him or her even though the characters themselves do not change.

Most scripts show radical shifts in the attitudes of the principal characters from the positions they held at the beginning to those they hold at the end. A character moves from ignorance to knowledge. Usually, the character sees the world in which he or she lives more and more clearly after the actions he or she takes than before. At the beginning, the character vows never to marry again. Guess what he or she will do two pages before the script ends?

At the beginning of a script we see the attitudes held by the principal characters toward the "world of the play" in which they take action. We learn their positions in this specific universe. Generally they either love the world they are in or are eager to change it—usually the latter. The plot that follows (the present action) changes that attitude in some way. If the characters can't cope with the change, they will probably take drastic action. The actions may destroy them, or it may mean a renewal of some sort.

Dialogue

While dialogue is obviously the conversation between or among characters, it is not so obvious that its primary function is to "contain" the dramatic action. Dialogue is the vehicle of dramatic action, the lifeblood of the script. Dialogue always exists in the present tense. Someone is speaking it at that particular moment. It is a building process: A says something to B, and B replies; so A answers back to B, and B to A, in a continuing cycle. The purpose is always the same: to seek response in another person as we do in real life.

Dialogue Is in Verse or Prose. Verse is not just décor—it is structure. It is heightened, more exalted language for conveying intense feeling and high actions. Shakespeare used verse for his more exalted characters and prose for his more "prosaic" ones. The obscenity in the dialogue of David Mamet[42] suits the characters he writes about and the world they live in. It is totally unsuitable for other worlds—a lot of other worlds.

Dialogue Is Usually More Connotative than Denotative. Dialogue is much more weighted with feeling and meaning than dictionary usage or definitive meaning. Think of the word "mother." You know the definition. But it is very likely that everyone you know puts a slightly different value on that word because of what it connotes. It probably connotes different things to you at different times.

Dialogue Is Heard Rather Than Read. When reading a script, you still must hear the dialogue in your mind. Do not just read it as you would the newspapers. You must learn to hear the dialogue—not just as words being spoken, but as it is spoken and felt by the particular characters. "You jerk" can be an insult or an endearment. It isn't just a two-word phrase. It's a two-word phrase said by a particular person under specific circumstances. That makes all the difference in what those two words mean.

Dialogue Is Structured for Effect. In good scripts, the writer usually constructs sentences so the important phrase—the actual point of each line—comes at the end of the line. This placement makes it climactic.

People who write for actors have to recognize certain problems actors may have. For instance, actors normally tend to get a little softer in volume at the end of a line as their breath runs out. A writer like Neil Simon will build the sentence so the punch line comes at the end. The punch line is usually made up of words with vowels rather than diphthongs, and plosives like "p," "t," and "k" rather than fricatives like "f," "v," and "j." This forces the actor to put more "push" on the word, so it is more likely to be heard.

Brilliant translators know both languages well enough to bring the same color to the new language as the old one. Often they must use very different words rather than translate exactly. Literal translations of great plays often seem boring because the translator has not captured the essences of the specific dialogue the playwright has written for that character.

So, in doing your analysis, you need to look at all the following and discover what they reveal about the characters and their situations.

1. Choice of words
2. Choice of phrases and sentence structures
3. Choice of images
4. Choice of peculiar characteristics (e.g., dialect, slang, jargon)
5. The sound of dialogue
6. Structure of lines and speeches (verse–prose)

Dramatic Action

Dramatic action is the continuous conflict between characters. The hard core of all scripts is (1) action and (2) characters. A director needs to understand the nature and mechanics of dramatic action because action is the life force of a script. Dramatic action exists only in the present tense. The characters are always in a state of "I do," not of "I did."

As a director, you need to understand the difference between dramatic action and an actor's activity. Acting is the process of illustrating the dramatic action through activity. Action is the clash of forces between the characters. All action, therefore, forces a reaction, or action in two directions with adjustments in between. The cycle goes this way:

1. A does something to B.
2. B feels the force of A's action (adjustment) and decides what action to take.
3. B does something to A.
4. A feels the force of B's action (adjustment) and decides what action to take.

All dramatic action is Wimbledon, not the Tour de France. Dramatic action is not a one-way road but always a returned action. It goes in both directions.

Every speech of every character contains a dramatic action. If a speech is more than three or four sentences long, it may contain additional actions. Do not worry about long speeches until you have mastered the technique of extracting the action from short ones. Then you will sense the shifts in action in major speeches.

Each *beat* has its own objective. Your job is to help the actors find the speech-by-speech dramatic action as well as the objectives of the beats. Emotion emerges from dramatic action.

A script is always a dialogue—action between two or more characters—and never a monologue. An interior speech is not a monologue. It's
an argument carried on between two opposing sides in the same character, frequently between his outside self (what others force him to be) and
his inside self (what he knows he must be). It could be an argument on
the merit of two choices, one more beneficial to her, one more beneficial
to others.

The subtext in a sequence of speeches, for example, could be recorded
in this way:

1. A requests.
2. B refuses.
3. A pleads.
4. B ignores, and so on.

Express each action in the present tense. Let each verb grow out of the
preceding verb. No adjective, no adverbs—just verbs. If you sense the
action, the verb will come.

Verbs that are too general don't work. Keep asking: Can the verb be
acted? Can it force another character to "do" something? You need to
search it for specific and not general verbs. Acting is specific, never general. Verbs that are too generic—for example, love and hate—don't
require the actor to be specific and will not work. Generic verbs, like love
and hate, are so broad they are meaningless to an actor. Since the point
is to energize the actor, only a specific verb works.

Avoid verbs that call up simple physical actions: run, jump, walk,
bounce, laugh, smile, and so on. Look for verbs of doing: rejects, begs,
retreats. They contain the basic passions and emotions. Directors point
out that the verbs must be *actable*. The character wants to hear the music,
to catch him in the lie, to go to the party, to drink a beer.

Character

Let's start with a peculiar distinction. When we talk about character, we
are talking about the person the writer constructed. When we talk about
characterization, we are talking about the person the actor makes out of
what the writer constructed. Get it?

The character is the house plan. The characterization is the finished
house, with variations provided by the owner. Even using the same house
plan up and down the block, the houses look different when they are finished. Some have shades; some have drapes. One has a lot of blue tile in
the kitchen. The other has a green slate roof.

So you see how much room you and the actor have when it comes to characterization. Staying within the character provided by the writer—the dialogue—the actors and director can come up with very different interpretations. During rehearsal, encourage your actors to play the scenes over and over, with new suggestions of action for each playing, rather than discuss the characters in an intellectual way. Let the good stuff come out of them. Read William Ball's book[43] again.

Over the years, we have done some of the same scripts more than once. One of us has done three different productions of *Tartuffe* using the same Richard Wilbur[44] translation. Each one came out quite differently, and we had good reason to be very satisfied with all three of them. We think a really good script can be done by the same director every seven years. By that time, you have changed enough and had sufficient new experiences to see it from a different perspective.

Seeing the same script done in different productions by different directors is immensely pleasurable if the directors are good ones. Each director brings something new and wonderful to the production, the cast, and the design team. The final productions are all different and all excellent.

Although a script focuses on all the principal characters, one character usually dominates the action. Since conflicts cannot exist without two forces—a *protagonist* and an *antagonist*—the action revolves around these two (or possibly three, if there is more than one antagonist). During your analysis, you need to determine whose play it is, along with the primary antagonist or antagonists. A character takes shape and is revealed in the course of the action. Thus, characters do not change as much as they unfold. In this way, aspects of character are fully illustrated in a series of climactic moments.

Analyze each major character on the basis of your own perception of the dramatic action. Give each of the following areas particular attention, and record your results in writing.

Directors and actors need to know the following:

- Desire is what a character wants most. Konstantin Stanislavski[45] developed the term *super-objective* for it. It is the term most actors and directors use today. The character's super-objective is the driving force behind all of the character's actions in the script. It is not the line-to-line or scene-to-scene motivation. It is the basis of the interpretation of the character, and it is the motivation behind all his or her actions.
- Will is a character's relative strength in attaining his desires. How hard is the character willing and able to work—or cheat—or

kill—to get what he or she wants? Sometimes there is a vast difference between how much we want something and what we are willing to do to get it.

- Moral Stance is the set of values the character cherishes. Is the character driven by love, money, power?
- Decorum is a character's physical appearance. The physical appearance of the character includes the attributes that are important regardless of the actor who plays the part. What manners and mannerisms, important physical behaviors, or other visible element must the character possess?

The next step is to develop a list of adjectives.

Adjectives

Now you can take all those adjectives you couldn't use in the previous list and put them to work here. Summarize all of the categories above by using adjectives only. Don't write a character's dramatic actions here. Just write the traits of character they reveal: lazy, charming, friendly, silly, sloppy.

It may also help to make a list of character-mood-intensity.

Character-Mood-Intensity

Character-mood-intensity is the physical or body-state of the character at the beginning of the play and at the beginning of each unit.

Each character in a play begins at a different character-mood-intensity because each character is independent by definition. Actors tend to "catch" each other's actions, attitudes, and intensities—like flu germs. Help each actor to remain distinct.

Idea

We will discuss *idea* more fully in Chapter 8. For now, we can say that the idea of a script is its basic meaning. It can be another word to describe theme, spine, or dramatic action. But in this chapter, we will use it to express the driving concept that makes this script different from others like it.

Tempo

Tempo gets a fuller analysis in Chapter 8 also. We can define it as the changing rates or beats (used in the musical sense, not as a substitute for unit) of the dramatic action.

Mood

We also saved the discussion of mood for Chapter 8. *Mood* includes the feelings or emotions generated by the dramatic action.

Homework

Homework is your responsibility. As we mentioned in the first chapter, you are supposed to do it at home, before you get together with all those other people and waste their time. Much of your preproduction time is spent alone at home doing your script analysis.

Ideally, you should sit with the script and do a written analysis of every aspect of the it. You need to know the script thoroughly so you can understand it and communicate that understanding. If you can't communicate your ideas because you don't really understand them, everyone working on the project will be doing a different version of the script. We have all sat through performances where that has been the case. The results vary from boring to painful.

Homework will help you to cut down on the amount of talking you have to do. Actors should be acting, not discussing seminar-style. Of course, you need to do a lot of discussing with the production staff. But conference time should be spent refining ideas, not trying to come up with them.

Your homework helps your staff do their work more effectively. You will know the material so thoroughly you can communicate it more effectively. Why write it down? So you'll think about it more clearly and won't forget important points. Writing it down will free you to use the ideas of others. This kind of collaboration will enhance the final product, instead of allowing each person going off in many different directions at once.

You can start the analysis anywhere, but of course it is better to be systematic. The two methods we described both will give you a complete analysis. As you read more, you may find other methods of analysis that work better for you.

Summary

Finding Your Own Method of Analysis

One good way to find the method of analysis that works best for you is to try as many as you can find. The ones that are really bad for you will collapse before you have gotten very far. Or perhaps you will collapse first. You never know.

So try another one. What we have described here are two good ways of doing it, very thorough and detailed. You don't want to get caught short when you have no time to adjust. Each director eventually finds patterns of analysis that work best for that particular individual. As Nike would say, "Just do it."

Suggested Reading and Viewing

Reading

Stage
Albright, Hardie. *Stage Direction in Transition*. See chapters 4–6.
Ball, William. *A Sense of Direction*. See "Objectives."
Catron, Louis E. *The Director's Vision*. See part 3.
Dean, Alexander, and Lawrence Carra. *Fundamentals of Play Directing*. See chapter 2.
Grote, David. *Script Analysis*.
Hodge, Francis. *Play Directing*. See part I.
Kirk, John W., and Ralph A. Bellas. *The Art of Directing*. See part 2.
O'Neill, R. H., and N. M. Boretz. *The Director as Artist*. See chapters 3 and 4.
Patterson, Jim. *Stage Directing*. See step 2, STAGE DIRECTING by Jim Patterson.
Shapiro, Mel. *The Director's Companion*. See parts 1 and 2.
Vaughan, Stuart, *Directing Plays*. See chapter 4.

Screen
Armer, Alan A. *Directing Television and Film*. See chapters 4 and 5.
Block, Bruce. *The Visual Story*. See the appendix, part I.
Katz, Steven D. *Film Directing Shot by Shot*.
Lukas, Christopher. *Directing for Film and Television*. See chapter 1.
Proferes, Nicholas T. *Film Directing Fundamentals*. See chapter 1.
Weston, Judith. *Directing Actors*. See chapter 7.

Notes

1. *Directing Plays: A Working Professional's Method* by Stuart Vaughn.
2. *Play Directing: Analysis, Communication, and Style* by Francis Hodge.
3. Peter Bogdanovich director. The cast included Carol Burnett, Michael Caine, Denholm Elliott, Julie Hagerty, Marilu Henner, Christopher Reeve, and John Ritter.
4. *Once Upon a Mattress* (2004) (TV) *Queen Aggravain, Noises Off . . .* (1992), "The Carol Burnett Show" (1991) TV Series, *Plaza Suite* (1987) (TV),

"Mama's Family" (1983), *The Four Seasons* (1981), "Carol Burnett & Company" (1979), *Friendly Fire* (1979) (TV), *The Grass Is Always Greener over the Septic Tank* (1978) (TV), *Sills and Burnett at the Met* (1976) (TV), *The Front Page* (1974), *6 Rms Riv Vu* (1974) (TV), *Pete 'n' Tillie* (1972), *Once Upon a Mattress* (1972) (TV) . . . Princess Winifred the Woebegone, "The Carol Burnett Show" (1967), *Once Upon a Mattress* (1964) (TV), . . . *Princess Winnifred, Calamity Jane* (1963) (TV), "The Carol Burnett Show" (1960) (TV), "The Garry Moore Show" (1958) (TV Series), and . . . Regular (1959–62).

5. Directed by Andrew Adamson and Vicky Jenson.
6. Directed by Andrew Adamson and Kelly Asbury.
7. Directed by Quentin Tarantino.
8. Directed by Andy Wachowski and Larry Wachowski.
9. Directed by Peter Jackson.
10. "The West Wing" (1999) TV Series (creator) (story) (executive producer), "Sports Night" (1998) TV Series (creator) (writer) (executive producer), *The American President* (1995) (written by), and *A Few Good Men* (1992) (play) (screenplay).
11. *NYPD 2069* (2004) (TV) (writer), *L.A. Law: The Movie* (2002) (TV) (television series), "NYPD Blue" (1993) (TV Series) (creator) (writer), "Cop Rock" (1990) (TV Series) (creator), *Columbo: Uneasy Lies the Crown* (1990) (TV), "Doogie Howser, M.D." (1989) (TV Series) (creator) (writer), "L.A. Law" (1986) (TV Series) (creator), "The Twilight Zone" (1985) (TV Series) (writer) (episode "Quarantine"), "Bay City Blues" (1983) (TV Series) (creator), "Hill Street Blues" (1981) (TV Series) (creator) (writer), "Delvecchio" (1976) (TV Series) (writer), "The Invisible Man" (1975) (TV Series) (creator), *Columbo: Mind Over Mayhem* (1974) (TV) (teleplay), *Columbo: Double Shock* (1973) (TV) (teleplay), *Columbo: étude in Black* (1972) (TV), *Silent Running* (1972), *Columbo: Blueprint for Murder* (1972) (TV), *Columbo: Lady in Waiting* (1971) (TV), *Columbo: Murder by the Book* (1971) (TV), and *The Counterfeit Killer* (1968) (TV).
12. Independent film directors of the 1960s and 1970s who controlled their own production costs with little studio oversight.
13. *Sleep* (1963), *Empire* (1964), *Harlot* (1965), directed by Andy Warhol.
14. Directed by George Lucas.
15. *Star Wars* (1977), *Star Wars: Episode V—The Empire Strikes Back* (1980), *Star Wars: Episode VI—Return of the Jedi* (1983), *Star Wars: Episode I—The Phantom Menace* (1999), *Star Wars: Episode II—Attack of the Clones* (2002), and *Star Wars: Episode III—Revenge of the Sith* (2005).
16. Sidney Howard director.
17. Orsen Wells director.
18. Joel Coen director.
19. French original, "Le Tartuffe ou l'imposteur," originally three Acts (1664 version), later five Acts (1667 and 1669 versions) in rhymed alexandrine couplets.

20. Considered by many to be William Shakespeare's greatest comic character, Falstaff appeared in "Henry IV, Part I" (1598), "Henry IV, Part II" (1590), and "The Merry Wives of Windsor" (XXXX).
21. USA Network 1997–2007
22. NBC Network 1971–97.
23. Written by Henrik Ibsen, one of Scandinavia's major playwrights.
24. Directed by M. Night Shyamalan.
25. Written by Henrik Ibsen, one of Scandinavia's major playwrights.
26. Directed by John G. Avildsen.
27. Directed by Sylvester Stallone.
28. Directed by John G. Avildsen.
29. Directed by Andrew Adamson and Kelly Asbury.
30. Directed by Sam Raimi.
31. Written by Edward Albee.
32. Directed by Mike Nichols.
33. Directed by King Vidor.
34. Directed by Michael Mann.
35. Directed by George Lucas.
36. Directed by written by George M. Cohan.
37. Directed by Michael Curtiz.
38. Written by William Shakespeare.
39. Pulitzer-Prize winning theater (1913–96), for *Commonweal, New York Herald Tribune, New York Times* in 1966 where he wrote theater reviews there for seventeen years.
40. Sam Raimi director.
41. Written by Arthur Miller.
42. Screenwriter and Pulitzer Prize playwright and known for his use of profanity; plays include, *Sexual Perversity in Chicago* (1976), *American Buffalo* (1976), *Glengarry Glen Ross* (1984) (Pulitizer Prize winner), *Speed the Plow* (1988), *Oleanna* (1992); screenplays include *The Postman Always Rings Twice* (1981), *The Verdict* (1982), *The Untouchables* (1987), *Glengarry Glen Ross* (1992), and *Wag the Dog* (1998).
43. *Sense of Direction: Some Observations on the Art of Directing* by William Ball.
44. A skilled poet, editor, and teacher, Richard Wilbur translated three of Molière's comedies: "The Misanthrope" (1955), "Tartuffe" (1963), and "The School for Wives" (1971).
45. Russian actor and director Konstanin Stanislavski, cofounder of the Moscow Art Theatre in Russia, compiled a series of principles and techniques which today are regarded as fundamental to both the training and the performance of actors and actresses who want to create believable characters on stage and screen.

4

Working with Actors

Earlier in the book we mentioned that the principal part of a director's job is working with actors. Later on in this chapter, we will discuss the casting process. But first, let's look at the actor from the director's point of view. Whether or not you had any say in selecting the actors with whom you work, you still have to do your best with them once they are cast.

We constantly stress that time is money, even on an amateur project where no one is getting paid. So your first responsibility is to be as thoroughly prepared as possible. Strange things will happen, unexpected things that will upset your plans. But the more prepared you are—the more fully developed your plan A—the less likely you are to need plan B.

Whenever possible, have a plan B for every plan A. Think of all the "what ifs" that you can, and try to figure out a way to cope with them. If something occurs to mess up plan A, see if you can manage to wait twenty-four hours before coming up with plan B and implementing it. Usually, the immediate solution to a problem is not the best one.

For instance, suppose you lose an actor unexpectedly, for whatever reason. Your first thought is to get J to do the part. See if you can stall long enough to think a little more. More often than not, K will appear—in person or in your mind—and you realize that K is a much better replacement than J. You are safe. You haven't contacted J, and K is available.

Plan B comes in handy in almost any situation. You're in the Helsinki airport, waiting to board your flight, when you realize you lost your plane ticket. You are in such a panic, you can't remember your name, let alone plan B. You carry a credit card with enough spending room that you can, if you must, buy a whole new ticket at top price. You are not doomed to spend the rest of your life in the terminal, like Tom Hanks's character.

As soon as you remember plan B, the voice on the intercom requests that you report to the airport manager's office. Someone found your ticket and turned it in. With all the counterterrorism measures, no one else can use it or cash it in, so you are saved.

Of course, the crisis that will occur is the one for which you don't have a plan B. Then try to get that twenty-four-hour window to come up with one.

An Actor's Responsibilities to the Director

In this section, we will look at what one should be able to expect from actors in the various media. Too bad—it does not always work out that way. But these expectations are reasonable. Note that we use the same four expectations, but for each medium we have to modify them.

On Stage

You have the advantage in stage work, most of the time, of having the final say in the casting. Since you selected that person, you saw something that made you think he or she was well suited for the role. In rehearsal, you find out it isn't so. If the actor is doing a good job, it is better to keep the actor and alter your expectations to fit the actor's competence. If you fire an actor because *you* made a mistake, every other actor develops acute paranoia and cannot function at the best level possible.

Of course, if the actor messes up, dump him or her immediately. You can be sure that the other actors already know the person is a screw-up and a detriment to the whole project. You are generally the last one in the group to figure this out. If the actor does not live up to his or her responsibilities, get rid of the person.

Showing up drunk for rehearsals, being late or missing rehearsals, being late learning lines, and refusing to work with someone to "catch up" are all mortal sins. You are well within your rights to replace the person for the good of the project and the morale of the cast and crew.

In addition to these basic requirements, you should expect the actor to do the following.

The stage actor should try to follow your suggestions and try to stay within the world of the script you envision. Even if the actor has done the role before, he or she has the obligation to step into your world for this production. It is *your* interpretation that is being presented. You are like a conductor in an orchestra—it is someone else's music, but you are responsible for the interpretation.

Recently we saw a production of a play that one of the actresses had done several years ago. Then she was the director, and we thought it was a fine interpretation with good acting. This time she was an actress. Like all the others in this production, she was way over the top and turned character into cartoon. We felt sorry for her because we knew she knew better. But she was respecting the prerogative of the director. The director wanted cartoons, and the director got cartoons. The actress and we were disappointed, but we were imposing our world of the play on another production of it. We still think our interpretation was right, but the actress was correct in doing it as the director wanted it—or leaving the show *early* in the rehearsal period.

The stage actor should bring something new into every rehearsal. The actor should be doing enough homework to have something to show you. A really good actor can be the best addition to your creative process. The actor should be able to see and think about the character in ways that you don't or haven't had time to do. If the actor says, "I want to try something today. Let me know what you think," just say, "OK." If the actor wants to talk to you about the experiment, say, "Don't tell me—show me."

The stage actor should leave the directing to you. Actors frequently have excellent ideas that will work. But they involve another actor or a scene this actor is not in. The actor should suggest it to you and *not* mention it to anyone else. Once the actor runs it by you, you can give the suggestion or even say, "L has a suggestion that might work. I'd like L to explain it to you, and then we can try it." If you find that an actor is "directing" the play, without your permission, put a stop to it immediately.

The stage actor should make no changes in his or her personal appearance without previous approval. It is fine for you to tell actors that they need to get their hair cut or change the color. But no actor should make any physical changes, however minor, without prior approval. Sometimes on stage, you can fix it if they do. But that is still not the point. You are hiring their physical appearance, and that should stay the same unless the actors have been told to change it.

On Film

Unless the director is hired by the producer or even one of the stars to direct the picture, the director will have as much to say about casting as the director of a stage production. Remember, film is the director's medium. If you are dealing with a film in which you as the director have not been involved from the outset, it may be likely that you had nothing to do with hiring the actor. You need to be able to work with this person anyway. You can only report improper behavior—the dismissal is not always in your hands.

The film actor should try to follow your suggestions and to stay within the world of the script you envision. It is highly unlikely that the actor has done this role elsewhere, so he or she is less likely to question your vision of the part. Even if the actor has done the role before, he or she has the obligation to step in to your world for this production. Just be consistent in your vision.

There have been several reincarnations of the Batman character in films. Each had a different director and a different actor playing Batman. But even if the same actor had been cast in two of the films, the new director would expect the actor to play his Batman according to the director's concept, not the concept established by the previous director. Perhaps that is why they keep changing the Batmen.

The film actor should bring something new into every rehearsal. This is less likely to happen in film. Most actors will be with you only on the days you actually shoot them. They will barely have enough time to do what you want. They may be able to give you a bit of variety but only what they can develop in minutes rather than days. Some of the major actors may have had some real rehearsal time and had the script long enough to get some character work done. But you need to be totally prepared because most actors have not had time to do any homework. You may need consistency from them more than originality.

The film actor should leave the directing to you. Film actors will get input from a variety of sources, so the rule here needs to be modified somewhat. They should take direction from authority figures only. If you told the actor to do X on the next take and the actor does Y, ask why he or she made the change. The answer may be that the DP (director of photography) or the producer or someone else gave the order. You can rescind it or confirm it, depending on the order. The same stage rule applies about the actor not giving "helpful suggestions" to another actor.

The film actor should make no changes in his or her personal appearance without previous approval. It is fine for you to tell the actors that they need to get their hair cut or change the color before the next shoot. But no actor should make any physical changes, regardless how minor, without prior approval. Particularly in film, minor changes in appearance mean that the shots won't match when the film gets edited. An actor may shoot two parts of the same scene weeks apart, but the continuity will be destroyed if the actor does not have the exact same appearance in the same scene. So, no getting heads or other body parts shaved just because the actor is drunk or should be in rehab but is too dumb, drunk, or stoned to know it.

On Television

You had, most likely, no input into hiring the person. You simply have to work with what—whom—you have been given. That means you won't have any power to get rid of the person if the relationship isn't working for you. Also, by the time you find out it isn't working, you don't have time to find a replacement.

The television actor should try to follow your suggestions and try to stay within the world of the script you envision. Even if the actor has done the role before, he or she has the obligation to step into your world for this production. Like film, chances are the actor has not done this role before. However, some of the actors may have been playing these same characters long before you were hired to direct this episode. The actors deserve to be heard. They should know the world of the script a lot better than you do.

The television actor should bring something new into every rehearsal. This is really unlikely to happen in television. Most of the actors will be with you only on the days you actually shoot them. They will barely have time to do what you want. They may be able to give you a bit of variety, but only what they can develop in minutes rather than days. Television schedules are generally so rapid that you have very little time to spend with the actor in any case. It is usually "blow and go." You may not even be aware the actor has made certain adjustments because your attention has to be in several places at once. So you need to depend on the actor for consistency. They should definitely clear it with you before they "improve" anything.

The television actor should leave the directing to you and the twenty-seven other people who will be telling them things. Pity the poor actor who has conflicting input . . . or is at least getting directions that seem to the actor to be conflicting. You told the actor to stand here; someone else told him to move there because of a boom shadow. The actor can cope with that sort of thing—minor, reasonable blocking changes. But it is very difficult and confusing for the day player actor when the chain of command is unclear and the new guy has to figure out whose word is law and whose is just interference. Still, an actor should not be getting input directly from another actor, unless the actor making the suggestions is the person whose name is on the show. The power goes where the money flows, remember.

The television actor should make no changes in his or her personal appearance without prior approval. This rule is equally important in any medium.

A Director's Responsibilities to the Actor

On Stage

You are the Great Ruler on stage. Your word is law. You also have an obligation to use that power for good rather than to prove what an ugly rat fink you really are. Don't confuse having power with abusing it.

A friend of ours was a Broadway dancer in the 1950s. He told us the story of a director–choreographer who was dreadful to the cast, particularly the women. He recalled that the chorus girls sat outside the stage door waiting for rehearsals to begin at 9 AM, crying in terror at the verbal abuse that would be heaped on them for the next eight hours. This director (no gentleman) is now dead, yet he is still revered as a demigod of the American theatre. Please!

Be patient. Everyone has a bad day once in a while. One of the best aspects of stage work is that you probably have enough rehearsal time to let the actor get past that bad day.

Be prepared. Even if actors are getting paid for their time, it's debilitating for people to waste it.

On Film

You are the busiest person there. You are constantly talking with someone and making decisions, and you never seem to have a minute to yourself. People follow you to the bathroom to get answers to questions that can't wait until you finish your personal business. Then, when you do leave, you have to go home and plan some more.

Be patient. Everyone has a bad day once in a while. With all the time and money that goes into a film, it is sometimes difficult to do this. But you can try.

Be prepared. You are spending an incredible amount of other people's money—or, in amateur filmmaking, your own. The time you spend at home doing your work is relatively cheap time. The time you spend on the set, doing what you should have done at home, is wildly expensive.

On Television

You do not have the implied power of director as in the other two media. Though you are doing your job well, others feel no qualms about re-directing for you. The work is relatively easy. The pay is good, and you generally don't suffer the blame when the show craters, so get over it. Take the money and do live theatre off Broadway for emotional rehabilitation and artistic satisfaction.

Be patient. Everyone has a bad day once in a while. Another friend of ours, an excellent, accomplished, older actress, was on a day shoot for "Law and Order" one time. For some reason, that day she could not manage to learn her lines. They went to every length to assist her. They sent someone to her trailer to work with her while they were shooting another part of the scene. When it was time for her—again—she still couldn't keep the lines in her brain. By this time, she had reached the terminal paranoia stage. She was a playing a psychiatrist, a judge, or some such part. They put her at the desk, spread her script in front of her and got her through the scene with her cheat sheets in full view—of her, not the camera. She was ready to quit the acting field. In fact, they have hired her again. They recognized she is a very competent, conscientious actress who just had a "senior moment" that lasted twenty-four hours.

Be prepared. Notice all the other people who are there in that studio? They are getting paid tons of money—many of them more than you. If you waste much of their time, they can get you fired. Do as much of your homework as possible at home. Of course, many of these other people will keep giving you new stuff to cope with—script revisions, and so on. You should expect a considerable amount of understanding when that is the case.

The Different Kinds of Actors

As a director, you will be working with a wide variety of actors. Some have years of experience, tremendous professional training, experience teaching other actors, and even experience directing. Others are just cute twins, nine months old, who are needed to play a single baby. You need twins because you can't work infants very long and one of them is usually crying. It is difficult to make up a set of rules to cover the range of actors, but what follows are a few generalizations about them.

What should you expect from different kinds of actors in each medium?

Stage-Trained Actors

If the actors have had considerable stage training and experience, they are usually dependable and learn lines quickly. They are used to a considerable amount of rehearsal and feel cheated when they don't get much chance to develop their character. They have, for the most part, received a great deal of training in a particular method of acting and may have trouble understanding you if you don't speak that language. It is nice if you are able to adjust to those factors, but if you can't, no problem. Ultimately, they have to learn to adjust to you, not the other way around.

On Stage

You want a stage-trained actor for a stage experience. Check their references. Actors lie a lot on their resumes. If you know and trust a director they have worked with, check with that director. It may take extra time to do the background check, but some quick phone calls save a considerable amount of grief.

Stage-trained actors should be adaptable. Expect them to have clear articulation and good projection. They should have sufficient training to comply with all the demands of the script. Usually, they can interpret ideas and language clearly.

They appreciate genuine praise but not the phony stuff. Most directors say that praise should be specific but not too specific. Saying "You really handled that beat with Bob and John well," is good. Saying, "I like the way you tossed your head on line seventeen," will leave them up all night wondering just what they did, and if they can ever repeat it. They can't.

On Film

Stage actors with no film experience will be so used to projecting and amplifying the performance that they will come across at first as manic. Stage actors are used to filling 1,500-seat houses, not speaking softly, and letting their eyes carry the message. They expect a great deal more interaction with the director—they assume you will tell them more about their characters, your concept of the production, and so on. They don't just grab on to a characterization and go with it.

They may fall apart if they see the rushes. As stage actors, they don't get to see what they or their performances look like. It takes quite a bit of time to develop that level of objectivity toward their appearance and work. They may even want to change things with which you are totally satisfied.

They may have a hard time learning the concept of hitting their marks. In theatre it rarely makes a difference if they are a few inches to the left or right. Sometimes you have to show them in the camera what a difference it makes.

On Television

Stage actors will behave much the same way they do on film. However, because television is shot a little differently, their performance is usually modified more easily. Because of boom placement, you will probably be grateful for the fact they have no trouble projecting. Since they are often on the set for just one week of shooting, they may not be aware of the story line of the production, but they are likely to develop more interesting characterizations during the course of the week (that is, they are more likely to grow into their part). They are also, as mentioned earlier, more freaked out by getting directions from so many different sources.

We have heard stories that some stage actors never learn the concept of hitting marks consistently, and a producer swore to us that she had to fire a major character from a soap opera because of it. Soaps have so much to do and so little time. The actor would almost inevitably rehearse going behind the sofa and then, when the cameras were rolling, go in front if it. In those days, the shooting had to be done within a few hours' time window so it could be picked up by the satellite.

He was a major character in the soap and had been built into the long line of the story, so the writers had to "burn" his character in a fire. His character was confined to a burn center, bandaged from head to foot, to finish out the story line. Then he suddenly "disappeared" from the show, the way they often do in soaps and some foreign countries.

Film-Trained Actors

Usually, it is more accurate to call them actors with film experience rather than actors who are trained to work on film. With the demise of the studio system, for a long time actors got no real training in film. Most film actors learned from experience rather than from having a great deal of formal education. Some businesses offered acting classes, but many of them were of dubious value.

Many theatre schools thought it was beneath them to mess with media acting. The realities of the business are beginning to edge their way into theatre professional training programs, and now some emerging actors have had some film training. One agent was interviewing an actor from a top MFA drama program for representation and asked, "Do you have a reel?" The actor replied, "A real what?"

On Stage
Film actors rarely need to project well. They generally learn a few pages of dialogue at a time and do not need to retain them once the material is shot. The film actor usually has trouble projecting and is not used to learning an entire script, so you have to give them extra time to learn their lines, the same way you do for older actors who can't memorize as quickly as their younger counterparts.

Memory is a lot like a muscle—if you don't keep exercising it, it gets flabby. Supposedly British actors can learn an act of a play in a single night because they memorize so much. But even young film actors can't absorb that much because they are not called on to use that "muscle."

When you see a famous film actor in a major Broadway role, you will be aware that many of them have become totally dependent on microphones for their projection. When Jessica Lange played Blanche in *A Streetcar Named Desire* on Broadway in 1995, the theatres were not amplified the way they usually are now. Not only was she hard to hear, but when she was on stage, unconsciously the other actors would slowly reduce their projection until they matched hers. By the end of the scene, the audience could hear hardly any of the dialogue. Fortunately, we knew the play well enough to know what was happening. But many of our seat neighbors were totally confused.

It's sad that every Broadway house is now rife with amplification. But between actors who can't project and audiences who can't hear—they are either old and deaf or young and hearing-damaged from loud music—all Broadway plays are amplified. Usually, in our opinion, they are overamplified.

Film actors tend to get dry mouth when they perform. When Timothy Busfield did the lead in the Broadway production of *A Few Good Men*, he carried a cola can throughout the entire production. From doing so much television work, the strain of projecting made his mouth go dry.

Kathleen Turner carried a cup of "coffee" upstairs to the bedroom when she went to change her dress on Broadway in *Cat on a Hot Tin Roof*. She had to do a lot of sipping to make it through the first act. It is a Maggie monologue with brief interruptions by Brick. But the next time she appeared in a Broadway play, she had mastered the technique. She didn't need liquid assistance to get through the part in *Dangerous Liaisons*.

On Film
They know the drill. They understand the peculiarities of the medium and what is expected of them. Often they are playing parts that are practically identical to the ones they have played before because of the tendency to typecast.

On Television
They have a hard time working as fast as TV demands. The more film they have done, the harder the adjustment.

Television-Trained Actors

Television-trained actors generally tend to behave more like film actors than like stage actors. Their range may be more limited, but they can usually work faster than film or stage actors.

Actor Types

Much to their dismay, actors are typed according to their apparent ages and other characteristics. The following are the most common terms for these types. Basically, the categories are left over from British and French stage terms.

- *Leading man* is usually 35–50. He is heroic, handsome, energetic, and manly. Good examples are Jimmy Smits and Tom Cruise.
- *Leading lady* is generally 30–45. She is elegant, attractive, and beautiful. Julia Roberts and Cameron Diaz are leading ladies.
- *Second man* may be 30–45. He could be a good guy, a villain, or a comedy type. He can be nice looking, often suave. In films, Benjamin Bratt might fall into that category. Even though he is handsome, he usually provides a contrast with the leading man. The second man comic characters are likely to be less attractive than the lead, like Brad Garrett ("Everybody Loves Raymond")
- *Second Woman* is also 30–45. She usually contrasts with the leading lady in looks. If one is blonde, the other is brunette. If one is outgoing, the other is reserved.
- *Juvenile* is in the 20–30 age range. He is generally boyish and handsome, like Tom Cruise in *Top Gun.*
- *Ingenue* is 18–30. She is young, female, and often the juvenile's love interest. Anne Hathaway is one example.
- *Character man* is 50+. He plays fathers, senior statesmen, and other authoritative figures. Sean Connery and Clint Eastwood are two examples. They often used to be leading men.
- *Character woman* is also in the 50+ age range. She is attractive, distinguished, and usually plays mothers and judges. Meryl Streep and Phylicia Rashad are two examples. They often used to be leading women.
- *Second character man* is also 50+, but he contrasts with the character man. Usually he is shorter, chubbier, and so on. He is frequently a comic, like Danny DiVito, and Peter Boyle.

- *Second character woman* is 50+. Like the character man, she is often a comic. Kathy Bates and Doris Roberts are two examples.
- *Low comedian* is noted for physical comedy, like Buster Keaton and Jim Carrey.
- *Soubrette* is a sexy, earthy, comedienne like Megan Mullally ("Will and Grace") and Sandra Bullock.
- *Character juvenile* is 18–30, with unusual looks, and is generally comedic like Adam Sandler, Andy Dick, and David Spade.
- *Character ingenue* is his female equivalent but is usually pretty, like Laura San Giacomo and Kaley Cuoco ("Eight Simple Rules").
- *Utility players* (in England, they call them walking gentlemen) are people who play small parts—aspiring actors and has-beens.

Actors come in two categories—those who always play themselves, like Jimmy Stewart, John Wayne, or Van Damme, or those who disappear into their roles, like Meryl Streep or George C. Scott. You can name five actors who fit in each category.

It is important to say a word about understudies. Since film and television do not use understudies, this is a stage problem only. Do you use them or not? Union rules govern their use on most professional stage productions, so this is a problem only for the amateur theatre director. It is strictly up to you, in keeping with any policies the particular organization may have.

In nonprofessional stage plays, using understudies has both advantages and disadvantages. The advantages are that (1) you always have a "spare" if anything happens to the principal and (2) more people get involved in the production. The disadvantages are that (1) it ties up a lot more actors, (2) it requires extra rehearsal time, which is frequently scarce, and (3) you either have to make special arrangements for the understudy to perform, which is difficult, or risk having some very frustrated actors hanging around waiting for an accident to happen.

Neither of us has used understudies in university productions, but we have colleagues who do. We have no definite rule for the situation. Just be aware of the pitfalls of whatever choice you make.

The Actor's Point of View

Generally, actors want to please. They would like to work again. If they get a bad reputation, it hurts their chances of future employment. They usually know that your job is to make them look good because they can make you look good by doing so.

If you would like to do a good job directing actors, you need to act once in a while yourself. The longer you stay away from acting, the easier it looks. Eventually you may tend to regard all actors as dumb clods just because they don't understand intuitively what you want and can't memorize forty pages of script in an hour.

Most people think they can act and frequently regard acting as a simple minor skill that requires little brains or talent—though looks seem to help. They seem to think that if you can talk, you can act. The less acting they do, the easier it seems to be. Bike riding is easy. Mountain biking is hard. Winning the Tour de France is practically impossible. Talking is easy. Acting is hard. Great acting is practically impossible.

Take a look at some of the crew people on certain stage, film, or television studios. Listen to the snide jibes and under-the-breath remarks. They can be very nice one-on-one with actors, but in some sad cases, they seem to enjoy belittling them from a safe distance away. Try to discourage that behavior in your crews—and in yourself. Actors are aware of it, even when they don't appear to be. It doesn't help the actor, and it doesn't help the show. You need to encourage an atmosphere of mutual respect and admiration. It does wonders for productivity.

Most directors don't get to see how other directors work. As a result, they get into a certain groove about the way they do things. This leads to the assumption that their way is the only way. Actors have to constantly adapt to every new director's method, which can be remarkably different from every other. They have to learn to adapt to your way. It helps if you have a little flexibility about recognizing the actors have their way.

What about Casting?

Many great stage directors have said that the most important part of their job is casting. In his book, William Ball says that 80 percent of his job is casting. At seminars, you may hear directors say that 90 or 95 percent of their work is casting. In fact, it seems that the stage directors we admire most give the highest percentage of their job description to the work of casting. When asked, we always say 98 percent so people will think we are extremely good directors. Particularly on stage, if you have a great cast, the show will be great. Even if the sets and costumes are not the most wonderful, a terrific cast will have the audience thinking they have seen a wonderful play.

Probably your most important asset as a stage director, then, is the ability to select a good cast and to communicate well with them. For many reasons—scheduling, other commitments—your first choice may not be available. Often one must select a person who is not the most obvious choice for a part. Every once in a while, the person who seems to be the best choice is someone with whom you simply cannot communicate in your role as director. You could be best friends in real life but not in a production situation. Bite the bullet—make the choice. You must be able to work with this person, not go out for coffee.

Most experienced stage directors will tell you that the person who is the most experienced is the best one for the job. Unfortunately for the newcomers, that is true. Even doctors will tell you that the best surgeon is the one who does that particular surgery the most often. One surgeon suggested that people never use a doctor who hadn't done that specific procedure at least 400 times. That's why they call it "practicing medicine." It takes the first 399 patients to learn to do it properly. We call it "rehearsing."

Ideally, you should never ask a person to do a role, particularly in academic or community theatre. Suddenly the balance of power shifts. The actor who is asked then starts telling you when and if he or she can get to rehearsal. After all, he or she is doing you a favor. Tell actors you think there are parts they should try out for, but don't ask them to do the part. Ask them to audition for the part. Make it clear you are not precasting.

You hear a lot of stories about actors who are so well known they won't audition for a part. That may be true for very famous actors, but you are still a long way away from working with them. Until you are begging Tom Cruise to be in your film, or Meryl Streep to come to Broadway for you, don't blow your right to casting choices. Suppose someone better comes along at auditions and you have given the part away? It's easier if you asked Bob to audition for you, and then you cast Bill. But once you have cast Bob in advance, you can't easily dump him and give the part to Bill.

Even famous actors will audition if they really want a part and the producers are not begging them to do it. If the part is that desirable, all actors will beg for an audition to prove they can handle the part.

Once you have your cast, think about how you can get the actors as much time as possible to learn their parts, work through them, and get to know the script and their role in it as well as possible. Time is money, and there is never enough. Even in amateur theatre, people have jobs, classes, or home responsibilities—or all of the above. They are doing something else for a living and doing theatre to make the living worthwhile. Be respectful of their time. Use their time. Don't waste it.

Casting privileges rarely come with the job of television director. You usually inherit actors selected by other people. So when you are doing student projects or independent ones, enjoy the luxury of selecting the cast members with whom you want to work.

When you inherit a cast, you have to learn to be adaptable in dealing with a group of people who may have been working on a project together far longer than you have. Imagine getting a job as a director on Friends during its sixth season!

Top Ten Casting Considerations

We covered a lot of this material earlier, but it bears repeating.

First, if you are primarily responsible for hiring that actor, never fire the actor because you messed up. Actors are insecure enough without your help. Some stage directors have total control of the casting process. They had the opportunity to carefully audition actors, to see that they fit the parts to the director's satisfaction. Then they get into rehearsal and decide that this actor, who is doing a great job and working well and conscientiously, is not quite what they are now looking for. So they fire the actor, thereby making every other actor a paranoid wreck.

Arvin Brown, a really fine stage director, once said that if an actor turns out to be not what he now wants, he tries to fit the part to the actor since he can't seem to fit the actor to the part. Brown realizes there is something about the actor that made him, as the director, hire the person in the first place. And he should go back to that quality and work with it.

Second, get rid of the actor who is screwing up. This idea bears repeating often. If you let one actor arrive late, soon most of them will. Actors should be early or on time, prepared to rehearse. Actors must learn their lines and blocking in a timely manner. You should not have to put up with people who have alcohol or drug problems or cannot abide by the rigors of rehearsal discipline. Just as you owe it to actors to keep them on if they are doing their best, you owe it to everyone to get rid of people who are doing less than their best.

The television industry is full of stories of actors who were cast in the pilot and then dumped because the "chemistry" wasn't right. Of course, the stories that you hear are about the actors who then were cast in another sitcom and ended up in a ten-year run with a million-dollar-an-episode contract. Why does that happen in film and television? Many people have had a hand in the casting process, so the actor was a committee decision in the first place. We all know how bad committee decisions are.

If you marry the best looking person you know and then dump that one when a better-looking person comes along, you indicate your superficiality and stupidity. The same is true of selecting actors. Take the time to make the best choice possible and live with it—as long as the other person is doing his or her best to make the relationship work.

Third, actors usually have to learn to adjust to you. As much as you can, try to adjust to them also. As you work with the actors, you can learn their little quirks and try to adjust to them. For instance, this actor may appreciate side coaching—getting an adjustment from you while he or she is in the middle of a scene. Other actors find this process so distracting that they tend to lose focus.

You can't be all things to all people. But if it doesn't interfere with the total body of work, it helps to be able to adjust. Sometimes the situations have nothing do to with the work itself. If an actor is uncomfortable with your sense of humor or your language, he or she may not feel powerful enough to ask you to stop. But he or she will appreciate your effort to curb your behavior.

Both of us are big huggers. We often hug friends. Many Latinos do so in this culture, and it is neither sexual nor offensive. But two of our colleagues are very uncomfortable with it, so we never hug them. Even though they see us hugging other colleagues, they appreciate the fact that we respect their different sensibilities.

The biggest complaint we hear about some of our talented student directors is their constant use of the "f-word." Some of them cannot finish a sentence without it. Some students are totally comfortable with that language style. Other people tense each time they hear the word.

The one word that drives us to distraction is "like." Can anyone in the United States under the age of forty get through a complete sentence without inserting it? You ask the time, and they say, "It's like 4:30." What is that supposed to mean? The "l" word is so irritating that we would rather hear the "f" one at times. But our students are unaware they have said it. So, if you give me a direction, please don't put the word "like" in it. It is the only word in the sentence I will hear.

Fourth, feel free to rely on the casting recommendations of other directors, especially if you know their work and directing styles. Actors are more likely to behave with you as they do with your peers. If three other directors tell you this guy has a terrible time keeping his lines straight, you are not going to affect a miracle memory cure. If you can give the actor the time to learn the lines, use him. If you are rushed for time, don't.

In academic circles, we see so many young actors who give a director a very hard time about something. We learn that the actor will do the same thing to all our colleagues, not just us. One young man is a joy to work with if he has the part he wants. But if he thinks the part is beneath him, he does all sorts of subtle things to sabotage the production. Yet, a younger, less experienced faculty director will come along and think, "I can shape him up." Not very likely!

We ask out student directors to share with us their experiences with actors, especially those who are new to the program. They often remonstrate, "He gave me a hard time, but you're a teacher. He wouldn't do that to you." Wrong! If this person is a jerk with you, he would be a jerk with Strasberg or Spielberg and with a faculty director as well. If the actor pulls that stuff in the professional field, the reputation will frequently get around so fast that the actor won't get a chance to pull it on a big name. People may change, but usually they do it over a long period of time and generally not very much.

Fifth, know what you need from the actor before you cast. Sometimes certain attributes take precedence over other considerations. Recently, we put on a play for which we were doing the world premiere. We used a professional actor, whom none of us knew, on the basis of the recommendation of others and an audition tape. Usually this is a bad policy. But we chose him for several good reasons. A—It is the leading part, and this person has done the workshops and concert performances of the show. So he knows the material thoroughly. B—The rehearsal time is unusually short, and he can come in knowing the role cold. C—The principal character is a very famous person, and the actor bears a nice physical similarity to the character. No one we know in our casting pool does. D—Having a professional actor in the role is a good publicity device. E—He can serve as a mentor to aspiring professional actors in the group. Yes, those are good reasons, but we could still have regretted our choice for a variety of reasons too awful to think about.

You always want to cast the person who can "carry the show." The part of the protagonist usually goes to someone the audience wants to "watch, believe in and invest empathy in for a whole evening," (109) according to Stuart Vaughan in his directing book. He has a list of attributes you should consider, which we have added to our list of casting considerations.

Sixth, does the actor own the role? We want to feel that the actor playing the character owns the character, not that the character owns the actor and is about to eat him alive. We call it "owning your space." Characters have a reason to be in that space, and the actor should demonstrate that the actor deserves to be there as that character. It doesn't make any difference if the character feels secure. The actor should make us secure.

In the film *Collateral*, Tom Cruise plays a character type rare for him—the bad guy. Cruise makes us believe the bad guy knows what he is doing. We don't have to like the character—we just have to feel secure that he is who he is supposed to be. Jamie Foxx plays a character who is totally insecure. Foxx has the same authority as Cruise because we believe the actor is carrying the part, and we believe the character is insecure. The actor is playing an insecure character with authority.

Seventh, does the actor have vocal clarity? We mentioned earlier the need for stage actors in particular to be heard and understood easily. If we don't hear the dialogue, we don't get the story. The person can have an accent, but if it is so thick we can't understand the ideas, we get lost. The vocal quality can be unpleasant, but it should suit the character and not be unbearable.

Obviously stage actors have to be heard and understood completely the first time the audience hears the words—there is no second time for live theatre audiences. Even on film and television, the audience has to hear clearly. If scenes have to be reshot or looped because one actor is a mush-mouth, costs go up considerably. That means fewer chances for employment for the actor—and possibly that director.

As stage directors, we hear the dialogue so often that we can lose track of the clarity. At this point, directors need a fresh set of ears to help them. We faculty directors often sit in on each other's rehearsals to be fresh ears for the director, letting him or her know what passages or persons are hard to understand.

All good actors make the dialogue sound as if it is being spoken for the first time. Consider the line, "Mos Eisley Spaceport. You will never find a more treacherous hive of scum and villainy. We must be careful." It is a terrible line, and even writer George Lucas knew it just before filming it on the set of the original *Star Wars*. He wanted to change it, if not cut it. But veteran Alec Guinness asked to do a take because he thought he could say the line, in character, and make it work. He proved to be correct.

That is the big difference between an actor and a civilian. A nonactor may be very believable the first time through a line but not after the tenth rehearsal or reshoot.

Eighth, look for an actor with intelligence. We have found that the more intelligence the actor has, the more tools you have at your disposal as a director. Your biggest task is to communicate. Obviously, it is easier to communicate with people who are intelligent, who "Get it." Of course, we also argue that intelligence in all the people in your work group enhances the quality of the work.

Many times, intelligence compensates for raw dumb talent. Just as it is hard to play a drunk when you are inebriated, it is difficult to play a "dumbbell" if you are not smart. One of our graduates was class valedictorian. He plays the "dumb guy" on a TV series.

Ninth, the actor needs energy. When we speak of the need for actor energy, we mean that there is a certain vitality about the person, not just a lot of twitching and wasted energy. If the actor is blah, he or she has a much harder time getting our attention. Even in repose, the actor should show this energy.

Energy does not mean going over the top. The best equivalent is that the actor's instrument should be in tune. An actor should be ready to play every note at any volume with appropriate feeling and sensitivity. He or she shouldn't be like some ancient computer that takes ages to boot up and never quite has the power for a job of any size or complexity.

Tenth, the actor needs "the look." We summarize the final attribute as "the look." Actors often have to be handsome or beautiful but not always. Actors should look like the characters they play. Danny diVito has a very different look than Tom Cruise, but they both have the right looks for the parts they play. Obviously good looks made life easier for Tom Cruise early in his career and hampered Danny diVito. But both of them have "the look," and neither has to worry about competing for the other's parts.

"The look" can also be interpreted as "the feel." The right actors emanate a kind of sensibility that makes you feel they will bring something special to the part. It's hard to describe and harder to find an analogy for it. We would even argue that it is not always the same on stage as on screen. Some actors "have it" in both screen and stage roles. Others have it live but not on screen, or on screen but not live.

Other Casting Considerations

We need to think about traditional versus nontraditional casting. Traditional casting assumes that every part ever written was designed for a handsome young white male. (Go back to the ancients. Even women's parts were played by handsome young white males.) Think again. Traditional thinking is still rampant in the professions, but that should not stop you.

Years ago, if a television script called for a judge, the part was automatically assigned to a white male over fifty with hair to match his race. Now we see judges of every ethnicity, both sexes, and a variety of ages. You may be so used to it, you are not even aware of it. We are so old that we still notice that the judge was cast nontraditionally.

Unfortunately, this traditional casting concept is still embedded in the minds of many of the people in power. A few years ago, we got a tearful phone call from a former student. He is an incredibly handsome young man, part African American, part Latino, with a rich, velvety voice. He was befriended by a famous New York agent, who used to talk about him as a sort of son. The agent seemed to have a very hard time even getting auditions for the actor.

One week, the agent's office was beset by absenteeism and the kind young actor volunteered to come in and staff the place. A casting breakdown came in calling for an intern, "handsome, beautiful baritone voice, good build." He realized that he hadn't been sent in for the role, though he was clearly perfect for it. He looked through the files to pull out his head shot and resume. He decided to submit himself. The reason for the tears? He was in the "ethnic file." This agent did not send a minority person out on a call unless the call sheet specifically called for that particular minority.

Another former student, now a very successful Latino actor, got sent on a call for a very popular sitcom early in his career. It was a one-line part for an air-conditioning repair man. The line was hilarious, and the pay was terrific. He did the audition and then said, "Would you like me to play it with an Hispanic accent?" They let him try it. He got the part—because he made a funny line funnier with his delivery. It was not because he was Latino, nor in spite of it. He was—is—a fine actor, and his agent and the casting people recognized that.

So, if you have a traditional mentality, get over it. Sometimes we are short of good male actors and heavy on fine female ones when we are doing classical theatre. So we have done the plays in a modern setting. A woman played Cassius in *Julius Caesar*, which gave some of her later speeches to Brutus a particular poignancy. A number of people thought we were doing Cassius as channeled by Hillary Clinton. It didn't occur to us, but that interpretation works, too.

In our classical productions, women have played lawyers and even Caliban in *The Tempest*. We have done a *Hamlet* with a Latino in the title role, while Hamlet's parents were Anglo actors. No one noticed because we didn't make a big deal out of it. Actors are actors, not ethnic persons. They can play nearly everything. Even though our university has a majority of Latino students, we have cast Anglos as members of Latino families. No one thinks anything of it.

Conversely, you can use nontraditional casting to make a point. Once we did *Zoo Story* and cast a white Peter and an African American Jerry. It added a level of racial overlay to the play that we thought made it interesting.

How to Organize the Casting Process

This next section assumes you are the person doing the casting. That is a given in live theatre and ought to be in screen projects.

When you prepare your cast breakdown for auditions, try to write descriptions that can attract the best possible choices. If the character is a white racist, then you want to cast a white person and have him or her act racist. If the character must have certain skills, like singing, the information must be in the breakdown or you will be forced to waste a tremendous amount of time.

The breakdown is the first step. In addition to containing information that should appear in your casting notices, writing the breakdown helps you decide how you see each character. Read the script over carefully, and note what attributes are absolutely necessary for the actors in each part. It will help you sort actors immediately. You can note on the actor's audition sheet: "Too thin to play Ruby, could play Veronica."

Even after you select the attributes you want in the character, you can always change your mind when an actor changes it for you. One classic example of this is supposed to be responsible for the original Willie Loman in *Death of a Salesman*.

Few people know that the part of Willie was written as a smallish man. He described himself at one point in the script as a "shrimp." Then Lee J. Cobb auditioned and blew everyone away. Arthur Miller changed several lines in the script to suit this tall, heavy man. Ever since, the word in the script has been "walrus."

Director Brian Warren wrote fairly extensive breakdowns for each of the many characters in his production of the stage version of *One Flew Over the Cuckoo's Nest*. This information was too much to be included in the printed breakdown that appeared in the newspaper, but it was given or sent to every actor who signed up for an audition slot. Below is a sample of the breakdowns he wrote for the female characters:

PRINCIPALS—WOMEN

NURSE RATCHED is a handsome, middle-aged woman whose age is "hard to tell." Though "ripe and womanly," she locks her sexuality inside an oddly-perfect face that is as smooth as flesh-colored enamel, a brilliant warm but artificial smile, and a white uniform that has been starched until it appears almost metallic. She walks stiffly, and when she is angry she seems to swell up like a giant octopus.

NURSE FLINN is a flat, stale, tedious young girl with apprehensive eyes, a gold cross at her throat, and a constant fear of being raped although she finds the prospect thrilling, too. She is deeply ashamed of her body.

CANDY STARR is a happy-go-lucky woman who walks "light-footed across the grass with her eyes green all the way up to the ward, and her hair, roped in a long twist at the back of her head, jouncing up and down with every step like copper springs in the sun."

SANDRA is a big, earthy party girl who got married right after McMurphy went to the Work Farm, but has now been separated from her husband.

The Interview

To us, at least, this step can be very important. It can be part of the audition or precede it. It is a brief job interview. The actor has a head shot as well as a resume to give you. You spend a few minutes getting to know the actor and ask any necessary questions. Then comes the audition. The difference between an interview and an audition is that the interview is a discussion with the actor in his or her own persona. In the audition, the actor reads for a part for which he or she is being considered. We think it is very important to get a sense of the actor's persona, as well as to see how he or she handles the character. We can probably get the actor to adjust the character. We won't have time to get to adjust the actor's personality.

The interview is a good chance to check things out from the actor's resume. A few well-placed questions can help to determine if the actor has padded it with false experience.

The Audition

The audition can be done in any number of ways. The important aspect is for you to hear (*audio*, meaning "I hear") what the character sounds like as the actor interprets it. Of course, you get to see the actor as well. We prefer to do the audition in the following manner. It is not necessarily the best way, but it works best for us.

We schedule audition–interviews in ten-minute intervals. Since we know many of the actors very well, the interview part is often very brief. We have each actor read separately and not with other actors being considered for parts. Often, with actors we know, the process takes much less than ten minutes. Then we can take more time with actors we don't know or see a walk-in or two.

Auditioning is a special skill for both the actor and the director. The following is a section we adopted and enlarged from material found in other sources and from our own experience as well.

Getting the Best Talent

Actors are given all sorts of advice about how to do well in auditions, and there are courses for actors to improve their audition techniques. But what about the auditors? How do we get the best results for the time and energy we spend casting?

Coaches constantly remind actors that we auditors need to find the right actors. They need to be reminded that we are more eager to cast correctly than they realize. Try to convey this attitude during the audition process. Do whatever is necessary to create a positive atmosphere so the actors will be able to show their best to you. This is no time for ugly power trips.

Performers spend time and money preparing for auditions, particularly professional ones. Be as specific as possible in your casting notice so the actors can show you what you want to see. If you get pictures, resumes, tapes, and so on, it is a courtesy to return them, even though you have no obligation to do so. But if you think you might have some use for them relatively soon, keep them. An actor is flattered when you say, "I have nothing for you now, but I'd like to keep this for my files. I may have something else soon."

Treat the resume as a confidential document. It should not get abused by lowlifes looking for a date or an e-mail pen pal. Most actors try to have agents or answering services to filter out people who use this material wrongfully.

Your *casting notice* is your best guarantee of getting the best actors to come to the auditions. It should contain all the information necessary. Include all the following ten items:

1. The *name* or working title of the project or production company.
2. A brief description of the project. Is it a student production, a workshop, an original piece? It is vitally important that your casting notice contains the fact that nudity is involved and, if it is, specifically how much (e.g., full frontal male nudity for three leading characters). Whether for screen or stage, the actors should have a clear idea of what the piece involves regarding physical exposure before coming to the audition. That also applies to physical exposure in the sense of physical danger involved.
3. A brief description of the audition procedure. Is it interviews only? Will you do physical or vocal typing out? Are you requiring a prepared monologue or two or more monologues? Should they be from a certain period or genre? Will you do cold readings from the script? If dance is involved, what level of dance ability and style (e.g., tap, ballet, jazz, modern, ballroom, street) are you expecting? Does the actor have to sing? If so, what style (e.g., legit, rock, pop, belt, lyrical, country)? If it's a published show, do you want to hear songs from the show or not?

4. The place. Be sure information on place of auditions is correct. Also be sure you say where the show will be performed or shot.

5. Specific character breakdown as needed. Gender, age, race, height, and hair color should be specified only whenever such attributes are required of the part. If casting is multiracial, say so. If you must have female dancers no taller than 5 feet 7 inches, say so. If the tenor has to have a clear B flat, say so.

6. The schedule. Why waste time auditioning actors who can't fit the schedule? Include if at all possible dates and times of callbacks, the date rehearsals begin, when the show opens, when and how long it runs, and video rehearsal and shooting schedules.

   In our university productions, we often have students with horrendous work and class schedules. Know before you cast what the obligations of each individual are. We make a tremendous effort to do so, yet we frequently complain that we have not been able to have a full cast rehearsal for three weeks because of conflicts. It is even worse with student projects.

7. Is any pay involved? Are any special requirements involved, such as being a duly registered student in a summer workshop? For film projects, will actors get footage for their reels? Is this a union or nonunion show?

8. How is the actual audition being handled? Is it an open call? Is there a sign up sheet? Can they make phone appointments? Be sure the phone is intelligently manned during the time phone appointments are being made. These days we always ask for e-mail addresses whenever appointments are being made. If something changes—for instance, the room floods and the auditions must be moved—you can contact everyone fairly efficiently as well as have signs at the old location.

9. If you are looking for only extras, replacements, or understudies, be sure to say so. Will they have a guaranteed chance to perform?

10. If certain parts are precast, say so in the audition notice. Don't let actors waste time preparing for parts that are unavailable.

Scheduling and sign ups. Be realistic on the time allowed. It's wiser to tell the actors five minutes but to actually schedule ten minutes apart. If you don't need the extra five minutes, the actor feels he has gotten the five you promised. If you need the ten, you have it, and the actor is flattered by the attention.

Open calls. Personally, we hate them. Either everyone comes at the same time, or they all come late, wasting everyone's time. Then the auditioners sit around and cause tension to mount and rumors to build. We have seen actors "work over" perceived rivals to undermine their confidence. At paid or professional auditions, all sorts of traffic problems can develop. We prefer scheduled auditions and think that open calls are generally not a good idea.

Location. Use a professional location. No sane person should go to a hotel room or private house they don't know. Borrow or rent a nice neutral space—a studio, an empty theatre, a bank conference room—anything that appears public and on the up and up. There should be sufficient light and air, a piano and dance space if necessary, a separate waiting area, and a toilet.

Be early.

Stay on schedule. You will still fall behind, but do your best.

Be brief. Introduce yourself, but don't do a life story. Auditions run smoother if your notice requires actors to bring their own audition material. If someone really interests you, don't keep them on, reading away. Schedule them for a callback. That is what callbacks are for. Auditions are really preliminary screenings. Never tell auditioners they have the part, but you can tell them that you will call them back on the twenty-second. Therefore, they should save the date.

Get help with your own auditions. Some people use their producers or stage managers. We prefer to have an audition secretary who may be the assistant director. We like to use the producer or stage manager as an extra set of eyes and ears sitting near us at auditions. Have someone else in the waiting area to keep track of who's next and to distribute cold reading scenes or collect any information necessary.

If you want someone for a callback, give that person a script to look at. Suggest any section to which the person should pay particular attention. Tell the actor to be prepared for whatever you will expect to see—tap and jazz steps, a lyric singing piece, a foreign accent, whatever. The actor has made an effort to come to your scheduled audition. You should make an effort to schedule the callback when it is convenient for the actor.

You need to give yourself plenty of lead time in casting. Don't waste time on tricky stuff like foreign accents at the first audition. See if the person looks right, speaks clearly, and can act, then find out about the other stuff at the callback. Let the actor know what you will be looking for at the callback.

Never cast on the spot. This is a law rather than a rule. But if you break the law, at least don't read anyone else for the part once you cast it. It's not fair to the actors.

Be professional. If you're a pro, people will want to work with you. They can't be expected to love working with rude or disorganized people.

Don't panic when you suddenly have to replace an actor. Wait twenty-four hours if possible before deciding what do. Your first idea or choice is usually a bad one, and it would have been better to wait. A great idea will come to you in twenty-four hours. If it doesn't, then go with that immediate panic idea. You may wind up playing it yourself or having the stage manager do it. But those should be your last choices, not your first.

Many of the preceding ideas came from an article by Andrea Wolper in the July 29, 1984, edition of *Backstage*, as verified by our own experiences.

Sample Casting Notice. December 11 and 12 are the new dates for auditions for UTPA University Theatre's spring musical, *Once Upon a Mattress*. This audience-pleaser originally starred Carol Burnett as the young princess and is the hilarious musical adaptation of the legend of *The Princess and the Pea*.

Anyone in the community may audition, although there are no parts for children in this show. Nearly all the parts require singing voices. People should be prepared to sing at least sixteen bars of a song, preferably one from a standard Broadway musical and not rock, gospel, or country. An accompanist will be present, but those auditioning should bring their own sheet music.

Auditions are held in COAS 107, the Studio Theatre of the Communication Building on the Sugar Road side of the Edinburg campus. They start promptly at 7 PM both nights, with call-backs scheduled for Wednesday, December 13.

According to director Brian Warren, people may audition on either Monday or Tuesday. On Wednesday, the finalists from the first two nights will be called in for further auditioning: "They should be prepared to sing and then we will ask them to move to another room to learn some brief, simple choreography. They don't all have to be dancers, but we need to know who can learn dance steps and who can't. Also, anyone with a head shot and resume is requested to bring them." Most of the characters are college age, with an equal number of men and women.

Parts will be assigned and scripts distributed before the Christmas break. Rehearsal begin in early January and will be scheduled for evenings, The play will run the first weekend on March.

Anyone needing more information about the auditions can contact Brian Warren at 381-2222 or Elva Galvan in the box office at 381-3333.

In Five Minutes, What Should You Look For?

For screen work, we suggest you videotape the person. Some people come across very differently on screen. We had a student who was, putting it kindly, a mediocre stage actress, but she burst through the camera. On film or video, she was immensely powerful. We rarely tell a student, "Go West, young person." She was an exception. In spite of our urging, and a reel that would make most professional actresses jealous, she never got up the nerve. But she did a load of student projects and had a reel to die for. From her stage work, you never would have guessed it.

As you work through this list with each actor, try to write a fast note—a word or two—in answer to each question. How soon we forget! The notes help to remind us later. These notes can be very cruel and curt. They are for private consumption, just to help you keep the auditioners straight. You don't want others to see them because often they are cryptic and can seem mean when you are just being terse.

In order to be sure casting notes don't "get out," we keep the notes locked in our office. After casting, we shred the evidence. After casting, if we have the time and think we may want to reference them later, we compile them and keep them in a secure place.

Try to remember to note the following:

1. What the actor looks like—tall, short, bright red beard, chubby
2. Voice and speech characteristics—great projection, slushy, raspy
3. Audition behavior—nervous, relaxed, smart Alec, focused, ditzy
4. The acting—phony, convincing, overdone, true
5. Movement skills—clumsy, graceful, awkward
6. To call back or not. Write it on the sheet so you don't forget.
7. Make up one that is important to you. These are important to us.

Also worthy of note: if you are doing screen work, put the auditions on tape. Many directors leave the interview and shooting to others. They then watch the tapes later and make their call-back list from the replay.

Most directors, rightfully, become uncomfortable if the actor plays directly to them as if the auditors were their acting partners. We just suggest to the actor, right away, "Please play to"—and give them a spot to look at. We can then take our notes in comfort without making ourselves or the actors uncomfortable.

Directors should at least say "thank you" as the auditioner leaves. If you are sure you will call the person back, you can say, "You'll hear from us within the next (day, week, whatever)."

A good technique, if you are not rushed for time, is to give the actor an adjustment and see if the person is a trained seal or can really act. If the person plays the scene sweetly and calmly, ask the actor to play it as if the other person is their worst enemy. It is not a matter of what the actor does. If the actor is incapable of change, you'll be in big trouble if you use him or her. We nearly always run short of time in the first audition, so we usually save the adjustment request for the call back.

Recently, we started asking the stage manager, who is in the audition room, to use our cell phone to take a digital photo of each actor, whether or nor the person has a head shot. It helps us to remember that individual when we study our notes later. They look exactly as we remember them from the audition and not as they appear in their head shots.

Call Backs

Call backs give you a lot of different options. You have a chance to do a bit of directing to see if the actors are responsive to your directing style. Feel free to guide them toward your specific interpretation of the part if they seem to be going in another direction. Often people at the call-back have had a chance to peruse the script. Now you get to try things with them and even to let them try things with you. If they have an idea for the characters, let them show you.

Note we say, "Show you," not "Tell you." In auditions and rehearsals, some actors fall into the trap of talking about acting rather than doing it. It really doesn't matter what the actor says he wants to do. You have to see it. Describing the action intentions shows you nothing.

You have to see what they want to do. "I want to play her as a deeper, more sensitive woman with a caring heart and a great concern for her daughter," is just a time-wasting device designed to keep the actor from having to do what she is there for—act. Let her show you a couple of lines in the new modality, and see if it does anything for you, the character, and the scene.

But never show the actor what you want. Otherwise you will have Mini-Me's instead of actors. It is the actor's job to act, not direct, and the director's job to direct, not act. Tell them what you want and let them show you something—not the other way around.

This is the point where you make sure they have the specific skills you need for the roles. If they must sing, you must hear them sing. If they must do an accent, you must hear the accent.

Steel Magnolias playwright Robert Harling told us about his experience with casting his play in England. The actress would come into the interview room and the director would remark about how good it was to see her since they had worked together in repertory or the Old Vic and so on. Then he would ask her if she could do a Southern accent. She would assure him, in her best Mayfair diction, that she could. Not once did he get to hear an actress do the Southern accent during auditions. In the U.S. productions, on the other hand, each actress demonstrated her ability to do the accent. Give us the U.S. audition method every time!

Sometimes the casting question can be a health issue. One of us has a weak ankle, the other a weak lung. One of us can't do simple dance steps, while the other would be taking a dangerous chance in a part that required heavy smoking. If you absolutely, positively, have to have an actor who smokes, I would refuse the role. I need the lung more than the job. If I can't dance, you would know it instantly and wonder why I wasted your time trying out for a dancing role.

So, if the part requires special skills, strengths (like carrying a corpse over your shoulder), or other problematic issues, clear it up at call backs by seeing that they can perform the task.

You can ask for a second call back. If you go past two, unions require payment, but it is not generous. An actress friend was called back several times for the same part in *The Sopranos*. There wasn't a lot of other work for her that season. Although HBO has a lower-than-network pay scale, it was a chance to work.

Rather than being flattered, she turned them down when they asked her to return for audition number four. "The callbacks are way out in Queens. It takes over an hour to get there, and I don't get paid taxi or limo fare. Also, it's night when I leave, and taxis are scarce in Queens. I don't need the part that badly. Besides, it was not a recurring part. How many times do they need to see me before they can make a commitment?"

So, remember—don't mistreat the actors. Even actors have limits for the amount of abuse they will take.

Suggested Reading and Viewing

Reading

Stage
Albright, Hardie. *Stage Direction in Transition*. See chapter 8.
Catron, Louis E. *The Director's Vision*. See chapters 11 and 12.
Dean, Alexander, and Lawrence Carra. *Fundamentals of Play Directing*. See chapter 12.

Hodge, Francis. *Play Directing*. See chapter 7.
Kirk, John W., and Ralph A. Bellas. *The Art of Directing*. See chapter 12.
O'Neill, R. H., and N. M. Boretz. *The Director as Artist*. See chapter 7.
Patterson, Jim. *Stage Directing*. See step 4.
Shapiro, Mel. *The Director's Companion*. See chapter 7.
Vaughan, Stuart, *Directing Plays*. See chapter 6.

Screen
Benedetti, Robert. *From Concept to Screen*. See chapter 6, pages 55–58.
Lukas, Christopher. *Directing for Film and Television*. See chapter 3.
Weston, Judith. *Directing Actors*. See chapters 6 and 8.

5

What Is Composition?

Composition

Composition involves arranging the actors and other visible materials in a visual plan to illustrate the dramatic action in the best possible way. As you look at any picture—stage, screen, painting, photograph—the complete set of visible elements in the picture and their relationship to each other make up the composition. The elements of the composition don't tell the story. The composition shows you the feeling, quality, and mood through color, line, mass and form.

Each kind of theatre has the same basic principles of composition, but the practices differ according to the medium being used. The principles of composition are, in many ways, the same as those in painting. But obviously the application of these principles changes with the medium. The principles of composition are the same for painting and sculpture, but the application is different. It is the same in the various sorts of theatre.

On stage, for instance, the different physical stages—arena, thrust, proscenium, and others—will dictate different applications of the principles. Since in film and television you have different tools at your disposal, you will also apply these principles in a different way.

Think of composition as the stage or screen picture you can see at any single given moment. It is a picture. What does that picture tell you? If I am putting out my hands to give you a present, that is one stage picture. If my hands are in about the same position but pointing a gun at you, the picture has radically changed. Everything you can see in a single frame is the composition.

In working on composition, we try to get the picture itself to tell or rein-force the story without the aid of dialogue or blocking (i.e., movement). We can achieve any single principle—putting the most emphasis on the most important person or thing in the picture, for instance—by a variety of means.

You can put the most important person or thing (let's call that A) in the foreground:

$$D B A C E$$

You can make A larger:

$$B C L A R D E$$

You can make A lighter or brighter than anything or anyone else:

$$B L G F A R C D$$

You can frame A in an emphatic position—like a doorway or a win-dow—to draw attention:

$$B L G F / A / R C D N$$

That is basically how composition works. At each moment in the pro-duction, you are deciding which methods available to you will work best under these particular conditions.

First, let's count a few basic kinds of visual frames with which a direc-tor may deal.

Live-Theatre Stage Configurations

In the live theatre, we generally work on three different stage configura-tions: (1) proscenium, (2) open-thrust, and (3) arena. These are usually spaces designed for theatrical purposes by architects. There used to be a configuration called the forestage-proscenium, but it is very rare these days.

We should add another space—the found space. This found space is any space not designed originally as a theatre that a director uses to pres-ent a production. Sometimes, people just do a play in a church, a garage, or even a barn, with little architectural adjustment. Other times, a build-ing is converted at great expense and with major design changes. Then we don't call it a found space any more. It's a conversion. At that point, the found space usually takes on one of the other three forms.

Proscenium

The typical theatre of the nineteenth century was the proscenium. The audience looks at a wall that has a picture in it. The actors are in a frame, and the entire audience sits nearer or closer to the frame. Most of the theatres you have seen have very likely had proscenium stages. Broadway theatres are proscenium houses.

Since the 1950s, other configurations have gained in popularity, but the proscenium stage is still the most common. A proscenium stage tries to create the illusion that we are sitting in front of it and everything we see behind the hole in the wall is happening as we watch. The curtains hide the light sources and stage mechanisms. The seating arrangement and the lighting force the focus on the stage and away from the other audience members. For most of today's audience members, it is just like the movie theatre so familiar to them.

Blocking Suggestions
Actors usually should maintain their places behind the wall and not appear to cross through the proscenium toward the audience or appear to be outside the prescribed lines of the setting. It would be as "shocking" as having a film actor come off the screen and walk toward us in the movie house. In recent decades, the rule is often violated for special effect.

Thrust

The thrust is a stage with a playing area that juts out into the audience. Some audience members see it from one side, some from another, and some from the front view. When you work on a thrust stage, you have all the staging problems of the proscenium and the added challenge of staging so that the side viewers are not disadvantaged. Thrust does, however, provide a greater audience intimacy and generally requires less scenery to be built.

In a thrust stage house, audiences are seated on three sides of a stage, with the stage backed by a wall on the fourth. No portion of the stage is concealed from the audience, Everything takes place before the audience. It is "thrust" because it juts out from its wall into the audience area.

Thrust theatres can be configured so the audience is raised, as in Lincoln Center, New York, and the actors are at entrance–floor level. Or the thrust can look like Shakespeare's Globe with a raised stage surrounded by audience. Thrust is the classical stage, the oldest form we know. A version of it was used by the Greeks in the fifth century BC, and it was also the stage of classical Chinese opera.

It is quite popular for a number of reasons. It gives a more real quality to the stage with its three-dimensional feel. It helps to segregate live theatre from the flat screen look of television, film, and the proscenium stage. It gives the designers a back wall so there is some scenery. It requires less scenery than a proscenium stage, so it is less expensive to capitalize a show scenically—there are fewer flats to build and paint. Actors and directors find it easier to block for visibility on the thrust than on the arena. They don't have to keep in constant motion to be visible.

At our university, we chose a thrust configuration for all these reasons when we designed our new theatre. When we first started using it, someone remarked, "It's like acting in the right hand of God the father." The stage space feels protective and has a positive energy about it that actors from other venues find energizing.

Lighting plays a stronger role in this kind of stage. With the lighting designer's expertise, audiences don't notice the lack of scenery that might otherwise bother them. On the open-thrust stage, light becomes the curtain, with actors entering and exiting in the dark.

The vomitory entrance became very popular with the development of the thrust and arena stage. The vomitory allowed quick entrances. A large number of actors could be "vomited" onto the stage area very quickly on to or off the stage. Some arena stages have several of these entrances.

Vertical playing space is very important in thrust staging. Designers and directors are always looking for ways to get levels on stage to make for interesting visual effects in blocking and scenery.

Blocking Suggestions

Composition and movement on this stage are a peculiar combination of proscenium and arena blocking. Blocking for this stage is excellent training for television camera blocking. Plays televised from a thrust stage come out better than those shot from a proscenium stage. The theatre naturally lends itself to a three-camera shoot. In fact, the thrust theatre at out university allows a six-camera setup—three in the top row and three on the floor.

Arena

An arena is a stage centered within a circle of audience members. Its chief advantage lies in its intimacy and the fact that there can be very little scenery. A boxing ring is an arena stage.

An arena is also called a theatre-in-the-round. This configuration has never been as popular as the proscenium. It came into fairly widespread use in the 1930s by groups wanting to produce plays on lower budgets. An arena stage can produce more seats and less scenery costs in the same square footage as a proscenium. It has been popular in community, educational and non-Broadway professional venues. Several famous regional theatres use the arena configuration.

At first, audiences and critics felt the effect of arena staging was more lifelike than proscenium staging. The audience was closer to the actor and could visually share the experience with other audience members. It was a more communal experience. Most early advocates loved the presumed intimacy.

Theatre-in-the-round can be a trap. It requires experienced designers and directors as well as capable, trained actors. Everyone involved must know the particular challenges of working in the arena space. They must all be aware of the fact that seeing is more difficult for the audience and blocking accommodations are needed. It's a major challenge for designers to make a realistic-looking set with no walls or major visual obstructions. Actors require greater projection, even for a small space, because some of the audience is always behind them.

Blocking Suggestions

First you must forget the one-sided view of the proscenium stage. You must work particularly hard on character relationships so the audience is clear even with the limited views they have. And you can't have two people sitting on a couch for a long time. Actors need to have more frequent and more varied movements than they would in a proscenium play.

In the 1960s, a few professional productions were done on revolving circular stages, but they were blocked proscenium-style with no back wall. The stage rotated constantly, like a theme restaurant on a tall building, only more rapidly. You were supposed to sit and watch the actors spin into various versions of the view, rather like watching your child on a merry-go-round. These buildings were fairly short-lived and expensive experiments.

If you must block for the arena, give directions as if the stage were a clock. Traditionally, the light booth is high noon and the other numbers radiate from there. Whenever we had to direct for the arena, we felt like navigators in a war movie: "Actors at ten o'clock, chief."

Screen Configurations

Working with cameras, we confront four major considerations: the recording medium, the display screen aspect ratio, the principle of thirds, and camera placement.

The difference in the recording medium—film vs. digital video—is significant. Each medium affects how the image will appear to the audience. From the perspective of lighting, film can deal with a contrast ratio of one hundred to one. As of this writing, the best digital recording can do is about fifty to one. This means that film is able to much more closely approximate what the human eye can see. And there is also the perception of the "look" of digital (the six o'clock news, soap opera, or porn film look) as opposed to the traditional film look. The ability to record and display major visual contrast variables is like a painter having a richer selection of pigments from which to choose.

Often budget dictates the selection of the recording medium. Digital video is certainly more within the financial range of beginning and independent filmmakers and producers. On larger budget productions, the cost of footage (e.g., raw stock, developing, transferring, negative cutting, and printing) is a minor consideration instead of a major one as it is on tight budgets. Ultimately, the goal should be to provide the audience with the best image the budget allows.

But realistically, cost drives production values on every level. Even when the choice of medium is film, the differences among the various film widths (16 mm vs. 35 mm vs. 70 mm) can have an impact on the audience. Simply put, the larger the canvas (16 mm, 35 mm, 70 mm), the more information—the more detail—the director can capture and display in the end product. Assume the director knows from the start of the project that the finished production is destined not for the big screen but for the video and home market. Then there is almost no discernable difference between 16 and 35 mm film and certainly no value whatsoever for a 70 mm stock.

Some digital editing programs will add a specific visual effect to the postproduction image, giving video a "film look." While this may fool some viewers, it does not add the missing degrees of contrast. It doesn't actually convert the quality of video to that of film.

The director wants to be able to make the choice of film or video based on strictly creative criteria. Realistically, that is not always the case. Therefore, it is in the director's best interest to know the abilities and the limitations of whatever medium the project is to be recorded and displayed upon.

The screen aspect ratio, or the size and shape of the screen on which the audience views the production, dictates the shape and content of the individual shots. Slow down and read this section carefully and you'll grasp the concepts and terminology that may have escaped you for years. Consider film and TV to be pictured in "landscape" instead of "portrait"—to use terms you will understand from dealing with your computer printer or monitor. Landscape is wider than it is high; portrait is higher than it is long. The image of film and TV is therefore wider than it is high.

1:33 to 1

When the motion picture industry was getting started, the aspect ratio was 1.33 to 1 (meaning the image was 1.33 units wide and 1 unit high). The units could be inches, feet, yards, or meters depending on the size of the screen the image was projected upon. It was typically written "1.33:1."

The 1.33:1 standard was the uniformly used format for film, although it was unofficial, beginning in 1903. This size, known as Academy Standard (Figure 5.1), was formally sanctioned by the Academy of Motion Picture Arts and Sciences when this industry-wide organization was formed in 1927.

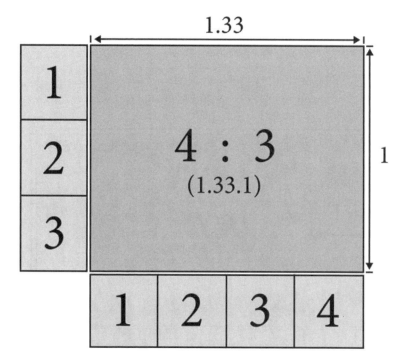

Figure 5.1   Academy Standard

3 × 4

When TV came along, it adopted this same size, roughly 4 by 3 (expressed as 3 × 4). Since TV began eating into film's audience, the motion picture business began experimenting with color forms and 3-D as well as different screen sizes as ways to win back its audience. The new image standard, called Academy Flat (Figure 5.2), was 1.66:1 to 1.85:1 (or a little wider in some cases), went under the titles of VistaVision, SuperScope, and Techniscope—all words you've seen on the credits of old feature films. This was soon followed by Cinemascope, Technirama, and TODD-AO—again, labels you'll find on old films that were also known as "anamorphic" because they required a special lens to morph or compact the image for filming and expand it for projection. The ratio was anywhere from 2.35:1 to 2.66:1.

16 × 9

Today the most popular anamorphic process is Panavision. This comes out at about 16 units by 9 units. It is the 16 × 9 shape that is the approved format for high-definition television (HDTV).

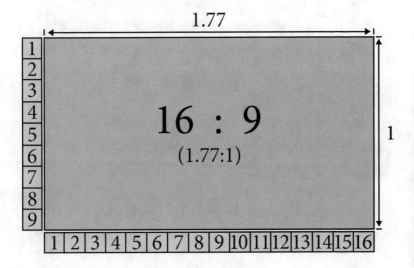

Figure 5.2   Academy Flat and Anamorphic Scope

Anything you film or tape now will ultimately be seen on a 16 × 9 size HDTV. The wider screen image is horizontally compressed when recorded on DVD and then stretched by the player for viewing. It is best to shoot for the new format because that's where part of the market is now and all of it will be in the future. Any director's viewer and the viewfinder of most midrange to higher-end cameras have marks indicating the part of the image to be captured within the major screen formats. This includes what is called "television safe," meaning that within these lines any image will be seen on the standard 3 × 4 TVs. Therefore, you should be familiar with the terms "full screen," "widescreen," and "letterbox."

"Full screen" is an image originally designed for 3 × 4 or cut off from any 16 × 9 or larger format to fit only within the 3 × 4 TV screen. "Widescreen" is an image that will either fully fit the 16 × 9 formatted screen or will be shown with a black area at the top and bottom of the screen called "letterbox."

High Def

High definition or "high def" video refers to the number of scan lines used to create each second of picture. The International Telecommunication Union (ITU) has set the standards as 1,080 active interlaced or 720 progressive lines at the 16 × 9 picture size. To grasp all the current technology and terms, here's what you need to understand. First, film is shot and projected at a rate of twenty-four frames per second. TV is thirty frames per second. Thus, when a film is shown on TV or converted to video, some frames of the film are dropped.

The terms high def or HDTV (1080i or 1080p) refer to the number of "scan lines" (lines of video dots, or "pixels") used to make up a complete frame of video as well as how these lines are linked. There are 1,080 (called "ten-eighty") scan lines per frame. The lines are laid out on the screen in two different ways. There are 1,920 pixels per line (or about 2.07 million pixels per frame).

In "interlacing" (the "i" in the 1080i), first the odd numbered lines [1, 3, 5, 7, 9, etc.] and then in the next half second the even numbered [2, 4, 6, 8, etc.] alternate to make a single complete "frame" of video. Each half second or each set of lines is called a "field." It takes both "fields" to make up a "frame." This method is linear and works with older TVs, even older projection sets (a system using an internal projector to enlarge an originally smaller image).

The other methods used to put the fields together are called "progressive scan" (also called noninterlaced scanning). This is where the "p" comes from in the1080p system that is marketed as "Full High-Definition." This method requires storing and transmitting matched fields of pixels in sequence. Also called 720p, this number refers to the number of scan lines per half second. Do the math: double 720 and you'll see that this number exceeds 1080, which is because there's actually more video information in the progressive scan technique than in the inter-laced system.

Whether the viewing screen is plasma, LCD, or high-end HD projection, all 1080p sets support the progressive scan technology.

Principle of Thirds

The *principle of thirds*, also called *the Golden Mean*, is a basic method of arranging material within the frame to accomplish the photographic intent. Any type of picture—stage or screen, motion or still—involves the exploitation of several elements. The picture should have simplicity and balance of shapes and use lines, patterns, texture, foreground, background, and tone. The picture should have a center of interest. By drawing a balanced tic-tac-toe design across the frame and then circling the four points where the lines intersect, you can identify four places on the screen where the center of interest could ideally be placed. With something important on two or three of these intersections, interesting shots are not difficult to compose.

Camera Placement

Film and television directors work with cameras as well as actors. The number of cameras used determines the style of shooting and the kinds of composition used. The decision to use one or more cameras is often a creative and a financial decision.

Single Camera

Single camera is the style most commonly used in filmmaking. This mode is not limited to feature film, however. The limiting factor is usually budget. A single camera allows for the best lighting and control of the production by building the product one shot at a time. Since feature films almost always are shot this way, single camera style is synonymous with "film style." The overwhelming majority of dramatic television series are shot in single camera/film style on film.

Multicamera

Multicamera style is often used even in feature films for expensive shots that are too complicated, dangerous, or costly to duplicate for different angles. Thus several cameras are positioned to capture a single event (for example, the crash of an airplane, the demolition of a structure, or the execution of a particularly daunting gag or stunt).

Desi Arnez and Lucille Ball were the first to shoot a television sitcom with multiple cameras ("I Love Lucy"). While this show and many that followed it were shot with film cameras, multicamera video has become the rule for most sitcoms and soap operas. There is still an occasional sitcom shot on multicamera film, but the technology of video has made it the recording medium of choice for such productions. "The George Lopez Show," for example, is a four-camera HDTV video setup.

Film directors most frequently use one camera. Each scene is carefully set up to be shot a number of times. It is likely that a scene will be shot at least five different times, each time from a different angle. There may be a master shot of the entire scene, a shot from audience left, one from audience right, a close-up of each actor, an over-the-shoulder shot of each actor, and so on. Our university's summer workshop films are usually done in movie style, even if they are captured on video rather than film.

The better your eye, the better you can be at composition. We have a friend who is a so-so director and a wonderful photographer. His great eye means that, when he directs a show, his composition puts the rest of us to shame. He lacks a few other skills that might make his work better, but his pictures are dazzling. When you have a good eye, you are always knocked out by the work of someone with a better eye. Until your eye is trained, you may not have any awareness of the qualities of composition.

Design classes are very useful for developing your eye, as are art appreciation classes and any other course that stresses the design elements. As you read stage or screen directing books, you will see they are filled with copies of paintings and graphics to illustrate points about composition.

In this chapter we discuss composition—the picture as an instant in time. Elsewhere we discuss *blocking*, which is the technique of moving actors or cameras around to accomplish your purpose.

Basic Principles of Composition

Emphasis

Stage directors have considerable concerns about emphasis because the stage audience gets to see everything on stage all the time. The problem is how to call attention to the particular thing or person that deserves more attention at this point in time.

Suppose you are directing a scene in which two people are equally important. They are having a conversation in which each speech is equally significant. On screen, you can achieve the emphasis by cutting between the characters either while you are shooting or when you are editing. On stage, the techniques are a bit more complicated.

The following are some stage rules that also apply to the screen.

Body Position
Body position refers to the position of the actor—which way the actor is facing. Full-front position gets more emphasis. The person who is standing directly facing the viewer gets more emphasis than people who are facing slightly inward or outward n the picture.

Area
Area refers to the part of the stage or screen space the actor occupies. Center stage or screen gets more. Whatever or whoever is in the center of the frame gets more emphasis than those in other locations.

Plane
Plane refers to the portion of the stage the actor occupies. Imagine the stage or screen area as slices, from left to right, each about a foot or two behind the one in front. Downstage planes, ones closer to the audience or camera, are stronger than upstage planes. The closer to the viewer, the more emphasis it gets. This is true in proscenium and camera work. It is not true in arena, since there is no downstage.

Level
Level refers to the height of the space on which an actor is standing. Whatever is higher gets more emphasis. If the person is taller or standing on a higher platform, he or she gets more emphasis.

Contrast
The eye goes to whatever is different from all the rest. If everyone else is wearing blue, then the person in red gets more emphasis. If everyone else is sitting and one is kneeling, the kneeler gets the most emphasis, and on and on.

Light
The eye goes to whatever is lighter in color—more lit or brighter in tone. The guy in the spotlight, or the girl in the white dress, or the red car will

get more emphasis than the guy next to him, the girl in the purple dress, or the black car. Why else would anybody buy an ugly yellow Hummer?

Volume
We pay more attention to whatever is heard better. Louder music or speech tends to draw more attention than softer . . . at least until your ear drums split.

Framing
We pay more attention to whatever is in a visual frame—a window, a door. If several people are in the scene, the one framed in the doorway is emphasized.

B:L G F / **A** / R C D N

Triangulation
The apex of the triangle gets the most attention. Stage directors constantly use triangles to block actors for reasons to be explained later. The one at the apex of the triangle gets the most emphasis.

Movement
Something moving draws attention. You can think of hundreds of examples.

Space
Something that has space around it draws attention. If one item is sitting on the shelf, it draws more emphasis than a stack of items on the shelf below.

I I I I I I I   I   I I I I I I I I I

Mass
Mass is something large. Duh! It's just easier to see. The bigger it is, then the harder it is to miss.

X X X **X** X X X X

Line
Something out of line with everything else draws attention. Think of chorus girls. The one not in line is the most emphasized. Either she is the star or she will get fired at the end of the week.

I I I I I I I I I I I I I I I I

More rules than these can be discovered. Also, these rules need to be modified for thrust and arena. In thrust, upstage is stronger than downstage because it is more visible to more people. So even rules are constantly being modified by circumstance—the set, the particular stage you're working on, and so on. A lot of these ideas will become more apparent when we study blocking.

Stability

Directors need to think about stability. Pictures need to have a base rather than seeming to float. Usually, all the things or people should not be clustered together but should be spread out so all the areas are used. All directors, regardless of medium, need to think of their stage pictures in terms of this attribute. Normally, you get it by having something rooted at the bottom of the picture—like the floor.

Balance

A picture needs balance in order to have visual appeal. Balance is a visual equivalency between the parts of the picture. The two sides are not mirror images of each other—that is symmetry. Balanced pictures simply appear to be about equal in visual load. For example, you might have something taller and thinner on one side and balance it with something shorter and thicker on the other. This concept will also become clearer as you learn blocking.

Line

Visual lines may be vertical, perpendicular, diagonal, straight, curved, or broken. Each kind of line evokes a different response in the viewer. In a stage or screen picture, you can have a variety of lines or allow a certain kind of line to predominate. A designer or art director will achieve this in the setting, and you will achieve it in the blocking.

Horizontal lines tend to be calm, stable, and relaxed. (You look relaxed if you are lying down, even if you are actually in turmoil.) A long fence line has that feeling.

——————— ——————— ——————— ———————

Vertical or perpendicular lines tend to appear strong, forceful, and even spiritual. Think of the look of a Gothic cathedral with its long vertical lines.

I I I I I I I I I I I I I I I I I I I I I I I

Diagonal lines tend to appear arresting, moving and vital.

I I I I I I I I I I I I I I I I I I I I I I I I I

Straight lines tend to express strength, simplicity, discipline, and rigidity. Think of a line of West Point cadets, palm trees, or Rockettes.

I I I I I I I I I I I I I I I I I I I I I I I I

Curved lines appear free, natural, and warm. Think of any natural form. It is almost always a curved line. Leaves, people, animals, clouds, bodies of water—it would be extremely difficult to think of a single natural object that was made of straight lines.

Broken lines imply tension, disorder, and informality. — — — — — looks more informal than ————.

Form

Form has too many different definitions to remember. But in this context, form refers to the qualities in the shapes of the visible objects and people in the picture that express mood. The mood evoked by a row of bottles is very different than a heap of mixed vegetables in a pictorial composition. Different forms tend to evoke different moods. Keeping in mind that rules are not laws, we can say that the mood effects of various forms seem to be as follows.

Symmetrical forms are very formal and artificial. Even the two sides of your face are not perfectly symmetrical. Nothing in nature is.

T XXT TXXT TXXT TXXT

Irregular forms tend to be natural, casual, or free. Shapes in nature tend to be irregular, as do human things in turmoil.

7 R G @ &

Shallow forms are those that seem to be flat, like a wall, rather than having depth. They tend to be only a single plane deep. They imply superficiality and artificiality. We think of shallow people that way for the same reason—they appear to have no depth.

Deep forms are shapes that extend over a number of planes rather than just one. A grand staircase is a deep form, compared to the wall example used before. Depth can be relative. An auto is a relatively deep form compared to a wall. A limousine is deeper, and a train is even deeper than those two.

Compact forms appear to be forceful and menacing. A bullet is a compact form, as is a basketball. The Hulk is more compact than a basketball player.

Diffused forms seem to be in disarray. They are scattered rather than compact. The spray of a large fountain is diffused. The base of a heavy stone fountain may be compact. A spider web is diffused. Fireworks are another example of a diffused form.

As you arrange the elements in the picture, your use of the principles of composition will give the audience a great deal of information that they may not process on the conscious level. However, it will still influence what they see and therefore what they feel.

The preceding discussion relates to any element in a picture—backgrounds, settings, furnishings, props, and people. Most of the time, we directors are very concerned with the people, as it is through them that we tell our stories. Even when other people have design responsibility for the nonactor elements, such as costumes and scenery, we have every right to be concerned about those elements and in charge of their planning. The contributions of these designers make or break what you are doing with the pictures.

Film and Video Direction and Interpretation

The viewers come first. Show them what they want the instant they want or need to see it, not before. Each shot or edit should support the meaning, mood, and form of the script. Interpret your material reliably.

The style of shooting should match the subject matter. A sitcom does not look like an action movie, nor does a mini series based on a Jane Austin novel look like a John Ford film. The general purpose and character of the material governs the treatment of the details.

Establish the scene, the location, or the set, as early as possible. This is done so the viewer will know who and what (e.g., windows, doors, furniture) is where. If you begin a scene with a close-up of a character or an object, the audience has no reference point as to where this person on thing is in relations to anyone or anything else in the scene.

Regulate the forcefulness of your picture statements to the relative degrees of importance of the program material. Some parts of the material are more important than others. Put your visual emphasis where it belongs.

Cross your camera angles. In a multicamera shoot, the camera on the left should be shooting across the set to the right, and the camera on the right should be shooting across the set to the left. On single camera or multicamera shoots, never try to look performers in the ear. Try to see both eyes if at all possible.

The pace of the editing or cutting should reflect the action and intent of the script. Misused rapid cutting gives a phony sense of pace to material that needs a slower rhythm.

The camera and the actor blocking should support the script. Artificial movement of either for their own sake distracts the viewer and becomes an obstacle to the telling of the story not an asset.

Do not jar the viewer unless you have a good reason. In expressing the nature of your material, encourage and do not inhibit the expressive abilities of your performers. Audiences tune in to see human beings doing something, not to see your camera angles. The more you use your performers for emphasizing points, directing attention from one another, and changing the picture composition through their movements, the more you can save your shot changes for moments when they really count.

Keep the viewer oriented. Do not cross the "axis" or take jump cuts. If you cross the axis, you will find you cannot edit together the shots. For a full explanation of crossing the axis, see Chapter 6.

Have a very good reason for changing shots. Cuts, dissolves, or wipes should be done at the artistically proper time (on action, dialogue, sound, or music). Your pictorial treatment should recognize and conform to the structural units of the material. Avoid calling or taking unnecessary shots or using effects just because you have them. If they don't do good, they do harm. Remember, a cut implies the next shot belongs with the one that preceded it. A dissolve or a wipe implies a change of time or place.

Composition

Composition is the physical arrangement of actor–characters in a ground plan. The director helps arrange actors in a series of still shots—a full stage production would require several hundred—that allows an audience to sense and feel basic forces.

Strictly defined, composition does not involve a movement (that it, a transit of the actor from one point on the stage to another). It is static—a caught moment.

An actor's body must be relatively, if not entirely, quiet during much of a performance, or an audience simply will not be able to hear what the actor says. A performed play varies between composition and movement. A large amount of movement during significant speeches overwhelms the important lines. Too little movement makes the scene static. Consequently, experienced directors and actors know to stand still and to hold composition at important moments. An important principle in acting is learning to hold the body and head still so that when they do move, they will say something specific.

Techniques of Composition

Body Positions

Stage right and stage left are the actor's right and left facing an audience. Now face the body to the major points of a circle, and you have the body positions. Directions are always given to the actor's right or left in any medium.

Levels

This describes the actual head level of the actor. He is at his highest level when standing. Any variation that takes his head toward the floor is a change of level (see Figure 5.3).

Figure 5.3 A set with levels

Planes

The stage and the camera have depth as well as width. When we talk about an actor "moving through the planes," we mean that he moves upstage or downstage. On camera we mean toward or away from the camera, which has shorter planes than the stage. Each plane is usually twelve to eighteen inches behind the one in front— twelve inches for cameras and eighteen inches for stage (see Figure 5.4).

Horizontal Locations

Horizontal locations demonstrate the position of an actor on the width of the stage or camera. The more off to the side the actor is, the more the character seems out of it also (see Figure 5.5).

Emphasis

A basic necessity in a good composition, emphasis is created with your use of the elements of composition (see Figure 5.6).

Figure 5.4 An illustration of actors on different planes in the same shot

Figure 5.5 An illustration of actors, one centered and others to the sides

Figure 5.6 An example of a shot with strong emphasis on one actor

Focuses

On stage and screen, we have two kinds of actor focus: (1) eye focus, in which one actor looks directly at another actor and (2) line focus, in which one actor (or more) turns directly toward another actor (see Figure 5.7). Body focus can get more emphasis when actors point with more elements of their body—props, arms, legs, torso, or all simultaneously. Both kinds of focus work on the principle of imaginary lines running from one actor to another.

Diagonals

Two actors in the same plane is not a forceful composition. This is a shared composition because each actor has equal emphasis. Two actors on a diagonal—different planes—is more emphatic (see Figure 5.8). The composition moves both horizontally and vertically in the imagination of the spectator. Directors use diagonal compositions to create or strengthen tension. It involves putting the actors on different planes.

Figure 5.7 An example of several actors giving focus to one actor

Figure 5.8 An example of actors blocked on a diagonal

Triangles

Compositions of three or more actors are arranged in triangles. Triangles are really double diagonals. The deeper the triangle, the greater the emphasis. Triangles should be at least two or three planes in depth. The following is an example of a two-plane triangle.

Mary

Bob   Sue

Space and Mass

Effective compositions can be made by isolating one actor on one part of the stage and contrasting that isolation with a number of actors on the other side. The single actor has emphasis and individuality, and the others grouped away from him make a mass or cluster. Foreground and background do the same on camera.

Mary/Bob/Joe   JIM
Fred/Sue/Sam/Dick

Repetition or Support

When four or more actors are used, the dramatic action frequently places them on two opposing sides. The supporting actors who stand behind the principal actors are said to repeat or support the principals, which gives the principals emphasis. More is less, and the bigger the group, the less the importance of the individuals.

Mary/Bob/Joe/Bill	Ann/Art/Moe/Jack
Fred/Sue/Sam/Dick	Lou/Nan/Tim/Jane
TOM	HAL

Climactic Compositions

Two actors may play at the extremes of the stage or lens or very close together with each composition having explicit meanings. When they are close together, they are in a climactic composition. Climactic compositions should be used only for extremes: extreme love or extreme hate, for example. Climatic compositions must therefore be saved for the climatic moments of a script. On camera, close-ups are always climactic (see Figure 5.9).

Figure 5.9 Two actors in a close-up

Next, let's look at several different ways we use bodies to tell our stories. In addition to the principles we have already discussed, the following chapter, discusses some more specific ways we "compose" people to tell the story. In fact, when you think about it, it's hard to tell where composition ends and picturization starts. Both are concerned with using a visual image, while blocking is concerned with moving the visual image.

Summary

As part of your work as a director, you will identify significant moments in the script where a certain picture or image is absolutely necessary for you to tell the story. These points are your major compositions. The other stage or screen pictures that you compose lead toward and away from those key compositions. The path that you follow to get there is called blocking.

Suggested Reading and Viewing

Reading

Stage
Albright, Hardie. *Stage Direction in Transition*. See chapter 7.
Catron, Louis E. *The Director's Vision*. See chapter 16.
Dean, Alexander, and Lawrence Carra. *Fundamentals of Play Directing*. See chapter 6.
Hodge, Francis. *Play Directing*. See chapter 10.
Kirk, John W., and Ralph A. Bellas. *The Art of Directing*. See part 3.
Patterson, Jim. *Stage Directing*. See pages 119–28.
Vaughan, Stuart, *Directing Plays*. See chapter 7.

Screen
Armer, Alan A. *Directing Television and Film*. See chapter 3.
Bare, Richard L. *The Film Director*. See chapters 5, 7, and 9.
Block, Bruce. *The Visual Story*. See chapter 3.
Katz, Steven D. *Film Directing Shot by Shot*. See part 2.
Lukas, Christopher. *Directing for Film and Television*. See chapter 6.
Proferes, Nicholas T. *Film Directing Fundamentals*. See chapters 3 and 4.

Viewing

Try watching the DVDs of the films discussed in these chapters, with the sound off, to see how well the composition conveys information.

6

What Is Picturization?

In Chapter 5, we said that composition gives the scene mood, not meaning. Picturization is the process by which we add meaning. It is a name for the elements we add to the scene—before we add dialogue or movement—to tell the story. Picturization tries to get across subtext— the meaning that may or may not be supported by the words.

Let's use *Spider-Man II*, but a hundred other examples would do. Think of a scene in which the girl wants to know if Peter Parker loves her. He does, but he can't admit it. It would blow his cover. How do we know he does, even if the dialogue calls for him to vehemently deny it? Picturization! The outer action has to convey the inner meaning, even if there is no dialogue.

Alexander Dean and Lawrence Carra state that composition contributes the rational arrangement of technique and the mood of the subject, whereas picturization contributes the meaning or the thought. They state that picturization is the concept and composition the technique.

Francis Hodge words it another way. He defines picturization as storytelling by a group of actors. He says, "It is brought about by the combined use of composition (the arrangement of the group), gesture (the individual moving within his own sphere) and improvisation with properties (objects added to composition and gesture) for the specific purpose of animating the dramatic action. *Picturization then*, is a still picture containing detailed illustrations, brought about by individualizing and personalizing composition though the use of gesture and properties to tell the story of the group."

R. H. O'Neill and N. M. Boretz, in another stage directing text, describe it this way. "*Composition* is the physical arrangement of actors with, or to, each other. . . . Picturization is the meaning that is being suggested through that arrangement" (R. H. O'Neill and N. M. Boretz, *The*

Director as Artist [New York: Holt, Rinehart, and Winston, 1987], 2).
Now do you get the picture?

Since composition and picturization go hand in hand, most writers
today talk about them as the one element—composition. So in this chapter, we will discuss how to record the pictorial elements you want to create on stage or screen. If you can make an accurate record of the elements
you want to create, you improve your chances of ending up with those
elements in the final project.

Ground Plan

A ground plan is a drawing of the set as if it is seen from above (see
Figure 6.1). It shows where the various elements of the set (doors, windows, furniture, etc.) are in relationship to each other. It is drawn to
scale, and it does two things for the actor and director. It represents the
given circumstances, and it helps to illustrate the dramatic action. The
ground plan makes the place and circumstance specific. As mentioned
very frequently in this book, the more specific, the better. As directors
and actors, we need to think in specific terms of space and of the necessary obstacles that break up that space. A director must, therefore, always
think in three-dimensional terms. Although the ground plan is two
dimensional, acting space is a cube and not a rectangle on the floor.

A ground plan is partially a visual design for an audience. Primarily,
it brings out the dramatic action through director–actor communication.
Any good ground plan gives actors physical obstacles they must overcome to reach their goals.

A good ground plan illustrates the action. We do this on stage very
differently than we do for television. For either medium, the ground plan
gives the actors and director the means to visualizing and illustrating
action.

For the stage, one technique is the sit-down rule. According to this
rule, an acting area consists of two or more locations where some actors
can sit that are at least six feet or more apart—two chairs, or a sofa and
chair, in different parts of a room. You often have a couch and chair in
one location and another pair of chairs some distance away. Generally,
you want various places on the stage to which your actors can move to
vary the picture or spread out the groupings. Generally, each acting area
needs at least five or six feet of space or the space looks cramped and the
actors look crunched.

Here is the second important part of this rule—a ground plan must
have a minimum of five acting areas. If it is film work, the ground plan

should have positions for at least five camera setups. If any ground plan has less than five areas, your opportunities to use composition for exposition are very limited and the stage or screen picture can be boring or repetitive—you don't have enough places to look.

For the television screen, the rule translates another way. There should be at least five locations, even for a twenty-four-minute show. If

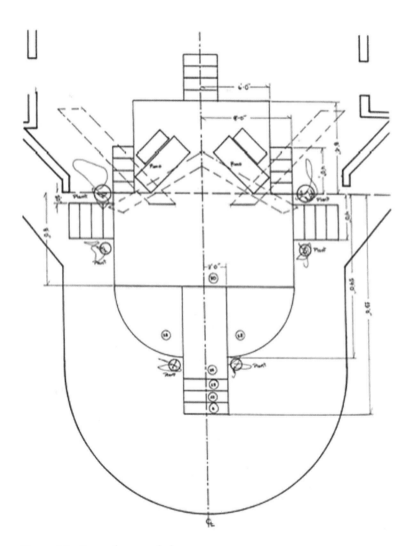

Figure 6.1 Copy of a ground plan

you look again at old sitcoms that you remember as having one set, you will see that the ground plan was arranged so that the cameras could be set up to get five different background views. Even "The Swamp"—Hawkeye's tent in "M*A*S*H"—had at least two acting areas in it. In TV, the areas are generally surprisingly small in dimension—much smaller than you think—but more varied in location. The principle is the same as for the stage, but the application of the principle is different.

Stage Ground Plans

Ground Plan on the Proscenium Stage

Here are a few rules to overcome the flat qualities of the proscenium stage. They will also help your audience see and hear better.

1. Open the side walls to the audience. As you look at the ground plan, the stage is not a rectangle. It is a trapezoid. The back wall is shorter than the proscenium line.
2. Open the set properties (furniture) to the audience. A couch facing the back wall doesn't do you any good as a seating area.
3. Mark the downstage corners of the ground plan with some object to indicate the edge of the space. If you want to create the illusion of a walled room, you will increase the illusion of depth by placing objects—furniture and props—there and blocking the actors to use them.

Ground Plan on the Arena Stage

These rules can help you to overcome the problems encountered by not having a back wall in an arena stage.

1. Use a center object that can be approached from all sides and will give you the necessary obstacle course. The object can't be very high or it will block sight lines. However, it must be approachable from every angle.
2. Use the outer rim of the circle as a backing so that you have someplace to put an actor who won't be able to move frequently. It is a good place for a low bench, for example. The actor draws less focus at the rim in a low position.
3. Think of the ground plan as a clock and use smaller groupings of props and furniture. Give actors more reasons to move and change

positions. The audience has to share "face time" with the various actors since not all of the audience members can see all the actors' faces at the same time.

4. The scene design must keep the actor visible the whole time he or she is in stage. Avoid long runways, once the character has left the scene. The actor must be in character the whole time he or she is in sight. It's hard to do when the actor has supposedly left and is still in audience view for a while.

Ground Plan on a Thrust Stage

These rules can help you take advantage of the thrust stage configuration.

1. Use levels—vertical playing spaces work very well in this configuration.
2. Keep in mind the rules of the arena. You need to keep 'em moving, but not as much or as often as in an arena configuration.
3. Use configurations that will prevent actors from lining up against the back wall. One of our rules is that actors tend to form straight lines no matter how you block them, and dancers tend to form crooked ones in spite of all your choreography. So try to prevent actors from slowly and subconsciously forming straight lines.

Screen Ground Plans

Ground Plan for the Television Screen

These rules can help you take advantage of the requirements of television.

1. Television is a very realistic medium, and whatever you put on the stage must look extremely realistic.
2. The acting place, regardless of period, should be designed as a series of small independent areas to allow whole scenes to played in the same space without pulling back the focus to reveal long, boring shots. Even a small kitchen should be designed so that a whole scene can take place in a limited space without requiring the actors to move more than a couple of feet.
3. The acting place should be designed to provide opportunities for scenes to be moved from one area to another. In a kitchen scene, the actors should be able to move from the table to the stove and counter area to change the background.

4. Provide a foreground and a background for each shot grouping so the effect is neither "heads in space" nor "up against the wall."

All directors, stage or screen, need to remember the following:

1. Make several ground plans and see which one gives you the most flexibility of placement for actors.
2. A ground plan is supposed to arouse the imagination of the actors and directors who must use it.

Test of a Good Ground Plan

Test your ground plan by answering the following questions:

1. Have you made several ground plans so you can see which one gives you the most flexibility of placement for actors?
2. Does it have strong upstage/downstage movement possibilities as well as stage right/stage left possibilities?
3. Are strong diagonals possible? Diagonals are very powerful movements for actors or cameras.
4. Have you created tension in the placement of your furniture pieces? Beginning directors have a tendency to "flatten" out the pictures.
5. Is it an obstacle course? As an actor works past furniture, he or she has opportunities to express the obstacles in the script.
6. What is the potential for strong compositions and picturizations? Can you get levels, variety, and so on?
7. Is it ingenious? It may be difficult, but designers have to overcome the tendency to do sets the same way all the time.
8. Will it provoke actors to make fresh and imaginative illustrations? Can they use the spaces and the furniture to more clearly illustrate the ideas of the scene?
9. Have you enough space to move actors around furniture instead of just in front or behind pieces?

Picturization for Screen Directors

Storyboards

Take a very good film on DVD or VHS—preferably DVD because the paused pictures are clearer. Stop frame it. Look at each picture. What does it tell you about composition and picturization?

Films like Stanley Kubrick's *Barry Lyndon* (1975), Ang Lee's *Sense and Sensibility* (1995), and Sam Mendes's *Road to Perdition* (2002) are simply beautiful to watch because of the composition of individual pictures. This is also true of Orson Welles's *Citizen Kane* (1942), John Ford's *Stagecoach* (1938), and David Lean's *Dr. Zhivago* (1965), among others.

Because storyboards are relatively new techniques, they are rarely used by stage directors. They are also less necessary in the theatre because the stage director is not concerned with camera angles and other considerations that are important in filming.

Stage directors are usually very good at picturization, but, because of the ephemeral nature of live theatre, it is more difficult to find good examples of stage picturization. Most texts use still photos of productions. If you can get the Broadway Theatre Archives DVD of *A Moon for the Misbegotten* (http://www.image-entertainment.com), the 1975 television production of the famous Eugene O'Neill stage play, you will find that, between the stage director, Jose Quintero, and the television director, Gordon Rigsby, the video has one elegant picture after another. According to Rigsby, the stage pictures were Quintero's, and as television director, he tried to capture them for the camera.

To achieve such photographic status, there has to be a union between the storytelling and the various arts of filmmaking. Ideally much of the actual photography will be in the hands of the DP (director of photography) and the key gaffer (head of the lighting department). Both will be on the same page with the director from storyboards and conversations they have had about the look and visual feel of the product.

Additionally the production designer and the art director will be critically involved in the visuals of the picture. Ultimately the director decides to accept or reject the creativity of the talented people—all aspects of each visual element (set and/or locations, costumes, and makeup as well as the placement of the camera and both the people and physical objects within a given frame). Good communication among visionary people will all come together on the screen. This is best done by way of storyboards.

Storyboards illustrate each individual camera setup of a screenplay or teleplay. Storyboards can be rendered in multiple boxes on each page or fill up a full page or two. They can be single color pencil drawings, multicolor marker sketches, or even full-color watercolor renderings. These pictures are in the proper aspect ratio in which the final product will be shot.

A storyboard is simply a way of writing down the plans for each shot that will be filmed or taped in the production. Like any other plan, it is subject to change as necessary. It is the best and clearest way of communicating plans to the various departments involved in each film shoot.

Look for storyboards on the special features of many major motion picture DVDs. You will see many examples of differing approaches to this step in camera storytelling.

The only wrong way to make storyboards is to make them so that they do not communicate with your staff, crew, and cast. Storyboards are a tool. Not all productions are storyboarded. Not all directors use them or even want to. If you are doing storyboards, they need to be as detailed as you need them to be. They are your tools. In some cases, you won't find them necessary. In many other cases, you will.

The storyboards may or may not be a creation of the director. Storyboards can be produced by a storyboard artist hired for that express task or they can come from the DP or production designer. Once storyboards are created and agreed to by the director, it is much easier for every member of the visual team to understand every requirement of every given shot.

All of the above are also true for the television production, only usually on a much tighter schedule and budget. The decisions about the look and feel of a TV series will be largely driven by the producer. A director handles and coordinates the visual story, while the script and the characters are more the province of the producer or show runner. Once established for a series, every episode and every director is expected to toe the line of the show's signature appearance.

For a MOW (Movie of the Week) or any single project, the director will have as much input into the visual style elements as the director of the pilot for a series. While this may be less than that of the director of a feature film, it is still substantial. The power the TV director wields is often tied to past successes or failures.

The film and video director has a toolbox of basic photographic elements. These elements are the visual words with which the director tells the story.

Shots

All camera shots, for the big or small screen, have the same ingredients and are known by the same basic elements, movements, and specific content requirements. A good camera operator will already understand these elements, but each director will have his or her own version of how much headroom, look space, and so on he or she wants in a particular shot. The movement of a shot with, before, or after visual action on the screen will also be a matter of individual discretion from director to director. Thus once a camera operator has composed a shot the director will often tweak it by calling for more or less of any basic element or, in the case of a zoom lens, requesting that the camera operator zoom or "z" in or out to get exactly what the director has in mind.

Basic Shots
- Headroom—A good picture leaves a bit of space above the head of the subject.
- Look space—A good picture has a bit of space in front of the subject's face.
- Focus—A good picture has the dominant element in clear focus.
- Triangulation—A good picture uses the triangulation principle, discussed in Chapter 5.

Moving Camera Shots
- Pan—The camera sweeps across the scene.
- Tilt—The camera head moves up or down.
- Zoom—The camera changes focus rapidly, either to widen the view (Z-out) or to close in on the view (Z-in).
- Dolly—This is a cart on which the camera can be mounted to be moved during a shot.
- Truck—A verb, this is the movement of a camera on a dolly (truck right, truck left, and so on).
- Ped—Ped is short for pedestal, the camera stand. The camera can ped up or down to change the viewing angle of the shot.
- Jib—The camera is mounted on a device that puts it at a unique angle.
- Crane—The camera is mounted on a crane to get an unusually high angle shot.

Specialty Shots
- ECU (extreme close-up)—very close in on the face, or eyes, or lips
- CU (close-up)—a shot of the head or even two heads close together
- MCU (medium close-up; also known as the loose close-up)—a little looser than the CU
- MED (medium shot; also known as the normal shot)—head, shoulders and chest
- OTS (over the shoulder shot)—the camera points over the shoulder of actor towards another
- Three-quarter—the shot of a person from the knees to their head
- 2FE (two faces east shot)—both actors face in the same direction, usually in two different shots, when instinct would tell you they

ought to be facing each other; usually the result of crossing the
axis unintentionally
- Carrying shot—a pan or zoom that takes a character from point A
  to point B.
- Down-the-line shot—a group of characters in a straight line shot
  from one end of the line, as if you shot a column of soldiers while
  they stood at attention
- Wide shot (also known as the establishing shot)—shows you the
  whole scene so you get a sense of place, where the action is occurring
- Pop zoom, fast Z-in, or Z-out—same as the zoom, only as fast as
  possible
- Swish pan (also known as a whip pan)—quick pan from one shot
  to another
- Aerial shot—shot from a very high position, as from a plane or
  some other high source

Combining the most basic elements with the moving and specialty
shots at the right moment, the director paints screen images that speak
volumes, with or without dialogue.

The Axis Rule

For the director, understanding the concept of screen direction and the
axis rule are mandatory. This refers to which way people on screen face
as well as what shots contribute to the telling of the story without confusing the viewer.

In your mind, draw a line between two people who are interacting on
a set or between the sole performer and a major object in the set (a door
or chair).

All camera setups, all shots from all cameras on a multicamera shoot,
should be taken from the same side of this line or axis. This keeps the
visual relationships between characters and/or objects consistent and,
therefore, keeps the viewers oriented as to who or what is where in the
scene. To take shots from different sides of this line will change the
screen direction of the action and confuse the viewer.

There are neutral shots—head-on shots or straight-away shots (think
of shots of a stagecoach or a car driving over the camera or a centered,
head-on shot of the driver). Even over-the-shoulder shots from behind
the driver can serve as a neutral shot.

After such shots, the next shot can have the people, vehicles, or object
moving in the complete opposite direction than they were before, and

the viewer will not get confused. See the famous car–train chase from director William Friedkin's *The French Connection* (1971) to examine this process in action.

Picturization for Stage Directors

Film and television directors tend to need to storyboard more than stage directors. Stage directors usually work in a physical setting that remains static for longer periods of time. From one short scene to an entire production, the director may be working on a single set that does not change. The director is picturing the scene from a single point of view; in most cases, dead-on. So usually the stage pictures are easier to notate by means other than storyboarding. To do the exact same production on screen, over one hundred different setups might be necessary.

But many stage directors and designers work with storyboards when the settings are complicated and the actor blocking is really difficult. While choreographers have elaborate systems, such as the Laban system, to record frequent rapid movements of dancer–actors, stage directors don't encounter such choreographing requirements very often. So the notation systems used by individual directors vary wildly.

Each stage director develops, as needed, some system of taking notes on the picture effect wanted at key points in the script. As directors move more frequently among media, many directors have started using a technique based on storyboarding to record their plans. Regardless of the technique used, all directors need to have a way of recording accurately the pictures they are striving to attain.

The following illustrations show several sample methods some stage directors use. In the first one (Figure 6.2), the director uses a floor plan and writes the code—usually the first letter of the character name for each character—on the spot where the character is at the beginning of each page. Then, as the character moves, the action is written next to the character name at the appropriate point in the script. But the director may also draw the motion with a line and then show with the arrow tip where the actor ends up when the move is finished.

Another method is to draw little stick figures. They usually have a point that sticks out like a carrot on a snowman. This point shows which way the character is facing. Some directors do this as one would see the actor from the audience (Figure 6.3); others do it as one would view it on the ground plan, from above. (Figure 6.4). Try the various methods you encounter to record the pictures, and then use the method that works best for you. It will most probably be a combination of methods that you find satisfactory.

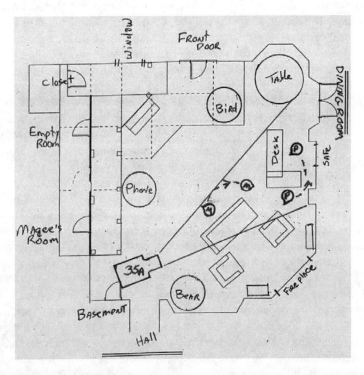

Figure 6.2 Letter-code blocking plan

Figure 6.3 Stick figures as viewed by the audience

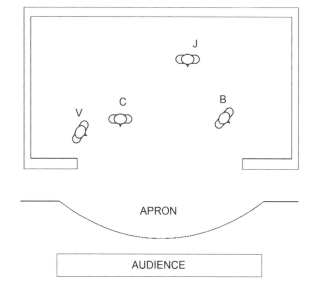

Figure 6.4 Stick figures as viewed on the ground plan

Suggested Reading and Viewing

Reading

Stage

Dean, Alexander, and Lawrence Carra. *Fundamentals of Play Directing*. See chapter 7.

Hodge, Francis. *Play Directing*. See chapters 12.

Vaughan, Stuart, *Directing Plays*. See chapter 7.

Screen

Armer, Alan A. *Directing Television and Film*. See chapters 6–8.

Benedetti, Robert. *From Concept to Screen*. See Chapters 6–9.

Block, Bruce. *The Visual Story*. See the appendix, part I.

Katz, Steven D. *Film Directing Shot by Shot*.

Lukas, Christopher. *Directing for Film and Television*. See chapter 6.

Proferes, Nicholas T. *Film Directing Fundamentals*. See chapters 2–6.

Viewing

Film

Try watching the DVDs mentioned in this chapter with the sound off to see how well the blocking conveys information.

Play

Broadway Theatre Archives. Eugene O'Neill's *A Moon for the Misbegotten*. Directed by José Quintero and Gordon Rigsby, 1975, ID14768BDDVD. http://www.image-entertainment.com.

7

Movement

Movement is the most powerful blocking tool. Movement is the actual transit of an actor or camera from one point on stage to another. In camera work, the camera movement has the same use and effect as actor movement between points. Movement takes place between compositions. In order to really see movement on the stage or screen, the actor, object, or camera must travel at least five feet.

An actor moving less than five feet is really making a very large gesture rather than a movement. You don't sense that the person or camera has gone to another space. This principle holds for both actor and camera movements. A camera moves, like another actor, to make the idea clear. Movement is climactic; it has a beginning, a middle, and an end. Since everything else already is there, the actor or camera movement becomes the most powerful tool of dramatic statement.

Movements of actors or cameras are the strongest dramatic choices a director can make. The size and direction of the movement gives it its strength. Movement has tempo values; it takes place in time. A play performed on stage looks like a dance. Just as a dance starts and stops, a play alternates between movement and composition, with gesture working continuously. On stage, compositions serve the same functions as close-ups, and movements are the stage equivalents of the long and medium shots. All movement should be determined from the dramatic action. It should not be applied for its own sake. It should be generated from within.

Correctly done, movement by an actor or a camera is not always obvious. It seems unnoticeable because it is so essential to the story, the character, the scene, and the moment.

Kinds of Movement

Writer's Movement

The writer dictates some important movements in a script. Entrances and exits are writer's movements. As directors, we must get the actor on or off at that point. The writer also puts in some movements so that an important piece of business can take place. The movement, "George goes to the desk, opens the drawer, gets out the gun and fires at Amy," is dictated by the dramatic action. In such cases, an actor is performing writer's movement. Some of these are vital and must be executed. Others may be used as you see fit.

Director's Movement

You may see many other movements described in the script. For a stage script, generally, these have been inserted, as we mentioned earlier, by the first people who professionally mounted the script for the stage. You are not obligated to follow these directions.

For film and TV, the movements described in the script are usually from the writer but may be from the director, particularly if you are reading the "shooting script" of a feature film. The shooting script is the very last draft of the script, often written by the feature film director before principal photography begins. In television it will be the script approved for production by the producer and is the one given to the director to execute. This rewrite will have all the actions, motions, and movements the director plans to or is expected to incorporate into the production. These same movements can be see in the storyboards if the productions has the budget for a storyboard artist or the director does this work him/herself.

Sometimes you hear blocking or movement described as choreography. Frequently, directors have a number of actors on view and need to provide variety, visibility, and other factors to keep the view from being static.

The director needs to know how to get actors on, around, and off the stage or screen quickly and efficiently. This need becomes quite a challenge when many characters are involved, so the director develops blocking. It should keep the action moving and make the significant characters and their business clearly visible. In addition, it must contribute to the mood of the script.

As the director, you must learn how to plan movements so they seem logical and smooth. Movement is choreography. It does not draw attention to itself. It looks natural even though it is artificially imposed.

Basically, then, all movements not required by the script itself can be labeled "director's movement."

Camera Movements

Each camera movement has a certain grammar to it. In other words, it shapes the ideas the camera expresses in the same way that the structure of a sentence expresses the ideas in the words. Any old shot won't do, just as any old combination of words won't express the idea you want to get across. Look at the previous sentence, with the words in random order:

> old just won't do, as any Any words across old combination express of idea get shot won't the you want to

The words above don't make much sense. If it makes any sense, it certainly isn't the sense we wanted in the original sentence. So camera moves help the story you want to tell make sense in the way you want to tell it.

The basic camera movements were discussed in Chapter 6 as a part of the film and TV director's basic toolbox of shots.

Ten Commandments for Camera Moves

1. Less is more—hide the art. Good camera work does not deliberately call attention to itself.
2. Like the stage, horizontal moves are restful or humorous; diagonals are strong and dramatic, especially if foreground articles are revealed.
3. Camera moves are great to begin or end a French scene. A French scene is a scene from which an actor enters or exits.
4. In balanced two-camera shots (OTS, or over the shoulder, for example), both cameras are equidistant from each other and each subject. The ideal position for this shot is close to180 degrees across from each other without becoming neutral or crossing the axis. Soaps tend to work better with tight twos, which means that two cameras are 90 to 170 degrees from each other. When actors are on a couch or a bench, you can get the angle flatter, which is

better. While this position can be difficult to adjust if the actor moves unexpectedly, such shots are pretty.

5. Cut dramatically—as little as possible—to give emphasis. Avoid the *jerky dance* video style that gives energy falsely, unless that happens to be your exact intent.

6. Avoid jump cuts. In a jump cut, the picture appears to jump because you have practically the same shot on both cameras. So when you switch shots, the actor appears to jump slightly. Do not cut from the same person to the same person unless one shot differs radically from the other. The camera setups in film-style shooting, or the camera positions in multicamera style, should be about 45 degrees different from each other as a rule of thumb. See Chapter 8 for more detail.

7. Lazy directors zoom—the good ones dolly and truck the camera. Zooms call too much attention to themselves and not enough to the scene. The zoom is an artificial movement, whereas the dolly or truck is more like a natural movement of the eye.

8. The shorter the lens—if you are using a fixed (prime) lens—or the wider the shot, the greater the depth-of-field (the area within the view of the camera that is in focus). Stay with the wide elements for the pretty shots.

9. When shooting an actor, focus on the dot of light that can be seen in the character's eye. This "light dot" is a reflection of ambient light that appears in the upper part of the iris.

10. Do not cut until you must. The challenge in directing is to cut as little as possible. Use your camera well. Don't show off moves just to prove you have them.

Moving the Camera

Cameras have three primary purposes. These purposes hold true whether you are doing a dramatic scene, a news broadcast, or a sports event.

- The camera covers the action.
- The camera creates the appropriate emphasis.
- The camera defines the mood and atmosphere. It always editorializes, intentionally or not.

Master shots cover all the action of a scene and are the continuity base for all the action covered by other shots. What you see in the master lets you know where the action is taking place. Master shots often serve as establishing shots.

Establishing shots establish set (rooms, buildings, etc.) or locations. They usually show the entire area of the particular location—the whole restaurant, office, living room, or campsite for instance.

Medium *shots* are "normal" shots—this is how we usually see the world.

Over the shoulder (OTS) *shots* are "eavesdropping" shots—they allow us to feel as if we are there but not necessarily confronting the person or action being shown.

Close-ups get the viewers very involved, pulling them into the scene or character.

The extreme close-up (ECU) is the most powerful shot in the director's toolbox—it makes the audience see something intimately.

Inserts are close ups shots of objects (i.e. guns, letters, signs, etc.) or characters to insure the audience sees clearly these objects or people at a particular point of a story.

Pickups are shots taken that did not work during the primary shoot. Often you realize when looking over the daily footage that you need a pickup of a piece of a scene to have the scene make sense.

Point of view (POV) *shots* are taken from the perspective of a person (or sometimes an object). On current "CSI"-type crime shows, viewers will see the corpse, and the next shot will be from the corpse's point of view—or the bullet's.

Multiple master shots are taken for different versions or views of the same scene.

A *montage* is a series of several shots or even scenes overlapped or cut together to form a new single image. Usually in a montage, the scenes change every few seconds in order to give the audience an emotional sense or idea instead of a rational one.

A scene is constructed like a paragraph and a particular shot can be the thesis sentence of the whole paragraph. The thesis sentence can come first, last, or elsewhere within the paragraph. It can be followed by examples, reinforcement, or restatements. This becomes an artistic/creative decision.

Camera Progression: How Many Setups?

The number of camera setups a scene needs is a matter of art and economics. A clever director can stage many scenes for a single setup. While this may sound ideal as far as financial outlay is concerned, it may not be. The single shot could involve the construction, leveling, and testing of a dolly track or the use of a Steadycam (requiring a special device and a specialized camera operator), a crane, a jib, and even a helicopter or other camera mounting equipment. Such a shot could also require extensive set construction and lighting and audio preparation. The end result could be a shot that takes hours or even days to get ready, as opposed to the standard twenty minutes to an hour per setup.

Artistically there is no finite answer to how many setups a director needs. Each director will see every scene in a unique way. This individual vision gets broken into the separate shots the director requires to bring his or her mental picture to the screen. Those mental pictures add up to the number of camera setups required.

Screen Directions

Screen directions are the side of the screen toward which a character or object moves. There should be look space in front of the character in this direction.

Changing Directions

Any change in direction of a character, object, or vehicle not portrayed in a neutral shot must be seen on camera. Think of the curve at the end of the race track. Without seeing the direction change on screen or having a neutral shot, the director has crossed the axis and confused his or her viewer by cutting from one shot with characters headed in one direction and the suddenly, on the other side of the track, headed the opposite way.

Complementary Shots

Also known as balanced shots, complementary shots occur when the director decides that one OTS deserves another OTS or one Medium deserves another Medium of equal value. Most of the time, you will try to get a complementary shot of each setup so you can edit smoothly. Complementary shots keep conversation or action shots equal to each other, particularly in an exchange of ideas or fight. It is awkward to go from a Medium of one character to a Closeup of another and then return to the Medium of the first character.

Dramatic Progression: Cheating Emphasis

The primary reason actors must hit their marks on stage or screen is because the resulting picture is designed for movement from one marked arrangement to another. Even when executed correctly, there will be times when the performer will have to "cheat," or move slightly and unnaturally, in order to achieve the correct blocking of the actors or to allow the cameras to work. Some examples of these cheats are given in the sections that follow.

Closeness

On screen, actors must be considerably closer together in certain shots than they would be in real life. On stage, actors usually have to stand farther apart than is natural in order to "dress"or balance a large stage space. On screen, actors stand or sit much closer together than in real life because the camera seems to magnify the distance. Think of how things look in your rearview mirror. The camera excludes the world outside the edges of the shot, and all the viewer has to work with is what is within the frame.

Separation

In order for triangulation or other concepts to work, the separation between performers sometimes may seem odd to the actor. But it is necessary for the dramatic point to be made to the audience. This is particularly true in blocking love scenes for the screen or stage.

Positioning

Body positions that feel odd may look totally comfortable to the viewer because of the message the total picture presents on stage or screen.

Duration
Actors usually have to hold positions for light changes, for curtain falls, or to allow sufficient time for the film or video editor to accomplish a slow wipe or fade at the end of a scene.

Variation
Sometimes arrangements are changed in order to avoid repetitious blocking. The director must come up with some justification for the change.

Visual Composition
All the elements of the visual composition are designed to satisfy the eye as well as achieve the best possible storytelling result.

Mood and Atmosphere

Position

The position of the camera or the actor may often give us an unconscious attitude toward the subject. The following shots may be used to convey our attitudes.

High Angle Shots
We look down on people and things we do not respect, those that we pity, or those we consider "beneath us."

Low Angle Shots
We look up at those whom we admire, respect, or fear.

Subjective Shots
Also known as POV shots, subjective shots show the viewer how a certain person sees a scene, person, or object.

Tilted Shots
Also known as Dutch angle shots, tilted shots tell the viewer that something is not right here; the world is skewed, off kilter, or no longer in balance.

Handheld Camera Shots
Usually used as POV shots, sometimes they are used to give a "You-Are-There" feeling.

Camera Movement

The way the camera moves gives us information and affects the way we view the picture.

Dolly

This is movement in toward or away from a person, place, or thing. This is the way we see the world when approaching or backing away on foot or in a vehicle.

Trucking

This movement is the same as a dolly but refers to movement left and right. A dolly movement gets closer or farther away, whereas a trucking movement goes left or right.

Tracking

Interchangeable with the terms dolly or truck, "tracking" is also used to indicate a following movement with a person or object. Tracking shots are a style characteristic in TV series like "The West Wing" and "Studio 60 on Sunset Blvd." by Aaron Sorkin.

Crane

Also known as pedestal or jib, this is an upward or downward movement of the camera beyond a simple tilt up or down. A crane movement usually occurs when a camera is mounted on a carrier with more range than a standard tripod.

Tilt

This is up or down movement of the camera on its tripod or mount. In a tilt, the camera moves but the pedestal is stationery.

Pan

A pan is a left or right movement of the camera on its tripod or mount. Truck refers to the movement of the entire pedestal, while pan refers to a movement of the camera only.

Lenses and Filters

Lenses and filters affect how much we see and demonstrate the relationship of the size of the shot to the importance of the shot.

- Wide angle: expansive view of a scene or location
- Normal angle: a medium shot; an "ordinary" way of seeing a person or scene

- Long angle: a close-up; seeing a person or scene telescopically from a distance

The Kiss Principle: "Keep It Simple, Stupid"

Don't be complicated just to prove you can. Make everything as simple as it can be for that particular purpose. Some things are naturally complicated, but as a rule, the simpler you can keep things, the better they work and the easier it is for viewers to "get it."

Moving the Actors

There are only two reasons for an actor to move:

1. The character is repelled from his or her present position.
2. The character is drawn to another location.

What is the character thinking at that particular moment in time? The character's thoughts are the basis for the character's movements. The "motivation" for any movement should either be clear at the moment it is made or else be revealed later. Movement without reason muddies the production and draws focus from the important elements of the production.

In many "living room" or "kitchen" dramas (the video and film equivalents of a stage play's "drawing room" drama), the audience may get a feeling of claustrophobia. In order to avoid this, many directors have the actors move often. In these situations proper motivation (or the lack of it) becomes evident to even the most casual viewer.

Since we now know the dangers of cigarette smoking, this device has fallen from favor, but there was a time when the need for a smoke (take a cigar off the coffee table, get a match from the mantle, and go to an ash tray on the bar) frequently served as a common motivation for movement in a small, enclosed set. The need for a drink (cross to the bar, get the bottle, get a glass, get some ice, pour the drink, stir the drink, then drink it) has long served the same purpose. Such casual movements are a form of "stage business" that has been used to add movement to long, "talky" scenes. These actions take on different meanings if they are done nervously or clumsily or with an air of calm or confidence.

Such movements must have a motivation (perhaps the character has a craving for nicotine or alcohol). These same actions can have other motivations (i.e., giving the character time to think of a way out a trap he has fallen into or serving as an attempt for someone to cover up guilt by casually performing an ordinary action that would be impossible for a truly guilty person). The right movements by an actor in character can convey a great deal of information about that character. The movement lets us know a great deal of information that would be awkward or difficult to put into words.

There is no wasted motion in a well-directed production. Even seemingly casual motions can have important meaning. A character who is seen scratching his nose, for instance, may turn out to be a cocaine addict. Seemingly unimportant actions such as patting a foot could ultimately be an action that sets off a booby trap.

Important Reminders about Stage and Screen Movement

1. Given a choice between watching something static or something in motion, the viewer will always look toward the motion. The eye goes to motion the way the eye goes to the lightest color in a shot (the whites of the eyes).
2. If an action is worth performing, it is worth seeing. Conversely, if it's not worth seeing, it's not worth performing.
3. A movement that does not contribute to the production detracts from it.

Major Actor Movement Principles

Do not block in movement just because you can. Think about the KISS principle. Let the move mean something. The character should move for a reason. The camera should move for a reason. Unnecessary movement is distracting.

The length of the move is information to the audience. The longer the move of an actor or camera, the more dramatic or important it is. Kisses should last no longer than necessary to convey the information needed. A kiss is a movement, and its length should be determined by the information the kiss is intended to convey.

Actors in motion should seem ready to stop. Actors not in motion should seem ready to move. Absolute stillness draws focus. When there are not a lot of distractions, it is easier to focus on the dialogue and ideas.

Actors should touch things or people only for a purpose. Movements and gestures of actors should be no bigger than necessary. Because of the distance of the image from the viewer, movements usually need to be bigger on stage, smaller on screen.

Stage actors need to move slightly when starting to say a line. Since there are a number of people on stage, the movement will call attention to the speaker. Screen actors do not need to move before speaking because the camera is probably on them already.

Rising and Sitting

For the camera, as a general rule, a performer should "telegraph" a rise or a sit-down. In "telegraphing," the actor makes a slight move or gesture to indicate the start of a major move. This helps the camera operator follow the action better. Telegraphing doesn't have to be very obvious. Merely taking hold of the arms of a chair prior to a rise, for example, is a way to telegraph it. The opposite is the case on stage. Moves should not be telegraphed to the audience ahead of time. Rising and sitting should be done as one continual motion, not a broken action. A well-trained actor knows how to stand and sit in a single fluid motion.

Crossing

To move an actor from one place on a set to another is a cross. On stage and screen, diagonal or curved crosses are more interesting than flat horizontal or vertical crosses. Unless there is a good reason, all crosses should be behind other characters who are speaking. To cross in front of a speaking character is to "upstage" him, drawing focus away. Obviously, on occasion, this is exactly what is required.

Turns

All turns should be "open" to the camera or stage audience and within the axis of action. In other words, a character should not turn his back on another (unless it's intentional) nor on the audience. This means that most turns will be made "downstage" or toward the camera. This is a stage and screen rule.

Entrances and Exits

Timing and speed are the major points to consider here. Consider the old "Laverne and Shirley" sitcom. Remember how Lenny and Squiggy would enter? Someone on stage would say something like, "Where are we going to find anyone that stupid?" The door would open and Lenny and Squiggy would enter with, "Hello." Timing is what made those jokes work, and they always worked. Time the entrance and exits of characters to achieve the best effect, be that a laugh, a cry, shock or fear.

The speed of an entrance or exit depends on the pace of the story, the action at the moment, and the ability of the camera to pick it up. Most performers will have a good feel for the speed of their entrance and exit. As the director, do not neglect these elements.

On stage or screen, never leave an actor hanging. An actor with an exit line should be positioned close to the door. As soon as the line is said, the actor should leave immediately, perhaps even slamming the door to punctuate the exit. If the actors, says, "I hate you, and I never want to see you again," and then has to cross twenty feet to get to the door, much of the punch of the line is dissipated by the cross.

Composition

Video and film differ from stage movement in that precise placement of actors is often important to achieve a particular shot. Actors must hit their marks exactly and on a certain line of dialogue for a certain shot to work. Stage blocking usually is not quite that critical, but many times it is.

For example, when two actors are both facing the camera, one behind and slightly over the shoulder of the other, this is a two faces east shot. It is a type of blocking that has been used on stage for centuries. But as it is used in video and film, the exact placement of both actors is critical. With this shot, both performers can be seen at the same time, the speaker and the reactor, or the camera can roll focus from one to the other as the scene progresses to achieve a particular effect.

An actor on stage or screen may be told to lean slightly one way or the other or to put his weight on one foot to slightly shift his position so that a particular composition will work.

Lighting

The lighting is always a major consideration. Actors must be conscious of their light and know when they are blocking the light of another performer. The director must watch out for actors who miss or block lights and direct the actors to make the stage scene or screen shots work.

Cameras

Camera blocking involves the placement and the movement of the cameras during a production. The director needs to decide what the major shots are and begin making blocking decisions after fixing these shots. If these shots are a must, which camera will cover each and where will these cameras be positioned when needed? Having decided that, the rest of the production can be covered with cameras available in other positions.

The cardinal rule in camera blocking is: a new shot must be more interesting than the previous one. At first glance, that sounds like an impossible ideal. However, just remember that the longer you stay on a shot, the more it is likely to lose interest. So, after a certain time, the shot needs to be changed to maintain interest.

The decision to take a two-shot as opposed to a group shot or a single shot must come from the director's evaluation of the action. There is no such thing as a "right shot" or a "wrong shot." These are artistic judgments as long as the audience is seeing what it wants to see at a given moment. If the shots lead rather than follow the action, the shots are likely to "work." In order to make a shot "work," the following details need the screen director's attention: carrying shots, zooming, and recomposing.

Carrying Shots

Any cross by an actor that is covered by a camera is called a "carrying shot." The camera is carrying the actor from one position to the next. There are several types of carrying shots: pans, trucks, dollies, zooms, and counters.

All carrying shots should have sufficient "look space" in front of the moving performer and "head room" over his head to give the impression that the action is a normal cross. If there is more room behind the actor than in front of him or too much "head room," the shot says that the actor is about to be hit from behind or from above. Thus the shot should always lead the actor across the set with normal headroom.

In a panning shot, the camera will remain stationary and follow the actor by pivoting on the camera head. A trucking or dollying shot will move the camera with the performer or it will counter the actor's move by moving the opposite direction.

An example of a counter would be the following. A camera is centered and facing a couch. An actor sits on the right end. As the actor rises and moves to camera left, the camera could truck right as the talent moves left. At the end of the couch, the actor might stop and turn back around, facing the camera. The camera would then be in the ideal position to zoom-in on the actor for a close-up. If the camera had remained centered and covered the movement with a pan only, the best shot the camera could get at the end of the actor's movement would be parallel or three-quarter shot and not the full face shot obtainable with the counter movement.

Zooming

The actor can also move from one position to another across the set and be covered by the camera zooming in or out, depending on which the movement requires. The important thing to keep in mind is that, as in all movement shots, the movement of the camera should be motivated by the action of the characters. An actor can move from a group or a single shot to the very opposite kind of composition by virtue of the action. A character standing with others can turn and come toward the camera or go off by himself to end up isolated both in his actions and on the screen. Likewise a character can go from being alone to joining a group while the camera covers the action by zooming-out.

Remember, however, that a zoom is an unnatural visual effect and should be used only for emphasis or to make subtle changes in a shot. If three actors are in a group shot and one exits, the camera should do a slow zoom-in as the third actor exits. The other two actors could slightly change their positions to better communicate with each other as a party of two instead of a party of three. Conversely, if a third actor steps up to two other actors who are being shot in a two-shot, the camera should slowly widen or zoom-out to allow this new performer to join the shot as actors number one and two adjust their positions. Again, this zoom movement should be casual and unnoticeable by most viewers. Watch almost any network sitcom or soap opera to see this type of composition in action.

Recomp

Whenever the camera shot is changed, the shot is recomposed or recomped. This recomp may involve zooming, a dolly, truck, pan, or tilt. The point is that the image changes with the characters action and so does the visual statement the camera conveys through its changing image.

All blocking of actors and of cameras should flow and "say" something through the following:

1. The point in the scene when the movement begins and ends
2. How the characters are seen before, during, and after the movement
3. How the characters relate to each other before, during, and after the movement
4. The distance involved in the movement
5. The dialogue and actions accompanying the movement

Size and Dynamics

If two actors move the same distance, the one using more gesture will seem more dynamic. Also, the one closest to the the camera will be larger on screen. If both actors are equal in the frame, the camera tracking of dollying with them, then it is the visual animation or vocal dominance that will determine which one is drawing more attention.

Rate or Tempo

The rate of speed of movements expresses mood values because audiences are affected by rate. Actors must move at their character's appropriate mood intensities.

Movements in Series

Ninety-five percent of all movement comes from the dramatic action—what the subtext tells the actors and the director to do. Actors who know their craft tend to move spontaneously out of their feeling about the script. The director can then suggest more or less movement, more specific movement, or a change in movement speed and specific destination of these movements.

Whether the actors develop movement on their own or you supply it, finding the movement inherent in the script depends on your talent and insight. Use verbs to express dramatic action. Avoid the ones that are obvious action verbs—run, jump, stab. Find verbs that show the wants and desires of the character.

Actors move every which way, but characters move in only two directions: they advance and they retreat. Movements have many mood values. They are constantly expressing the wants of the character. Movements have space, time, size, and variety. The long cross is a major move. It takes time; it is a large movement, and it can vary in mood a great deal.

Length of a Movement

All actor or camera movements, if they are to be recognized as movements, must travel five feet or more. Remember the following rules of movement:

- *Time*: The more time it takes, the stronger the move seems to be.
- *Size*: The bigger the movement, the stronger the move seems to be.
- *Variety*: The more varied the movements, the stronger they seem to be.

Summary

The basic rule of movement is: Don't work for the movement. Let the movement work for the script.

Suggested Reading and Viewing

Reading

Stage
Albright, Hardie. *Stage Direction in Transition*. See chapter 12.
Dean, Alexander, and Lawrence Carra. *Fundamentals of Play Directing*. See chapter 8.
Hodge, Francis. *Play Directing*. See chapter 13, Analysis.
Kirk, John W., and Ralph A. Bellas. *The Art of Directing*. See part 3.
Vaughan, Stuart, *Directing Plays*. See chapter 7.

Screen
Armer, Alan A. *Directing Television and Film*. See chapter 3.
Block, Bruce. *The Visual Story*. See chapter 3.
Katz, Steven D. *Film Directing Shot by Shot*. See part 2.
Proferes, Nicholas T. *Film Directing Fundamentals*. See chapters 3–4.

8

Idea, Rhythm, Pace, and Tempo

Idea

We use the term *idea* in two different ways in dramatic analysis. The first use, taken from college English texts for reading purposes, means the same as theme. In our case, for production analysis, the idea of a script is its basic meaning. The writer puts together characters and actions so that the actions result in an idea.

The writer doesn't usually come straight out and say—in big bold letters—what the idea is. Many times, but not always, one sentence said by one character contains the writer's idea specifically. More likely, the writer may never actually state his or her idea directly in words. Usually, the idea is expressed indirectly or with some subtlety. Do not be upset if you find it relatively difficult to discover. You will find it—it is there.

You can use a variety of means to find the idea. First, look at the title. What clues does it give you? Not all titles are clues, but it is a good place to start. What does *Death of a Salesman* mean? *Star Wars*? *A Raisin in the Sun*? *The Maltese Falcon*? *Roosters*? *It's a Wonderful Life*?

Some script titles contain a philosophical statement. That is not very common, especially in modern stage and screen scripts. Most writers do not like to come out and beat you over the head with the message. We save that technique for politicians and commercials. Scriptwriters consider that too obvious. Usually writers prefer to reach us through indirection. Intellectual statement is too obvious, too self-conscious.

Start looking at the dramatic action of the principal character or characters. If you can make a simple sentence combining the characters and the main action, you probably have the idea. The sentence will be the idea stated in action: "This script is about a shy college student who, gifted by extraordinary powers, feels he must fight evil when he would rather pass math." That is our made-up idea for *Spiderman II*.

Flat-out philosophical statements, although occasionally pinpointed in specific speeches, are not very common in plays and screen scripts. Most dramatic writers shun obvious statements of meaning. They want to reach audiences directly on the most primitive level of understanding. Intellectual statement is too obvious, too self-conscious.

Film studio head Samuel Goldwyn liked to say, "If I wanted to send a message, I would send a telegram." We tend to feel cross and irritated when we are "preached at." A lot of well-intentioned religious dramas preach so much, we can't tell if we are in church or at a play or film. A good dramatic script gets its message across with subtlety. That is why inexperienced directors may have trouble locating it. The idea of a script should not beat you over the head and shoulders. The reader or viewer should have to discover it.

In the way we use it here, *idea* is not quite the same as the *theme*. The theme is a generalized idea, something that can be applied to more than this script. Earlier we discussed that a good theme for *Oedipus Rex* could be "It is better to be physically blind than to be spiritually blind." The *idea* might be "Oedipus is the story of a man who, by trying to avoid a terrible fate foretold to him by an oracle, made it come to pass."

The best means of uncovering the idea, then, is to examine the dramatic action of the principal character or characters. One of the easier ways to see an idea is to place it in a simple sentence combining characters and action. As we have said, this sentence will be the idea stated in action. For example, "This play is about a childlike woman who refuses to grow up and tries to live in her 1950s version of reality." That is an example of an idea for a script we are thinking about writing.

Now that you have analyzed your script and done all the homework, you have certain other tools at your disposal to shape the finished product and give it the final sense you want it to have.

Tempo

Tempo can be described as the changing rates of the dramatic action. When the varying beats of several consecutive units are strongly felt, you have identified the pulsations of a production, or its rhythm.

Some of these terms are confusing because frequently they are used interchangeably. They are adapted from their musical origins. Even there, musicians don't always agree on what the terms mean. A musical dictionary will tell you that rhythm is everything relating to the duration of a sound, while tempo is the rate of speed of the piece. Therefore, our definitions here are a bit arbitrary.

Because all scripts are made in units of action, each unit has its own particular tempo. A script is made up of varying tempos, or unit beats. Therefore, a musical sense is one of the marks of talent in the director. Without a change in the tempo, the show becomes boring. Whether it is too frantic, without any breaks, or too static and still, it is boring. Even in a good script that is generally slow-paced and leisurely in its development, there are passages where the tempo picks up for a change to highlight the slow, gentle sections.

Have you seen a production somewhere that you thought was boring? A bad director can ruin a great script. If the script is a good script, then the probable cause of your boredom was the tempo of the play. Each scene chugged along, the same as the last. Perhaps the director played each scene as if it were life and death, or dragged it out, trying to milk every moment. Boring! Either way it lacked tempo.

The following are four characteristics of tempo: surges, rhythm, pace, and pause. These features—surges, rhythm, pace, and pause—are the elements of tempo. Frequently you will hear many of these terms used interchangeably. Don't let it bother you. Even professionals use many of these words interchangeably. You get the idea.

Surges

Surges can be seen as an increase in pace and rhythm leading to a climactic moment. A surge will often lead to a crisis, and a story may have several surges resulting in a final climax.

Think of a storm surge that accompanies a major hurricane. When a storm (the major conflict in a script) is coming, the waves increase in size, and their pattern becomes less regular than before. Local channels go live on camera. A script is made up of such surges, retreats, and new surges, all with accumulating force that finally culminates in a climax (the storm). A script doesn't just have a weatherman.

The 2005 movie *War of the Worlds* has some excellent examples of surges. The scenes build with increasing intensity, each event following the preceding one, faster and faster, until it reaches a crisis. The sky darkens, the wind picks up, we see strange lights in the sky, and finally everything comes crashing down. Then the pace slows down as we start to build another set of incidents toward another crisis, in a slightly different tempo, then move toward yet another crisis.

As excitement builds in the scene, the pace may quicken, the speaking volume may rise, the camera shots may cut more rapidly, and the background music may pick up tempo. A long period of excitement usually builds to a climax, and then we expect a return to a somewhat calmer state. A good director recognizes and capitalizes on these surges, no matter what the medium.

Rhythm

Rhythm can be described as the total effect of the unit beats. Most writers use the term "rhythm" rather than "surges." Rhythm is a way of describing multiple tempos brought together. It is similar to pace. A group of surges establishes the rhythm, and a group of rhythms establish the pace.

So, after a surge, we generally see a period of relative calm, then another surge of a different duration, and so on. These changes in the tempos of the scenes establish the overall rhythm of the work. Some scripts demand a generally faster pace than others. But a dull script has no changes. A dull production is one in which the entire show is played at the same pace, whether the pace is very fast or very slow. Every production needs variety.

Look at *War of the Worlds* again. Chart the rhythms. If you are a musician, you can actually name the movements of this "symphony"—allegro, andante, furioso, and so on.

If the tempos of film and television shows are correctly established in the editing process, then they don't change with each viewing. Even with no change, a different audience will feel "the show is too slow" or "that scene moves too fast." The changes lie in the audience, not in the production.

On stage during the performance, the actors control the tempo of the production. They control the tempo with the pace with which the dialogue is delivered. Actors control tempo with the number of times they "take a moment." A "moment" is a pause when the actor wants to have the focus totally on him or her—usually while he or she "suffers in silence." (The audience usually suffers too, but not in the way the actor imagines. The audience is usually suffering from boredom.) All these changes contribute to the tempos of the production.

Still, on stage the tempo is likely to change from performance to performance. At times the changes can be found in the differences among the different audiences. Also, tempo changes with the way the performers are feeling from day to day; therefore it is possible to see the same play by the same company on different days and see a very different production. Yet nothing may have changed but the tempo.

Actors will often come backstage and say, "We seem slow tonight." A good stage manger can tell right away when the tempo has changed and can remind the actors to move to the correct tempo. Sometimes actors may misjudge the tempo of the production. Often in a long running play as they repeat the performances, the play seems to the actors to slow down, so their tendency is to pick up the rate of the performance. Controlling the tempo in a stage play is a difficult, ongoing task.

Pace

Pace is the same as the gait of a horse. It is the rate at which a particular action proceeds. Some scripts are more fast-paced than others. A play by Anton Chekhov is usually slower-paced than a Jerry Bruckheimer film. But even so, each piece has some moments that are faster or slower than other parts. Most scripts include changes of pace for variety. In any production, the pace may vary considerably in different sections of the script.

One of the directors at our university is noted for the fast-paced comedies that mark his directing style. This person does really well with material that requires comic action and timing. Another has a different style and shines with material that requires subtlety and depth. He works best on slower-paced productions.

Several of us sat through Kill Bill: Vol. 2 and moaned about the fact that the well-choreographed fight sequences went on, and on, and on. To us, they lost pace. We had no such complaint about the sequences in *Million Dollar Baby* or *Cinderella Man*. Our responses show as much about our attitudes as their editing.

Pause

Pause is a silence—sometimes indicated by the writer, sometimes inserted by the director—that the actor must take in a particular spot. The pause can have a very strong effect because its tempo values can be very moving.

We all know that what is not said can sometimes be more important than what is said. The duration of the pause gives us a lot of information. (Propose marriage to someone and count the beats without a response. That really long pause ought to tell you—forget it.)

If you, as a director, want to use pauses, you should study the script and mark in the ones you want. In his plays, Harold Pinter does it for you. Then you have to sit there and try to figure out why the heck the pause is there. Of course, it's there for the reason just described—silence some-times has more punch than words. But then you have to figure out what is *not* being said in each particular pause, and there are bunches of them.

Film directors control tempo in the editing suite. Television directors can have some tempo control in postproduction. But usually the televi-sion director must see that the tempo is "in the can" before it goes to postproduction. The timing of the actors during the actual shoot is cru-cial to a good finished product.

On the opening night of a stage show, the tempo or pace is as close to the director's ideal as is humanly possible. But as the show plays, week after week, stage directors can see their carefully planned tempo settings destroyed by performers. The stage manager's job is to maintain the orig-inal pace set by the director.

In commercial theatre, the director may be long gone from the scene when the tempo of the production slowly shifts during the run. Stage directors may tell you of the trauma of returning to a production to find the pace has shifted drastically. In fact, a famous Broadway legend con-cerns the time that George M. Cohan, himself a master of timing as a performer, came back to see a show he had directed. He was so upset by the way it ran, he posted a notice for a special rehearsal "to take out the improvements."

Two traps await the stage director. Early on, with amateur performers, the tendency is for actors to be slow as they fight to remember their lines, causing long pauses between each speech. So the director bugs the actors to "pick up the pace." The amateur actor almost inevitably tries to rush the lines during the speech. Picking up the pace involves shortening the time between actor A's line and actor B's response, not in rushing the internal dialogue so that the audience has trouble understanding it.

Then, as the show runs for a week or more, actors discover little places in their lines where they can pause effectively, giving themselves another micromoment of focus. Soon the play develops into a drag race. In this case, each actor is dragging out his own speeches to get more audience focus than the others.

Mood

Mood includes the feelings or emotions generated by the various pars of the production. Mood is the result of the action, and the various moods in a piece give it the *tone*. As a director, your job is to find the tone for the work that is most appropriate. We can feel the emotions generated by the characters in action. We can feel so much empathy that we can actually change our pulse rates and breathing patterns. We may even feel we are spending as much physical energy watching a production as performing it.

Moods can be recorded in words in two different ways: through mood adjectives and through mood metaphors.

A *mood adjective* is usually one word that gives you the sense of the mood you wish to communicate—glowing, frantic, whatever. A *mood metaphor* is a phrase that invokes the sense of the mood. An example of a mood metaphor is "a moth fluttering around a lamp," or "a mouse caught in a trap," or "a dog with a fresh bone." Learn to use metaphors because they are the way of bringing to the surface your subjective feelings as the director.

Metaphors are a good way to talk with actors and designers to convey something that can really exist only in the doing. If they get the metaphor, they can then explore it in their own interpretation rather than simply aping what you have given them. Finding the right words to communicate your ideas is really a wonderful method of shorthand. The right metaphor can open up a raft of ideas to the actors and designers in just a few words, and everyone is still on the same track.

If three people were handed the same script, the results could and should be very different. Each of the three should find a somewhat different tone, or mood metaphor, for the work. Metaphors are ways of talking to actors and designers in order to convey something that can really exist only when it is accomplished. Metaphors communicate your idea while giving the other artists the greatest artistic latitude in bringing it to reality.

Tone

Tone is the *achievement of the appropriate moods* in a script. Tone is what the director is striving for, and it is very likely what the writer felt. It is the actual purpose of the production. Unless the director achieves this state, he or she achieves nothing. If you think you are directing a tragedy and the audience thinks it's a silly spoof, something has gone wrong with the tone.

Someone told us the following story:

> Once I had a ticket to the Broadway production of *Guys and Dolls* in the revival with Peter Gallagher and Nathan Lane. I was so sick that night I told my friend I might not be able to stay for the whole show. I thought I had the flu. We had standing-room-only tickets. So my plan was to slip out quietly when I got to feeling really bad. Two and a half hours later, I was still standing, still engaged in the show, and feeling so good I suggested we stop and have a drink afterward before heading home.

Talk about a mood-changing theatrical experience!

Tone can cause the audience members to change their personal moods. People who feel bad may attend a happy, lighthearted musical and come out feeling happy themselves. One of the joys of live performance is the way the tone of the play can transfer itself to the audience by the end of the evening. Of course, it happens in a great film also.

Art directors and production designers on films usually do a great deal to set the tone. The director may choose what the tone will be and the art director employs the means to attain it. Think of "CSI" (Las Vegas, Miami, or New York), *Road to Perdition* (2002), or *Pleasantville* (1998).

On screen, the tone and the mood are impacted not only by the performance but also by the cutting or editing (cutting refers here to the switching from shot to shot by the director in a multicamera production) and the music.

Cutting or Editing

You have two main ways to cut or edit—as you shoot or in postproduction. In multicamera video (as opposed to multicamera film) you usually switch or cut (or edit) on the fly—as you are shooting the scene. This is the way live news shows, sitcoms, and soaps are done. You can't do this with multicamera film. The film has to come out of each camera and be developed if you're actually using celluloid or downloaded to an editor if you're using digital video. In these cases, you must edit in postproduction.

So when and why do you switch, cut, or edit? While the following guidelines were developed for multicamera live video, they hold true for multicamera film as well as single camera film-style productions.

We start with TV because if you can direct multicamera live video, you can direct film and stage. The reverse is not true. Multicamera live video requires the director to make fast, confident decisions and to think ahead while staying focused in the moment. In both stage and film directing, there is time to consider options and make corrections. Now you know why directors prefer the latter two media. It's nice to have time to think.

When the director is working with multiple cameras and calling the shots as the production progresses, there is very little room for error. Directing multicamera productions demands a sense of timing that is anything but thoughtful, considered, or leisurely. Thus a director who can cultivate the arts and skills needed to succeed in multicamera live TV is most likely to do well having the time to make creative decisions at a more measured pace in either of the other two media.

Reasons to Cut, Switch, or Edit Shots

The following items are listed in order of importance.

1. To give the viewers a better view of what they want or need to see
2. To punctuate or emphasize by use of quick close-ups
3. To capture a quick reaction
4. To change the pace by changing the rate of cuts
5. To make it possible to set up the next shot in advance
6. To get out of trouble
7. To give variety (the least worthy of all reasons)

Many beginning multicamera directors use these reasons in reverse order. Since it is so easy to change shots and to switch images, inexperienced directors may fall into the trap of doing so. how many films or TV shows do you watch because the director has taken a lot of shots?

Editing is an excellent training ground for a director in film or TV. Just as everyone who edits a manuscript does not make a good writer, not all video or film directors can master the challenges of editing.

It is said that a film is written three times: once as a script, again when the script is brought to life on location with the cast and crew, and a third time when the picture is finally edited into the finished product. Directing multicamera video requires the director to handle the second and third writing of the script on the fly.

Regardless of when or how the production is cut or edited, the same requirements are in place as to when exactly to make the change to the next shot—when to say, "now look at this," "now look at this," "now look at this."

When to Cut

- Cut on action: You can cut at the beginning of an action, such as when a character starts to stand up, or you can cut at the completion of an action, such as when a door closes. It is also possible to cut in the middle of an ongoing action, such as when the character is crossing a room or going around the room.
- Cut on dialogue: You can cut at the beginning of a question, statement, answer, or line of dialogue or at the end of a question, statement, answer, or line of dialogue.
- Cut on a reaction: You can cut as a person turns his or her head or cuts his or her eyes to a new direction.

- Cut on music or a sound effect: A good place to cut is to the start of a beat with a piece of music. The cut can come at the beginning or end of a phrase or a piece of music or on a sound cue, like a scream, laugh, car crash, and so on.
- Cut on a light cue: You can cut as lights are turned on or off or as lightning or electricity flashes.

Stage Directors Edit, Too

The stage director has the same job of focusing the audience's attention that the directors have in the other two media, only the stage director has no camera or screen to use as his or her central canvas. Still, the stage director depends on the same principles the TV and film director use in order to get and keep the audience's interest. Stage and screen directors are both very concerned with having the following:

- A good story with engaging characters
- Fascinating action
- Striking dialogue
- Interesting sets or locations
- Arresting performances by appealing actors
- Actors whose very presence demands that they be watched
- Surprising, charming, or frightening portrayals
- Costumes and makeup
- The light and movement rule. (The eye always goes to light and motion.)

Take the seven reasons for cutting listed earlier and change them a little for live theatre. These are points in the script where you need to use your stage directing—that is, blocking—skills.

Reasons to Change Stage Focus

The following items are listed in order of importance.

1. To give the viewers a better view of what they want or need to see
2. To punctuate or emphasize
3. To capture a quick reaction
4. To change the pace by changing the rate of dialogue and movement
5. To make it possible to set up the next important idea in advance

6. To get out of trouble or make an action safer for an actor
7. To give variety (the least worthy of all reasons)

Stage directors have the same problems as directors in the other media—they just have different techniques for solving them.

Pointers for which There Is No Stage Equivalent

The Jump Cut

The term jump cut has two totally different definitions. The first refers to any shot that is jarring, odd, and unexpected while still being an effective storytelling device. This kind of jump cut is employed to stir the pot, to punctuate a moment, or to keep the audience slightly ahead of events as they unfold.

The second definition refers to a shot that is a mistake. When you are shooting a scene or program with three or more people in it (A, B and C, for example), people who are sitting or standing in a line or semicircle must be aware of the jump cut. The director who takes any successive two-shots in succession with the same person—person B, for example—in both shots, has "jumped" B from one side of the screen to the other (for example, shot 1 has persons A and B, and shot 2 has persons B and C). With person B being on the right side of one shot and then suddenly on the left side of the next, the viewer will get instantly disoriented. "Wasn't he on the other side?" they will ask themselves. In other words, with three people, the director cannot take successive two-shots with the same person in both shots but in different parts of both shots.

As soon as you do this, you jerk the viewer away from the scene and cause him or her to wonder about things that should be invisible. It is possible, however, to *pan* from a two shot of A and B to a two-shot of B and C. In this instance, the viewer sees person B move from one side of the shot to the other as the camera pans across. This is acceptable.

Editing Programs

Most film and video editing is done these days on nonlinear computer editing systems. To be sure, some TV stations, production houses, and even small studios still use cassette-to-cassette video editing and physical celluloid splicing to assemble a screen production. Nonlinear editing currently rules, and it is the way all editing is going.

There are stand-alone systems like Avid, but there are also systems that can use off-the-shelf computers, monitors, and software (for example,

Final Cut Pro and Adobe Premiere). Regardless of the type, all these systems pretty much work the same. The terminology is slightly different for each machine and even from one platform to another (Mac to PC), yet the essentials are almost identical. From edition to edition, the software will leap forward and offer new features and innovations. Then, within a matter of months, their competitors have caught up and maybe even passed their rival.

To the director, the particular editing system rarely matters as long as the editor has mastered it. The director needs to know what the finished picture is supposed to look like and be able to communicate this knowledge to the editor.

Music

Music is the final element at your disposal to shape the script with your sense of its ideas, tempo, and mood. In both stage and screen directing, music and sound effects add tremendously to the ideas, tempos, and moods of the production. Powerful film and TV scores become works of art of and to themselves—justifiably so.

The majestic orchestrations of John Williams (*Jaws* [1975], *Star Wars* [1977, 1980, 1983, 1999, 2002, 2005] *Schindler's List* [1993] and *Harry Potter* [2001, 2002, 2004]) have deeply moved audiences just as the scores of Henry Mancini ("Peter Gunn" [1958], *Hatari* [1962], *Charade* [1963], *The Pink Panther* [1963]), Max Steiner (*King Kong* [1933], *A Star Is Born* [1937], *Jezebel* [1938], *Sergeant York* [1941], *Casablanca* [1941], *Key Largo* [1948], *The Caine Mutiny* [1954]), and Erich Wolfgang Korngold (*Captain Blood* [1935], *The Adventures of Robin Hood* [1938], *The Sea Hawk* [1940], *Of Human Bondage* [1940]) have done in the past. The sometimes-quirky yet melodic scores of Randy Newman (*Three Amigos* [1984], *Maverick* [1994], *A Bug's Life* [1998], *Seabiscuit* [1903]) and "Monk" (2002), are examples of different directions in screen music that help the director tell stories in totally unique ways.

The total absence of music, as in Sidney Lumet's *Fail Safe* (1964), can have a chilling, documentary effect. But this is the very rare exception rather than the rule. Those who have seen Hugh Hudson's *Chariots of Fire* (1981) without music say that the film was dull and destined to be a box office flop. With the imaginative synthesizer score of Vangelis, who also scored Ridley Scott's *Blade Runner* (1982), the film became a major hit.

The second time you see *War of the Worlds*, you should be able to pay more attention to the music. John Williams's film score really sets the moods. The first time through the film, you may have been too busy absorbing all the other elements to be conscious of it. In your second viewing, as you chart the rhythms and surges and so on, listen to the way the score states, supports, and enhances the film. The music drives our emotions, even our heartbeats, as we watch. On the second viewing, you will notice how well the sound effects and the score are so integrated that at times it is difficult to tell if a sound is a sound effect or a musical effect.

Ideally the director will be able to work with the composer to spell out the ideas, tempos, and moods of every moment in the production where music is needed. The combined creativity of the director and the composer can unite for a finished product that captures all the director's aspirations and touches the audience in ways both fundamental and memorable.

A stage director must have the same relationship with the sound designer in live theatre. As you look at program credits in stage plays, you will more and more frequently see a credit for the sound designer. Our film experiences as viewers have conditioned us to expect a more complete sound track when we are playgoers.

Until a director is in the position or has the budget to hire an original composer, there are still a couple of options available. Stage directors, unless they are working on musicals, have to rely on the sound crew. The following are some stage and screen options.

1. Create the score yourself. If you play any instrument, it is possible to record yourself and use music you compose to use in your production. There are even programs that can turn your computer keyboard or a synthesizer keyboard of any kind into an entire orchestra.

2. Find local musicians or friends who will be willing to contribute their original music to your score. To be fair, it is only right that you make sure the musicians retain the rights to their music and allow you the performance rights only for your production and any ads that might be made for it.

3. Use prerecorded, canned music from a commercial music library (http://www.partnersinrhyme.com/FreeMusic.html or http://www.firstcom.com), for example.

4. Use computer music generation programs like Digital Performer (http://www.motu.com) and Logic Pro (http://www.apple.com/logic) that will enable the almost musically illiterate to create a professional sound track.

Summary

All directors, regardless of the medium used, must see that the production expresses an idea. The audience sees what the director intended when the director uses the elements of tempo, mood, and tone to reinforce the idea. Each medium needs to take advantage of its own strengths and compensate for its own weaknesses to do this effectively. In this chapter, you have made an early encounter with some of these methods. You will spend the rest of your professional lifetime exploring and enhancing your use of them to get an effective production.

Suggested Reading and Viewing

Reading

Stage

Catron, Louis E. *The Director's Vision*. See chapters 7–9.

Dean, Alexander, and Lawrence Carra. *Fundamentals of Play Directing*. See chapter 9.

Hardie, Albright. *Stage Direction IN Transition*. See chapter 13.

Hodge, Francis. *Play Directing*. See chapter 5.

Screen

Armer, Alan A. *Directing Television and Film*. See chapter 7.

Block, Bruce. *The Visual Story*. See chapters 5–8.

Katz, Steven D. *Film Directing Shot by Shot*.

Proferes, Nicholas T. *Film Directing Fundamentals*. See chapter 9.

9

What Is Blocking?

We put the chapter on blocking next to movement because they are essentially the same thing. Blocking is a term that can be used several ways. Blocking refers to the written instructions of a director, as in "The blocking calls for Bob to sit after that line." It also is the means by which the process is developed, as in "This afternoon we will finish blocking scene three." In theatre, the term staging is often used to convey these ideas. Blocking in TV and film also refers to moving cameras (or actors) in a screen scene. Often in sitcoms, for example, one day may be set aside just for camera blocking after the cast blocking has been refined in a camera-less rehearsal hall. We prefer to use the term blocking because it covers the movements of cameras as well as actors.

The Great Blocking Debate

Some directors argue that it is better to wait until you are into rehearsal to block—this allows them to rely on creative juices and group input to get exciting results. They will argue that if you really know the material and the people you are working with are top-notch, wonderful results will occur as the movements and so on are worked out in the rehearsal process.

This process can work for both stage and screen, but only for the most experienced directors. There are noted examples from every medium of directors who function in just this fashion and do so very well. The key to their success, however, is experience. It is a trap for beginners.

Beginning directors who attempt such practices quickly discover themselves lost—unable to deal with the questions from their cast as well as the technical demands of their production. Limited experience gives a director limited options when problems arise. Such directors quickly lose the confidence and respect of both their cast and crew. Everyone figures out in a big hurry that the director is grasping at weak and peculiar suggestions. That underlines the fact that the director simply is not prepared. Nothing undercuts a production more than an unprepared director who is not truly ready to direct.

The director has to have a target. Without any preblocking, the director is taking a trip without a map. You can always change directions, but you need to have a clear idea of where you are going before you start.

Time gets eaten up very quickly as a number of different moves for both talent and equipment are tried and discarded. It is like sitting around waiting for lightning to strike. We say that blocking is part of your homework, part of the preproduction preparation the director should do. Noted stage director Stuart Vaughan and others have some excellent reasons that we have amplified and adapted.

1. You get to try out a bunch of ideas before you get to rehearsal. You can play with several choices without wasting group time or possibly running into "interference." You can make your worst mistakes in private.

2. You can always get input later without dealing with ego problems early on. If you need to cut a line or scene before you rehearse, the actor is not offended. But once it becomes "his" line, he resents our stealing what is his.

3. You can get information to the actors about what is right for the scene without having to worry at the initial blocking rehearsal about what they "feel" they should do. At early rehearsals you should know the material and its needs much better than they do.

4. You can save an incredible amount of time that you can put to good use later. As everyone becomes more familiar with the scene as a whole, his or her input will have real value. Then you can make the changes.

5. You can help other departments to find out early on what they need so they can provide the support you need. You make it easier for them to do a good job. It will make them think you are a good director.

6. You can still make changes later in the process. You can always change a good plan A for a better plan B, but spending a lot of time when other people are "on the clock" can be very expensive. Remember what we said about "time is money"? Then, when you take their excellent suggestions and incorporate them into the scene, they will think you are brilliant, creative, and smart.

7. Especially when doing film and television, time constraints are usually severe. Coming in with some plan is really important. Otherwise, massive overtime costs will eat up the budget.

So, if you get the idea that we say you must preblock, you clearly are brilliant, creative, and smart.

Now, armed with the information you have been busy collecting, all that wonderful research you have done, you are ready to fill in column four of your prompt book.

We always teach—and were taught—that blocking should be done in pencil, but now many people enter a great deal of their work directly into their laptop and desktop computers. We have seen promptbooks in process that look suitable for framing. But even if you are still doing blocking with number twos instead of G-6s, you have to be neat and legible.

Figure 9.1 is a sample of a short classic scene from the play *The Importance of Being Earnest* (1895) by Oscar Wilde that student Ruby Ortiz did on her computer. The method works so well that many of our students use it, and we do, too.

Our theory is that a really good director makes himself or herself disposable. By having as much as possible written down, if you miss a rehearsal, someone can carry on in your absence as if you were there. We don't recommend it in practice, of course. Like sanctity, it's an ideal to strive for, not necessarily an attainable goal.

Always have an accurate drawing to scale of the sets you will be using so you can perceive the actors' relationship accurately before you start to block with them. This is a ground plan. It shows, as if looking from above, where everything, except the actors, is placed. You should get this from your set designer. If it's not possible, make your own using graph paper.

It's a good practice to use a template or a ruler. Several companies make thin plastic templates with cutouts in the shape of the lighting instruments, furniture pieces, a camera, and talent. For the director it is important that the template be cut to the same scale as the ground plan.

Do not think of ground plans as a stage requirement only. Any video or film production requires a blocking diagram. This, along with the marked director's script and the storyboards, tells the story of what is to happen at any given moment of the script. Shorter forms, like commercials, require storyboards only for clients, but blocking diagrams help the cast and crew. (Test your ground plan by answering the questions for testing a ground plan in Chapter 6.)

Scripts (see Figure 9.2) can be very sparse on the amount of stage directions and blocking information they contain. Even if the script is

Motivation	Character	Dialog	Movement
Is a witty old woman who is very concerned with whom her daughter marries.	LB:	You can take a seat, Mr. Worthing.	Sitting down. Looks in her pocket for a notebook and pencil.
Has a sense of humor as well but thinks the interview is ridiculous.	JK:	Thank you, Lady Bracknell, I prefer standing.	Stands and watches her.
Tries to make fun of the fact that Jack is not on the list.	LB:	I feel bound to tell you that you are not down on my list of eligible young men, although I have the same list as the dear Duchess of Bolton has. We work together, in fact. However, I am quite ready to enter your name, should your answers be what a really affectionate mother requires. Do you smoke?	Glances at her notebook. And then watches every move Jack makes.
Sarcastically	JK:	Well, yes, I must admit I smoke.	Nods his head to gesture that he does smoke.
	LB:	I am glad to hear it. A man should always have an occupation of some kind. There are far too many idle men in London as it is. How old are you?	Smiles as she speaks.
Hopes it is a good age for LB.	JK:	Twenty-nine.	In a serious voice.
Approves of Jacks age.	LB:	A very good age to be married at. I have always been of opinion that a man who desires to get married should know either everything or nothing. Which do you know?	Waves her left hand in the air as she speaks.
Tries to make a good impression.	JK:	I know nothing, Lady Bracknell.	Smiles and winks at Lady Bracknell.
LB thinks she's so smart.	LB:	I am pleased to hear it. I do not approve anything that tampers with natural ignorance. Ignorance is like a delicate exotic fruit; touch it and the bloom is gone. The whole theory of modern education is radically unsound. Fortunately	She lifts her head up high as she speaks

Figure 9.1 A sample stage script with columns

detailed in this way, it is up to the director to decide on the blocking of cast and cameras as a part of his or her job. To have this information in a different notebook, as the storyboards often are, makes for problems in keeping track of the dialogue and the action. The director will have marked camera shots on his or her script according to directorial decisions made with the text of the dialogue and its pace. It is easier for the director if the blocking diagram is kept in the same notebook, page for page in sync with the script. But if different pages are used for both script and blocking diagrams, this can make for a bulky script.

In TV, directors who have an assistant director (AD) they trust may allow the AD to mark the script based on the director's blocking in rehearsal. The director checks over the AD's marks to ensure they do reflect the director's ideas. Because the AD's marks are in pencil, the director can easily make changes and corrections before shot sheets are made for the camera operators. This practice is the exception rather than the rule, but some directors and ADs work this way.

In film, the director writes the shooting script with as much or as little detail as the director wants or needs. This script and the storyboards allow for the director to capture on film every movement of the cast and the camera that has been envisioned (see Figures 9.3 and 9.4).

The easiest way to keep blocking and shot marks together is to have the set plan (for only that set in use for a particular part of the script) copied on the back of the previous page of script. That way, the director can open up his or her script to a given scene and have the camera shots and all production movement there at one glance. Make sure all blocking marks (except those of the set diagram) are made in lead pencil (number two or darker). Changes can easily be made if and when they are required.

Shortcut Notes for Actor Blocking

X	cross	L	left	R	right
C	center	U	up	D	down

- X usually contains more information, such as X to chair UL.
- L, R, or C can mean the left, right, or center of the stage or another marking, such as X R of couch, X L of Fred, sit C of couch.
- U, or up, refers to the back of the set or the stage.
- D, or down, refers to the front of the stage or the area on the set closer to the cameras.

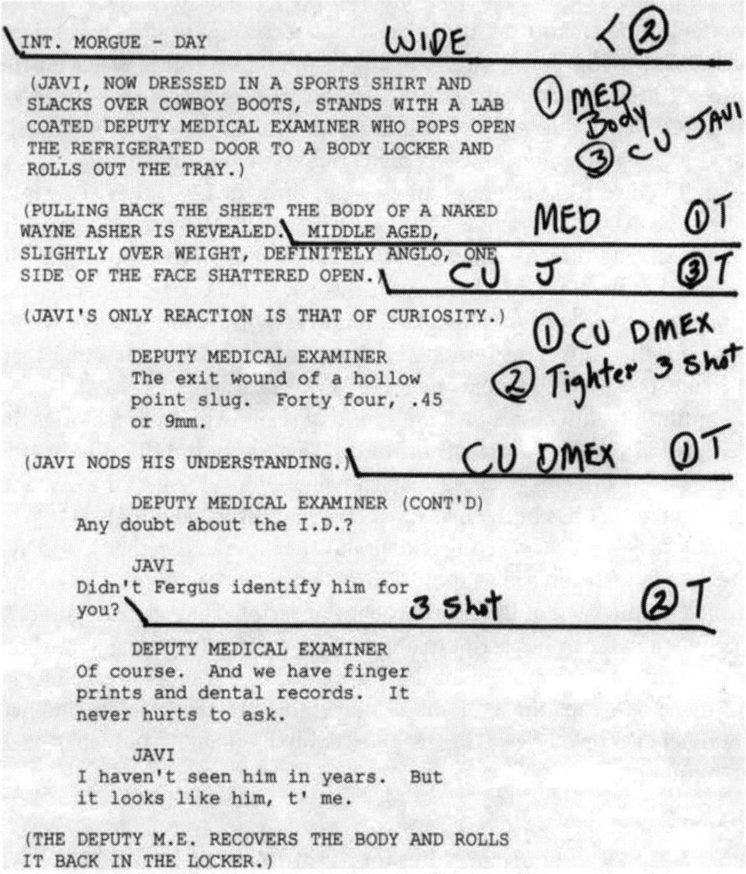

INT. MORGUE - DAY   WIDE   < ②

(JAVI, NOW DRESSED IN A SPORTS SHIRT AND   ① MED
SLACKS OVER COWBOY BOOTS, STANDS WITH A LAB   Body
COATED DEPUTY MEDICAL EXAMINER WHO POPS OPEN   ③ CU JAVI
THE REFRIGERATED DOOR TO A BODY LOCKER AND
ROLLS OUT THE TRAY.)

(PULLING BACK THE SHEET THE BODY OF A NAKED   MED   ① T
WAYNE ASHER IS REVEALED. MIDDLE AGED,
SLIGHTLY OVER WEIGHT, DEFINITELY ANGLO, ONE
SIDE OF THE FACE SHATTERED OPEN.)   CU   J   ③ T

(JAVI'S ONLY REACTION IS THAT OF CURIOSITY.)   ① CU DMEX
                                                 ② Tighter 3 Shot
          DEPUTY MEDICAL EXAMINER
          The exit wound of a hollow
          point slug. Forty four, .45
          or 9mm.

(JAVI NODS HIS UNDERSTANDING.)   CU DMEX   ① T

          DEPUTY MEDICAL EXAMINER (CONT'D)
     Any doubt about the I.D.?

          JAVI
     Didn't Fergus identify him for
     you?   3 Shot   ② T

          DEPUTY MEDICAL EXAMINER
     Of course. And we have finger
     prints and dental records. It
     never hurts to ask.

          JAVI
     I haven't seen him in years. But
     it looks like him, t' me.

(THE DEPUTY M.E. RECOVERS THE BODY AND ROLLS
IT BACK IN THE LOCKER.)

Figure 9.2 Sample TV script

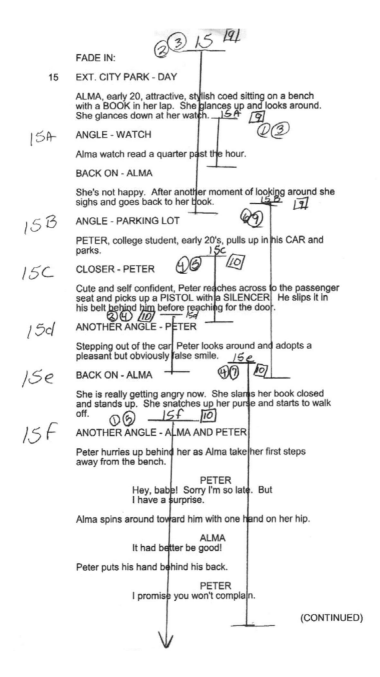

FADE IN:

15   EXT. CITY PARK - DAY

ALMA, early 20, attractive, stylish coed sitting on a bench
with a BOOK in her lap. She glances up and looks around.
She glances down at her watch.

15A   ANGLE - WATCH

Alma watch read a quarter past the hour.

BACK ON - ALMA

She's not happy. After another moment of looking around she
sighs and goes back to her book.

15B   ANGLE - PARKING LOT

PETER, college student, early 20's, pulls up in his CAR and
parks.

15C   CLOSER - PETER

Cute and self confident, Peter reaches across to the passenger
seat and picks up a PISTOL with a SILENCER. He slips it in
his belt behind him before reaching for the door.

15d   ANOTHER ANGLE - PETER

Stepping out of the car Peter looks around and adopts a
pleasant but obviously false smile.

15e   BACK ON - ALMA

She is really getting angry now. She slams her book closed
and stands up. She snatches up her purse and starts to walk
off.

15f   ANOTHER ANGLE - ALMA AND PETER

Peter hurries up behind her as Alma take her first steps
away from the bench.

                        PETER
        Hey, babe! Sorry I'm so late. But
        I have a surprise.

Alma spins around toward him with one hand on her hip.

                        ALMA
        It had better be good!

Peter puts his hand behind his back.

                        PETER
        I promise you won't complain.

                                        (CONTINUED)

Figure 9.3   Sample film script with blocking

1. Wide EXT. SUBURBAN NEIGHBORHOOD

A MAILMAN, in his early 30's, wearing a U.S. Postal uniform, walks down the sidewalk from a house to his U.S. MAIL TRUCK parked at the curb. He climbs in the vehicle, STARTS the motor and proceeds to the next house.

Figure 9.4 Sample storyboard

Shortcut Notes for Camera Blocking

Camera Shots

CU (close-up): An intimate shot of the head and or face of a character or a shot that isolates an object for careful examination or dramatic impact.

DTL (down-the-line shot): A diagonal shot of a group of characters or objects in a row with the most important character or object usually (but not always) being closest to the camera. (A comic effect would be to have the important character in the middle on the end of the line, further away from the camera.)

ECU (extreme close-up): The most intimate shot possible of a person or object, usually including the eyes only or perhaps the eyes and mouth of a person. This is the most powerful shot in the screen director's toolbox and is not to be used lightly or often but rather only on very rare occasions.

Est (establishing shot): Often the same as a wide shot. It helps the audience fix in their minds the location and relations of objects and people in a scene (the location of the doors and furniture, etc.). This is usually the first or one of the first shots in any scene.

GS (group shot): Any shot showing multiple characters over three in number and relying on the principle of triangulation or careful placement of each character for the maximum effect of the shot.

Med (medium shot): Also known at a bust shot. It is a "normal" view of a character from mid chest to just above the top of the head. This is the way the eye sees people in normal conversations.

OTS (over-the-shoulder shot): A two-shot from behind one character (B) and focusing on the other (A). The shot is named after the character whose face is seen (e.g., OTS A).

2FE (two faces east): A two-shot with both characters facing the same direction—toward the camera.

2S (two-shot): Two characters or objects or one character and one object in the same shot. This may be a "tight" or a "loose" two-shot.

3S (three-shot): Same as a 2S with the addition of another character or object.

W (wide shot; see Est shot): A shot that includes as much of the set, scene, or location as possible.

Camera Movements

Arc: A left or right semicircular movement of the camera around characters or objects.

Boom: Also known as a crane or jib. A large up or down movement of the camera on a mechanical device such as crane, camera, boom, or jib.

Dolly/tracking: Movement of the camera into or out of the set (dolly) or parallel to the set or action on device (camera dolly) or tracks.

Pan: Horizontal pivoting the camera head left and right on the camera mount without moving the camera mount. (The term is often misused when unknowledgeable directors say "pan up" or "pan down." A pan is *not* an up or down movement, it is a left or right movement.)

Ped: Short for pedestal. The vertical movement of the camera up or down without tilting; often used to raise the camera with a character as he or she stands. This term is commonly used only in studio TV, where cameras are typically mounted on pedestals.

Tilt: Vertical pivoting of the camera up and down on the camera mount (A tilt is *not* a left to right movement. This is the term knowledgeable directors use as opposed to the incorrect "pan up" or "pan down.")

Other Camera Directing Commands

Carry: To follow a performer across the set with proper headroom and look space.

Center: To move the character or object to the center of the picture frame.

Comp: Short for "compose the camera shot."

Defocus: Also called a "roll focus." Changing a focused shot to a blurred picture.

Focus: To adjust or correct the focal point of the camera lens using the focus ring on the lens or the focus handle on the back of the camera.

Frame up: The same as comp or recomp. To correct the existing shot to the prescribed composition.

Head room: The amount of space between the top of a character's head or an object and the top of the picture frame. This is an artistic call by the director as to how much space this shot actually requires. It is important, however, that headroom be consistent throughout a production.

Lock in: Adjust pan and tilt locks to secure the shot so it will remain stationary.

Look space: The space between the person's face and the edge of the picture frame in the direction the person is looking or facing. There should typically be more space in front of a character than behind him or her. Like head room, this is an artistic judgment call on the part of the director.

Recomp: Short for "recompose the camera shot."

Roll focus: Also called focus or defocus. Changing a shot to either blur out of focus or come into focus.

When space is short, as in printed scripts, put a number in a circle at the point where the move occurs and write the move in full on the facing page. Actually, this is the second best method. You should scan and copy the script so you have the room necessary to show blocking clearly and close to the text.

When preparing your prompt script for stage, leave large margins on each side of text. Many directors write emotional and motivational notes in the left side of the text page and put actors' blocking notes on the right. They leave the facing page blank, then divide it into columns for cues (e.g., lights, sound, fly)

Cue actors in relation to a piece of furniture or another actor, particularly if the blocking has to be precise. This type of direction can be needed for both stage and screen. In a tight blocking situation, say, "Stand behind Bill so your left shoulder is just brushing his right shoulder," if that is what you mean.

Telling an actor to "stand up left" means he or she should fill in the space in that area of the stage that is empty and should "dress" (position) himself or herself so that part of the set or stage area looks occupied. Dressing a space means putting someone in a place that would otherwise look unoccupied.

Often, on stage or screen, the blocking gets tight and the directions may require slight adjustments. Sometimes all that is needed is to tell an actor to "Put your weight on your left foot," or "Hold your pipe at the level of your third button."

Many of the same rules of blocking apply for both stage and screen. Just remember that the whole stage is your picture in theatre, while the whole frame is your picture in television and film.

Since film and TV will often have many more sets and locations than plays, screen blocking must take into consideration both the previous and the next scene when blocking both cast and camera or cameras. Each edit, cut, wipe, or dissolve from one shot to another is the screen director's way of saying to the audience, "Look at this. Now look at this. Now look at this."

Therefore, shots should be changed only when they give the audience new information. The new information may only be dialogue from another character, but hopefully it will involve something more than that. Remember the term, "motion pictures." If there isn't meaningful movement of either characters or camera, why isn't this production on radio or in print?

For long-running stage plays, do all blocking in pencil until the show is "fixed." At that point, the markings can be transferred to ink so they will stay neat and clean for the run of the production. The same is true for soap operas, sitcoms, and films for all markets. Pencil gives the director an opportunity to tweak blocking decisions up to the last minute.

Keep in mind that script markings are used in rehearsals to keep track of what is already done and worth keeping as part of the production.

These marks then become a reference guide for future rehearsals. When all script markings are set, they then become an action guide for all performances, so final marked cues and blocking notes should be clearly and accurately recorded.

For the single-camera, film-style director, part of the marking on the script occurs during the production. The director can make notes on the script to himself or herself about (1) how much of a given page was covered, (2) which camera position was used, (3) on which tape, reel, or disc it was recorded, and (4) which takes were the keepers.

One method of doing this is to use a simple code such at this: use squares with the correct number to keep track of the tape, reel, or disc being used and circles with numbers inside to indicate keeper takes. Later, in postproduction, this director's script, along with continuity notes from the script supervisor and the camera reports will save a great deal of time and confusion when shots are misplaced, misnumbered, or simply can't be found.

To get in a little practice, copy the sample scene, Make up a simple ground plan and use a system that works for you to block it, first for stage and then for screen.

(A BEAT THEN AMY ENTERS FROM THE HALLWAY AND CROSSES TO THE NURSE'S STATION. EVERSON ENTERS THROUGH THE HOSPITAL'S FRONT DOORS AND CROSSES TO AMY. THEY EXCHANGE LOOKS AND EVERSON CROSSES TO A CHAIR IN THE WAITING ROOM WHERE HE SITS. DR. WARD ENTERS A MOMENT LATER FROM THE OPERATING ROOM HALLWAY AND GOES TO EVERSON.)

WARD
I'm sorry. If I had known—I wouldn't
have been so encouraging.

EVERSON
How much of this does Brenda know?

WARD
None. She's still out.

EVERSON
Good.

(WARD REACTS)
Don't tell her, Doc. Not the—not about
being deformed. If she knew—.

WARD
I understand.

EVERSON
Just say th' baby—died.

(WARD NODS)

Actor Blocking

Although, as a stage director, you expect to aim toward the goal of controlled improvisation with actors, you must practice paper blocking as a necessary step in learning all the tools of communication. Paper blocking gives you options, since a dozen suggestions are far better than one. You work over choices in your mind and on paper before you have to bring them to life with a group of actors.

The promptbook is your original design for a live production of a script. A director, like any craftsman, is known by the condition of his tools. Yours is the promptbook. Therefore, try to be as neat and accurate as you can while building your promptbook. You will use it constantly, so try to protect it. Always make an accurate drawing to scale of the sets you will be using. Ultimately, your promptbook will contain all the information about the production—a complete record.

You must perceive the relationships of the characters accurately before you start to block the actors. Time is money, and in any medium, you can't afford dozens of people sitting around playing pinochle while you figure out what you are going to do next or where you will put the actors or cameras.

A three-dimensional perspective sketch of the ground plan is needed from the designer at this point. It needs to show more clearly what the ground plan looks like, as a cube. A ground plan is two-dimensional. Now you need to think in three-dimensional terms. New computer programs are coming out that enable a designer to turn a two-dimensional ground plan into a perspective drawing so we directors can see what the set looks like in three dimensions.

Here we're talking about programs such as Vectorworks, AutoCad, and Sketch Up. From the screen perspective, there are programs like Frame Forge Studio 3D, which is a storyboarding program. It will allow you to create three-dimensional sets with characters and a camera or cameras to give you an idea of what you want on paper before you have to bring it to life.

The designer, whether with a computer program or by sketching, should always have a perspective view of the sets—or the art director of the scenes—so the stage or screen director can visualize what the space actually looks like before blocking on it.

Theoretically, then, a director should do a rough blocking of a production before talking with the designers. A stage director can say, "Look, I need at least three doors in the Act I set, and two of them should be very close together so actor A can run in one and out the other in as little time as possible." Then the designer has important information to work with before coming back with the final design. Now that you have the final design, you can do all your homework, as far as blocking goes.

At this point, you may discover that you forgot something important. Usually, there is still time for the designer to change it before the scene shop has gotten into building it.

Doing blocking is a lot like building a house from scratch. As the homeowner, you need to make a list, technically called a program, for the building. How many bedrooms? Do you want a laundry room, a separate dining room, a large Jacuzzi in the bathroom? That sort of thing. Then you talk with the designer—the architect. When you and the designer have worked through the final plans, then the building—or blocking process—starts for sure. At this point, mistakes and changes get to be expensive. If you decide you want to move a door, in the house or in the set plan, it is much more expensive when the thing is being built than when you all were still doodling on paper.

Blocking is like a chess game—you always project five moves ahead. As you start blocking a scene, you have several critical points in your mind that you have pictured—points that you know where you want or need the actors to end up. Usually these are the key compositions discussed in Chapter 5. The rest of the blocking just gets everyone in positions that lead to those significant points.

The blocking you "see" at home during preparation time will meet its crucial test only when you suggest it to the actors (and camera crew). That advance planning puts you in a flexible position. The better the homework you have done, the less likely you are to get on the set and discover a costly mistake.

Here are two sets of suggestions for recording blocking. There are many other techniques. Find a system that works for you and is clear enough to be read by others in case you must miss a rehearsal. The idea is to keep such scrupulous notes that someone can carry on in your absence or in case your brain takes a little holiday when your body goes to work that day.

An Approach for the Stage

Number each movement on the page consecutively in the script. Then, in a separate place, write down the number and write out the movement in as many words as you need. By setting down the movement you will automatically imply the compositions and also, at least in your imagination, some sense of the picturizations. Now prepare a small cutout (a template) of your ground plan. With your computer, you can insert the ground plan any place you need and as often as you want. Traditionally, people do it at the top left of each page of script so they know where they are each time they turn the page.

Indicate each character by a symbol that works for you. A lot of people use a triangle with a different initial inside for each character. If several characters have the same initial, give one a circle, the other a triangle, the third a square. Show the direction of each movement by arrows on the lines and by the same number of the movement you have used in the written directions and in the text. When all the detailed blocking has been done for each page of text, enter all movement on a single ground plan. This time you can use large dots to show positions and colors to show movements.

An Approach for the Screen

On the back of each script page, photocopy the ground plan for the scene or scenes for the next page. Sometimes this will mean you will have two or three or more pages of ground plans between pages of script. Each ground plan should be labeled with the correct scene number.

Using a plastic template, mark the beginning and ending positions of the talent, using arrows to indicate the direction of movement. Include the position of the camera for each setup on the ground plans, too. With the edge of the template or a straight edge of almost any kind, indicate what you expect the camera to be shooting.

If you are working with a video script, the precise camera shot will be indicated in the director's marks in the director's column of the script. On a film script, unless you have produced a clearly defined shooting script with exact camera angles included, the only way this information may be transmitted to others is through the storyboards.

Some directors keep a separate binder of storyboards. Each picture is clearly labeled as to scene and shot number. Other directors like to keep their storyboard with their ground plans. Either system will work. The decision often comes down to how heavy the director is willing to have his or her notebook be or how many binders he or she wants to keep track of on the set. Many times a production assistant keeps track of the director's script and binders. Other directors prefer to keep the materials in the director's chair or in a saddlebag attached to it.

Not all scripts you direct will be shooting scripts. Some will be master scene scripts with numbers only for each scene. Whether you direct from a shooting script or not, you will need a numbering system. A true shooting script will have each shot numbered already by the script-formatting program.

Often you will find that you are adding shots you hadn't intended as you planned the shoot. Or you have to go back and pick up shots once the editor has seen the footage and knows what problems exist that are not covered with any existing shot. When adding shots or getting pickup shots, your numbering system should be constant so both you and the editor will know where the shot is expected to fit.

Master scenes will be numbered (like Figure 9.3). Shots within this scene, if not numbered by the script formatting program, should be related to by using an alphanumeric system, sometimes with dashes and even subscripts, to keep track of everything. Shot 9K-3 would go in scene 9, following shots 9J, and shot 9K-3 would go after 9K-2.

One little trick of the trade we always employ is to only use the letter X for sound. Thus 9X might be a sound bed recording of thirty seconds to one minute of what the natural sound of the set was without any dialogue or other sounds. Shot number 9X-1 might be the isolated sound of a door slam or even a character's laugh or scream.

Notice the difference between these two methods. The stage method concentrates on the performance of the actor to bring the role to life, whereas the screen method deals more with the technology of the screen. The screen method works only if it includes an understanding of the stage method as well as using this method as a part of the director's preproduction.

As you read other books, you will come across other systems. Find the one that works well for you and is sufficiently clear for your assistant to read as well.

Strive for freshness and ingenuity in the movement of both performers and of cameras. Anything trite and dull is sure death as far as director–actor communication with the ground plan is concerned. Try for a good number of properties—things actors can touch, use, or sit upon. If there are too few, a scene may be underillustrated. But too many can distract an audience by throwing emphasis on the properties themselves.

Multicamera TV Blocking

Place your camera from revealing angles. Select the angles so they can reveal material in an interesting manner instead of flatly. When performers are interacting with each other, cross your cameras. The camera on the left can shoot the actor on the right, and so forth. The camera closest to a performer is not always the one with the best shot. When actors are facing each other across the set, the camera farthest away may have the best angle.

Remember the need to show faces when devising your floor plan. Try to be able to see both eyes of the actors as opposed to one eye and an ear. When we talk to people, we talk to their faces—not to the sides of their heads. Work for the most revealing camera angles when planning your shot alternation.

Relate the action to the proper camera. Be sure the performers understand their relation to the camera so they can act and move properly. Keep your camera plan as simple and consistent as possible. Your want the audience to understand the picture as you present it. Their job is not to try to decipher your intent.

Prevent masking the subject from the camera. Be particularly aware of the position of the actors' hands. Performers' hands should not mask essential information. Keep performers from covering other performers in the scene. Since you see the picture accurately, you need to keep the significant actors in proper view. Merely having an actor shift her weight from both feet to one foot in particular may be enough to accomplish the desired framing.

Keep the subject in frame. When framing, keep important elements away from the edges of the picture. Work with performers on hitting their marks and keeping in frame.

Framing also depends on the camerawork. Rapidly moving subjects are difficult to keep framed properly. Don't hesitate to use wider shots when needed. Keep in mind the desired flow from one shot to the next.

Lead your subjects with the camera (the look space) when they are moving laterally. When subjects split and move different ways, follow the most important subject. Don't try to change focus to follow both.

It is *not* always important to keep all actors on camera during a cross. Allow an actor to cross out of frame and then back in when this achieves the desired effect.

Keep the subject in focus. Two ways to increase the depth of field are to add illumination or to shorten the focal length. Change camera angles to keep more than one subject in focus. Give camera crew time to rehearse difficult moves.

Frame closely enough to reveal important details. Every thing in the picture is not as important as everything else. Restrict the wide shots. On very small screens, wide shots can turn actors into ants. Rely principally on medium shots and close-ups. Frame only what is meaningful at that particular moment.

To shoot close, either move the camera in or change the focal length. It is always preferable to move the camera unless it is going to hurt the surrounding shots.

Proportion your subject, whenever possible, to a three-by-four ratio or a nine-by-sixteen ratio. Bring performers as close together as possible. Shoot wide subjects from an interesting angle. It's too easy to just zoom out wide to a shot, which is uninteresting.

Keep your lighting adequate to the task at hand. Keep the Kelvin temperature of your lights in mind. Be sure to light-balance each camera on each light change.

Keep the image elements from mixing so the key of a person's name does not appear on screen across his or her face, for example.

Take out all unnecessary detail. KISS again applies here. Keep it simple, Sugar, or the camera can't pick it up properly.

Use the far diagonals of the set because they will give the feeling of occupying the upstage areas and the far corners of the downstage areas. If the movement zigzags with interrupted stops, it will appear to occupy space. When you squeeze a scene into a small space, you create a different mood value than spreading a scene over a large space. Try to use each appropriately.

Reminder: All movements, if they are to be seen as movements, must traverse five feet or more.

Single-Camera, Film-Style Blocking

All of the multicamera considerations should be taken into account shot by shot, camera setup by camera setup. The key differences between multicamera and single-camera blocking is that the lighting and audio can be adjusted from shot to shot on a single-camera production, while these two technical elements will remain constant on a multicamera production.

Additionally, keep in mind that each individual camera setup for a single-camera production can take ten minutes, several hours, or even days to accomplish. No production is better for having a multitude of camera shots unless each shot contributes to the totality of the story. The old rule "less is more" is true here, as in so many other aspects of filmmaking. No one goes to a film because there are lots of shots in it. The point is to tell a story. Once you make the audience aware of shots, through angles that are too clever or shots that call attention to themselves as works of art, you've lost the focus of the audience's attention. You are in effect shouting, "Look at me! Am I not a great director? Can't I take fantastic pictures?" If that's your goal, still photography should be your art, not motion pictures—or you should be making music videos or travelogues.

What If It Doesn't Work?

Sometimes as directors, we want a special effect through blocking, but we can't get it. Don't worry. Blocking is the easiest and cheapest tool in your director's kit. If you can't get the effect one way, you most likely can get it another. You want a certain effect from the shot, but for some reason that camera can't go there. You can get the same effect by using an entirely different camera setup. You want some effect from an actor's position or line reading on stage. It just doesn't work, even after repeated rehearsals. Your job is to come up with something new that will accomplish the same effect. You can. Here are some tips.

The Action Is in the Reaction

Once we had a dreadful actress with a good voice playing the part of Katisha, the fearsome woman in *The Mikado*. She was supposed to strike fear and trembling in the hearts of the citizens of Titipu. The actress must have hated the part. She seemed to do everything in her power to avoid getting the effect we wanted. She was terrible, but the music department would not let us recast her.

So instead, we blocked the song so that at her slightest movement, the villagers went into giant, dying, tumbling pratfalls. Two dozen noble music and drama students went through death throes that left them sprawled in heaps all over the stage by the time the song was finished. The effect was better than anything any actress we know could have achieved. Their fear reactions made her far beyond ferocious. Sadly, many in the audience congratulated the actress on her wonderful performance, which was still flat. We gave purple hearts to the twenty-four chorus people who made her look great with their delightful antics.

In another production, a stage director was forced to cast an Oedipus who was somewhat less than dynamic. As we watched the show in production, we were aware that the character fell far short of kingly. Later we realized the fault wasn't only in the Oedipus actor—the other actors didn't treat him like a king. Physically, they treated the king character as a colleague rather than as a world leader. At one point, a lesser character put his arm around Oedipus's shoulder, buddy style. Even a much better actor would have had a hard time overcoming that behavior.

Film and television stories are legion about directors pulling out of bad situations with a good blocking direction or suggestion to an actor. One of our favorites concerns a well-known midcentury actor named Judy Holliday. She always had a weight problem. Each time she was in a film, she had to go on a strict diet. The director needed her to look at a man with blazing passion in her eyes. She just couldn't get it.

Finally, the story goes, the director said, "Judy, think of a hot fudge sundae, made with fresh homemade vanilla ice cream, with homemade rich chocolate fudge all over the top, and a giant blob of homemade whipped cream perched on top." The cameras rolled while Judy thought about food. The shot was full of passion and longing, just what the director needed. If this story isn't true, it should be.

For stage or screen, it's not what really is but what seems to be that is important.

Movement Overrides Speech

If there is movement and speech in the same frame, the audience will be more aware of the movement than the speech. On film, the director has a number of ways to direct focus. On stage, we need to be sure no person or thing is moving that would distract the audience from the important line being said.

Generally speaking, film will contain more moments when the visual is more important than the audible. On stage, the lines are usually more important than the movement. So, if you are in doubt about which is more important, assume that on stage the line trumps the action and on screen the action trumps the line. But remember, it's a rule, not a law.

First Things First, Important Things Last

Let's say the blocking calls for Al to offer Bob a cigarette to tempt Bob to smoke when Bob is trying to quit. That means three different points of action. Al has to say the line and show the cigarette, and Bob has to indicate acceptance or rejection. Using the principles we are discussing, the order chosen will indicate the significance of the action.

Al can pull out the cigarette and say the line, and Bob can react. That means Bob's reaction is the most important. Will he take the cigarette? Will he break his word to his dead mother? Tune in tomorrow to find out.

Al can say the line, Bob can react, and then Al can pull out the cigarette. That means Al's act of temptation is the most important. Al really wants Bob to smoke for some reason. What could that reason be?

Al can visually offer the cigarette, Bob can react, and Al can then say the line. Then the line is the most important. This last plan doesn't make much sense normally, but it would if the line were a trigger for the hitman to attack Bob when his attention was distracted by his moral struggle over the cigarette.

So, a lot of your blocking decisions will be made over which is more important in the piece—the lines or the visuals. Normally, in a play like *The Importance of Being Earnest*, you don't want a lot of movement. If the actor is moving, it is then harder for the audience to concentrate on the line. The dialogue in this play is funny only if heard and understood correctly and completely. The humor is in the language, not the action. Obviously, in many films, the action is paramount, and the dialogue is minimal.

Because many books contain excellent practical help in learning how to do blocking, we suggest you consult the list at the end of this chapter for additional help in learning your craft.

Summary

New directors are always worried about blocking. They want a lot of rules to guide them. Many directing books have these rules, and they are good to follow until you feel comfortable doing something differently.

We also suggest another way to learn about blocking. Look around you, or look at shows with the sound off. What do the pictures tell you about the situation? Each of them is an example of blocking in action, even if they are accidental groupings like people sitting on a bus. What do their positions and relationships express about themselves and their situations? These are the rules of blocking!

Suggested Reading

Stage

Albright, Hardie. *Stage Direction in Transition*. See chapter 12
Catron, Louis E. *The Director's Vision*. See chapters 17 and 18.
Dean, Alexander, and Lawrence Carra. *Fundamentals of Play Directing*. See part 3.
Hodge, Francis. *Play Directing*. See chapters 7–12.
Kirk, John W., and Ralph A. Bellas. *The Art of Directing*. See part 3.
O'Neill, R. H., and N. M. Boretz. *The Director as Artist*. See chapter 9.
Vaughan, Stuart, *Directing Plays*. See chapter 7.

Screen

Armer, Alan A. *Directing Television and Film*. See chapters 6–8.
Bell, Mary Lou, and Phil Ramuno. *The Sitcom Career Book*. See chapter 5.
Benedetti, Robert. *From Concept to Screen*. See chapters 6–9.
Block, Bruce. *The Visual Story*. See the appendix, part I.
Lukas, Christopher. *Directing for Film and Television*. See chapter 6,
Katz, Steven D. *Film Directing Shot by Shot*.
Proferes, Nicholas T. *Film Directing Fundamentals*. See chapter 26.

Viewing

Try watching the DVDs listed below with the sound off to see how well the blocking conveys information.

Play

O'Neill, Eugene. *A Moon for the Misbegotten*. Opened, 1947. Samuel French DVD. José Quintero and Gordon Rigsby, directors, Norton Simon, Inc., Producers, 1975.

Film

Darabont, Frank, director. *The Green Mile* (1999).
Kubrick, Stanley, director. *Barry Lyndon* (1975).
Lee, Ang, director. *Sense And Sensibility* (1995).
Mostow, Jonathan, director. *U5-71* (2000).

10

What About Organization?

In this chapter, we will deal with many aspects of organization. We will go over the typical organizational structure in plays, television shows, and films. We will give you suggestions and guidelines about organization—how to stay on top of the plethora of details that will plague you in your work. We will also touch on ways to organize your time.

The Devil Is in the Details (How to Keep Track of All the Little Devils)

It is vitally important that accurate records be kept. You have too much on your mind to keep anything in it that is not recorded elsewhere. Never expect to remember something—always have it written somewhere. Someone's job is to do that. Whoever that person is, you must be sure to pass along that information. Frequently, we mess up because we fail to inform the record keeper of a change in information that should be recorded.

Keeping track of things is an art form in itself. Fortunately, most of us can now use Excel, so we can develop charts easily to record information that we need. With the help of the computer, we can keep our records constantly updated with little difficulty. Some people like to keep a printed copy of each version for archival purposes, while others just alter the materials as they go. Either way, the most important element is keeping everyone current.

When you're working professionally, record keeping is one of the aspects of directing most directors hate. However, the bean counters, who have to see that the bills get paid and the money is expended properly, will hound you until you do the required paperwork. So, get used to it. Make it something you do a little at a time. Don't try to put it off until the end, when you can't remember everything.

Students often look at the paperwork of a production on stage or screen as one of the *last* things they *have* to do. In fact, the reason behind most paperwork is to help prepare the production. It should be done early on or as the project is under way, *not* as a chore to be finished at the end.

Calendar

Start with a production calendar (Figure 10.1). Working backward from opening night, build a calendar that lists the purpose or main thrust of each rehearsal, when casting will occur, when preproduction will start, television and film shooting dates, and so on. Below is a sample calendar from a stage production, and one from a film shoot.

Contact Sheet

The contact sheet is very important and must be correct at all times. It should include the following categories:

Name   Production role   phone/cell phone   e-mail

Everyone concerned needs to be kept up to date on every aspect of the production that affects him or her. The fastest way to do it in writing is with e-mail. This list is also the hardest to keep accurately. Does the address contain underscore (_) or dashes (-)? Frequently, when people write e-mail addresses you can't tell one from the other, even if their handwriting is clear in other respects.

If some in the group do not have easy e-mail access, then the phone numbers are the most rapid means of communication. If people have cell phones they keep on at all times, it helps the person in charge of notifying everyone about everything. Most TV and film directors expect everyone to have cell phones on and available for receiving their calls. But phone messages are not the best way of communicating long or complicated instructions. E-mails are best for those messages.

Time Is Money—A Guide to Spending It

Whenever you are doing a budget, at home or at work, you need to start by estimating that 10 percent of the funds will be available for a contingency fund—an unexpected expense fund. No matter the family, project, or business, budgeting is more likely to succeed if you start the project with a reserve fund for expenses that were unexpected. Sometimes you will need less money than you planned in a certain category, but you will always need more money in a certain category—that's a guarantee.

If you have never made a budget before, get help from someone who is familiar with the kind of budget you need to prepare. Whether you are budgeting for your first high school drama production or a major studio film, you must have a budget.

The Stage Production Book

The production book is the bible for the play or television show or film. While each person has certain responsibilities, for live theatre the stage manager's production book becomes the repository for every record, as a safety measure. Often, in practice, these lists are all kept separately and

LET THE EAGLE FLY

REHEARSAL GROUPINGS

GROUP A

2, 5, 6, 10, 12, 15, 22, 25, 28, 28A

GROUP B

14, 17, 24, 24a, 27, 27A, 29, 30

GROUP C

7, 8, 10, 11, 26

GROUP D

3, 4, 16, 20

GROUP E

1, 9, 13, 18, 19, 21, 23

Sunday	Monday	Tuesday	Wednesday	Thursday	Friday	Saturday
5 Company Meeting 2:00	**6** Day Off	**7** Music Rehearsal 7:00	**8** Music Rehearsal 7:00	**9** 6:30 - Music 7:30 - Read Thru	**10** 6:30/Group E Script Work 8:00/Group A Script Work	**11** 12:00/Group C Script Work 12:00 Group D Music 2:00/Group D Script Work 2:00/Music TBA 4:00/Group B
12 12 - 2:00 Group E 2:00 - 4:00 Dance	**13** Day Off	**14** 7:00 Music & Dance	**15** 7:00 Music & Dance	**16** 7:00 Block Act I	**17** 7:00 Block Act II	**18** 12:00 - 5:00 Run Show for Blocking
19 12 - 4:00 TBA	**20** Day Off	**21** 7:00 Music & Dance	**22** 7:00 Music & Dance	**23** *OFFSCRIPT OFF MUSIC* 7:00/Group C 7:00/Music 8:30/Group E	**24** 7:00/Group B 7:00/Music for Group D 8:30/Group A	**25** 11:00 Group D 12:00 Working Run of Act I

Figure 10.1   Stage production calendar from *Let the Eagle Fly*

Time Code	Shot	Decription	Characters
	2	Pan and Dolly	W, S, M
	2–1	CU - Front Door Lock	W
	2a	2 Shot - pan, carry M, pick up W	W, M
	2a-1	Med S as she Exits the room and starts down the balcony	S
	2b	2 Shot - pan, carry M, pick up W	W, M
	2c	Tight 2 Shot, W, S	W,S
	2d	Med M, Carry, pick up W	W, M
	2d-1	Med S Exits into Room	S
	2e	OTS M	W,M
	2f	OTS W	W, M
	2g	Med M, Carry, pick up W	W, M
	2h	OTS M	W, M
	2i	OTS W	W, M
	3	OTS S, Carry S, dev 3 shot (3C)	S, W, M
	3a	OTS M	W, M
	3b	OTS W	W, M
	3c	OTS S (pan for other OTS)	S, M, W
	3d	2 F E M	M, W, S
	3e	2 Shot W,S, pick up M, pan to door	W, S, M
	3 E-1	cu - s	S
	3f	cu - M	M, W, S
	3g	cu - W	W
	3i	3 shot at Front Door	M, W, S
	3j	CU lock	M
	3K	Pan, carry M	M
	3L	Med M	M
	45	Med fireplace	
	45a	Med M, pan, carry to top of stairs	M
	45b	Med M, dolly, Z out to 3 shot Ft. Door	M, W,S
	45c	MCU S at couch	S
	45d	OTS M	M, W
	45e	3 shot M, W, S,	M,W,S
	45f	Med W at registration desk	W
	45g	Med M	M
	46	2 Shot M & S, S exits from room	M, S
	46a	Med W, carry around desk to phone	W
	46b	Med M	M
	46c	CU W on phone	W
	46d	Med M goes to Phone, S to room	M, S
	46e	Loose Med M X's to W, S at Ft. D	M,W, S
	46f	CU M in dark	M
	46g	CU S in dark	S
	46h	CU W in dark	W
	46i	3 Shot all exit	M, S, W
	46j	Hi angle wide shot - set in the dark	

Figure 10.2   Daily film shot schedule

not one set of complete notes exists. That's reality. But ideally, the production book should be a total compilation of all records of a production.

The stage manager's principal concern is the prompt book. It is a complete copy of the script with all the performance and production notations on it. It lists actor cues, actor blocking, light cues, and sound cues, plus dance, music, and fencing notations if there are any. The prompt book also must have a contact list that includes everyone associated with the production; program copy, such as correctly spelled names and assignments; biographies if they will be printed in the program and any people who most be acknowledged or thanked for supplying props or other materials; accurate and up-to-date production and performance schedules; and special effects notes or lists. Stage mangers also may keep extensive rehearsal notes, copies of all memos related to the production lists, to remind people what needs to be done, and so on.

Other department heads maintain lists pertaining to their jobs, and these people should provide two copies of their lists for the stage manger's master production book. For instance, all the notes about costumes may be kept by the costume crew, but the stage manager should have copies as well. The lighting, prop, scenery, and sound crews need to have a record of every item, where it is placed, who uses it, where it came from, and so on. It is good practice for the stage manager to have copies of those lists also.

Once the stage manager starts to gather production notes, plots, cue sheets, and so on, the problem becomes how to keep and organize them. Use a three-ring notebook, since pages cannot slip out of order and they are safe if reinforced. Materials can be added, divided, or removed easily, and everything is in one place. A good stage manager keeps two copies of everything. Each copy is kept in a separate location so that if one is lost or accidentally destroyed, the other is still safe. Materials that have been replaced in the working production book can be stored in the back of the "safe" book.

For convenience, the *prompt script* may be in a separate notebook. A full production book can contain the prompt script plus one copy of every written record that relates in any way to that particular production. Again, the production book is considered the bible of the production, so anything anyone needs to know about any aspect of the production should be recorded there. Each group or organization has its own system for keeping records. The important requirement is to have a system.

TV and Film Paperwork

In TV and film, the workload is divided between the director and the producer. The production manager and the department heads (e.g., the art department, camera department) all are responsible for major paperwork that they produce and submit to the director or producer or both depending on the nature of an individual production or that of the studio or production company. In other words, everybody does it their own way. There are some generalities, but in any project, studio, or production company, what follows may be subtly or radically different from what you see here. All this paperwork is completed by someone at some stage of the production. That is important to realize.

Budget

The TV/film breakdown is most easily seen by looking at the budget cover page from a production. A TV or film budget has two parts: creative and technical. They are separated on the budget cover page by a horizontal line across the middle of the page. This line is a significant demarcation in the structure of the project.

Above the Line

"Above the line" costs are the creative costs. This includes the script, director, producer, cast, and a very few select staff members. Who the people are depends on the production and how an individual has negotiated his or her contract.

Below the Line

"Below the line" costs are all staff, crew, sets, locations, equipment rental, raw footage cost, and so on. In TV and film "above the line" is considered more prestigious than "below the line." There are times when directors of photography, costume designers, or art directors will take less money in order to be carried on the budget above the line.

To simplify the idea, look at it this way. In a network or studio, the people hired by the individual television show or film producers as artists on that production are usually considered above the line. They are paid for by the producers. People employed full time by the studio and the costs of running the studio are considered below the line.

The producer will have his or her own collection of information, contracts, permits, and script changes and personnel over which the producer has direct control. Similarly, the director will have certain material, script, script changes, storyboards, schedules, and casting and character notes that directly impact his or her job. Together, the producer's production book and the director's notebook will contain the material discussed in the next two sections.

The TV/Film Producer's Production Book

The production book is the producer's bible and diary as well as the one place where *every* element of the production is documented. The production book stays with the producer wherever he or she goes from the beginning to the end of the production and is used as a file for names, addresses, and important documents should the need for any of them occur long after the production is over.

There are sixteen basic categories under which forms, notes, records, and legal documents are collected and filed for quick reference. Ideally, the producer will tab index the production book to make it easier to use.

Note that this is not a "busywork" assignment for student producers to be thrown together at the last minute to meet a grade requirement. This is a day-to-day working volume that will make the production better and the producer's life a lot easier.

The TV/Film Director's Notebook

This book is to the director what the production notebook is to the producer. Here the director has at his or her fingertips all the information that is likely to be needed during preproduction, rehearsal, taping, and postproduction.

Some very specific items will be included in the TV director's notebook. Jotted notes, reminders, receipts, and other information are collected here for future reference. The director must be constantly rethinking the theme and images (both visual and audio) that will make up the finished product. The notes, sketches, and random thoughts are all kept here so they are available at any time.

This information may not be formalized by some directors. But if it is not categorized, the director's notebook becomes a collection of scattered facts, figures, lists, notes, and odd scribbling. When that's the case, the notebook becomes of very little value.

One Director's Challenge

Director Ricardo Gutierrez gave us many of his directing tools from his production of *Let the Eagle Fly* at this university. We have included some of the materials he used in casting and directing the production.

Let the Eagle Fly is a new musical play about the life of the famed César Chávez, founder of the United Farm Workers union. Gutierrez was invited to this university to direct the world premiere because he was already familiar with the piece. He had directed a concert reading at the Goodman Theatre in Chicago.

He flew in from Chicago each week to work with the cast and production team from Thursday though Sunday. He left late Sunday to return to Chicago. This was his schedule for the first few weeks of preplanning, casting, and production. After the French scenes were fully rehearsed, he stayed on campus for the last two weeks of the production process.

He was working with a new production team of people with whom he had no prior experience. He was casting from a talent pool with which he was totally unfamiliar. Therefore, accurate records were particularly crucial in this situation.

Some of Gutierrez's records are shown in Figure 10.1. First, he drew up a list of characters with spaces under each name. Then, as various people read at auditions, he wrote their names in under the character they most seemed to fit in his view. The musical director used the same system to write down the names of people who could sing these roles.

After the callbacks, they compared notes and selected actors who best fit the needs of the roles, vocally and physically. One actor, for instance, was an ideal choice for Simmons but did not have the low G vocally that the score required. So the man chosen to play Simmons, a good actor, had the G vocally but was not as visually close to the character as they would have liked.

To show what a casting block would look like, we made up the sample in Figure 10.3 for a production of *The Importance of Being Earnest*.

French Scenes
In order to maximize the limited rehearsal time available, Gutierrez cut the play into French scenes. Usually, a French scene is a scene that lasts until someone enters and leaves the stage. So a play, for instance, may have two acts with three scenes in each act. But each scene could have a dozen French scenes. If you break your script into French scenes, then you can work on it in the most efficient way possible.

Some of the actors had time conflicts—classes or jobs that interfered with the full rehearsal schedule. Even in professional theatre, this happens. By using the French scene chart system, you know which actors you need to work on any section of the play.

The French scene chart helps when you need to rehearse one group of actors for a dramatic scene and another group has to learn a dance sequence. If the costumer wants to pull actors from a rehearsal for a fitting, using the French scene chart can let him or her know when it's the best time to schedule a fitting. It is not unusual to have two rehearsals and two fittings occurring simultaneously.

THE IMPORTANCE OF BEING EARNEST			
JACK	ALGY	LANE-MERRIMAN	CHASUBLE
Mark. W. Brian W. Fred G. Tom G. Bill	Kent S. Larry B. Trey M. Eric W.	Kent S. Bill Albert G.	Kent. S. Tom G. Jim H. Doug C Albert G..
BRACKNELL	GWENDOLYN	CECILY	PRISM
Dana S. Linda D. Pat M. Pat L.	Araceli Betty R. Susie S. Salma B.	Mikki Nicole Dorothy Dora S.	
CASTING POSSIBILITIES			

Figure 10.3   A casting block for *The Importance of Being Earnest* based on the Gutierrez method

Figure 10.4 shows a French scene chart Brian Warren used in his production of *One Flew Over the Cuckoo's Nest.*

Gutierrez used a different system that works well when the play has numerous scenes, both large and small. In his play, a steady stream of characters entered and reentered. He gave each scene a title and listed the characters needed. Then he divided the scenes into groups to maximize the use of the various actors. When actors were called, they were used a great deal of the time with little sitting around waiting for their scenes. Only one actor was in all four groups, the man who played Cesar Chavez. Other actors could look at the rehearsal chart and know whether they were called for that rehearsal at that time.

Developing a Play Rehearsal Schedule

Table 10.1 is a chart to help plan your stage rehearsal schedule. Many factors come together when the director plans a rehearsal schedule. The length, difficulty, or intricacy of certain scenes may require more intensive work than others, so it is vital to complete preparations (i.e., do your homework) before developing the rehearsal schedule.

This chart can be used for three standard rehearsal periods. These are (1) a six to seven-week rehearsal schedule of thirty-five rehearsal periods, (2) a somewhat briefer four-to five-week rehearsal schedule of twenty-five rehearsal periods, and (3) a typical and compressed summer stock schedule of sixteen rehearsal periods. Obviously, the amount of time devoted to each part of the play during rehearsal depends upon the number of available rehearsal periods. A typical rehearsal schedule might follow the plan for a thirty-five-period rehearsal schedule and three-act play, each with two scenes.

Be sure to consider the play carefully before developing a rehearsal schedule. This planning is useful to help you to reduce the constant adjustments that may be necessary even in the best-planned productions. We prefer to use the calendar format instead. We enter our rehearsal schedules on a calendar. When a substantial number of changes are needed in the plan, we issue a second or third version of the calendar that supercedes the first.

Note that three hours is the optimum time you can rehearse in a given period without being counterproductive. A four-hour rehearsal block usually requires a fifteen-minute break. For a three-hour rehearsal, a five- to ten-minute break is sufficient. Rehearsals (except for difficult techs) that start at 7 PM and go on till 2 or 3 AM may be the sign of a poor director. Neither actors nor directors can be productive. In stock or professional situations, it is possible to hold two or three rehearsals (with two-hour breaks between) per day.

	*Enter on p.41 ACT I												ACT II							
	CHIEF/PILLS (1-8)	CARDS/MAC (9-18)	GAMBLE (18-22)	THERAPY 1 (22-32)	PECKIN' (33-36)	THE BET (37-41)	OLD GLIM (42-44)	BOXERS (44-49)	THERAPY 2 (50-58)	ELECTRIC (58-61)	CANDY (61-67)	W. SERIES (68-76)	B-BALL (76-82)	CHIEF/MAC (82-89)	PUNISH (89-93)	SHOCK (93-97)	MACS BACK(97-105)	PARTY! (105-119)	RATCHED (120-127)	FINALE (127-136)
CHIEF BROMDEN	X	X	X			X	X	X	X	X	X	X	X	X	X	X	X	X	X	X
AIDE WARREN	X	X		X		*X	X	X		X	X		X		X	X	X		X	X
AIDE WILLIAMS	X	X	X	X		*X	X	X	X		X		X		X	X	X		X	X
NURSE RATCHED	X	X	X	X		*X		X	X	X	X		X		X	X	X		X	X
NURSE FLINN	X	X		X				X	X				X		X	X	X			X
DALE HARDING	X	X	X	X	X	X		X	X	X	X	X	X		X		X	X	X	X
BILLY BIBBIT	X	X	X	X	X	X		X	X	X	X	X	X		X		X	X	X	X
SCANLON	X	X	X	X	X	X		X	X	X	X	X	X		X		X	X	X	X
CHARLIE CHESWICK	X	X	X	X	X	X		X	X	X	X	X	X		X		X	X	X	X
MARTINI	X	X	X	X	X	X		X	X	X	X	X	X		X		X	X	X	X
MR. RUCKLY	X	X							X				X				X	X	X	
TABER	X	X							X									X	X	
COLONEL MATTERSON	X	X							X									X	X	
RANDLE MCMURPHY		X	X	X	X	X	X	X	X	X	X	X	X	X	X	X	X	X	X	X
DR. SPIVEY			X			X										X				
AIDE TURKLE					X												X			
CANDY STARR											X						X	X		
SANDY																	X	X		

Figure 10.4 French scene chart from *One Flew Over the Cuckoo's Nest*

The kind of rehearsal schedule shown in Table 10.1 applies to a college production. A stock projection would do the same thing in half the time, generally by holding two rehearsals a day. A professional show would have at least two rehearsals a day but would probably spend additional time working on parts of the play that had to be redirected because of script changes.

Be specific about what needs to be accomplished in each rehearsal. It helps the actors considerably to let them know why the rehearsal is being held. Saying "Today we need to concentrate on getting used to the props. Actors should concentrate on familiarizing yourself with handling the props for this run-through" frequently helps them to do better on every other aspect as well. Most of us are less resentful of an activity if it appears to be specifically purposeful rather than generally necessary. When you can think of no other purpose for a rehearsal, run for continuity and check on where the rough spots are. You'll find them. See the sample given in the rehearsal calendar in Figure 10.5.

Table 10.1 Basic stage rehearsal schedule

- 35 Rehearsal Period Schedule
- (3 Hours Each Period)
- (16 rehearsals for summer stock plays, 25 for nonmusical professional shows)
- Director's Name
- Play Title
- Author
- Number of Acts
- Estimated Playing Time per Act
- Number of Scenes (Total)
- Anticipated Running Times

ACT I	Scene 1	Scene 2
	Scene 3	Scene 4
ACT II	Scene 1	Scene 2
	Scene 3	Scene 4
ACT III	Scene 1	Scene 2
	Scene 3	Scene 4
ACT IV	Scene 1	Scene 3
	Scene 3	Scene 4
ACT V	Scene 1	Scene 2
	Scene 3	Scene 4
Total Playing Time		

Developing a Half-Hour TV Show Production Schedule

Generating the production records for a half-hour television show sounds like a simple exercise in organization. Yet the amount of paper work generated in one episode of a simple TV comedy show is a marvel to behold. Every piece is necessary to keep track for the sake of continuity, to see that bills get paid, to see that people get paid, and to see that union and safety regulations are followed.

September 1995
ROOSTERS Rehearsal Schedule

Sunday	Monday	Tuesday	Wednesday	Thursday	Friday	Saturday
10 7:00 PM - 10:00 PM Block Act I	11 7:00 PM - 10:00 PM Block Act II	12 7:00 PM - 10:00 PM Carter -- run through of rough blocking	13 7:00 PM - 10:00 PM Run Act II -- Clean Up Act I	14 7:00 PM - 10:00 PM Run Act I -- Clean Up Act II	15	16
17 7:00 PM - 10:00 PM Run Act I & Act II	18 7:00 PM - 10:00 PM Run Act I -- Polish Act II	19 7:00 PM - 10:00 PM Run Act II -- Polish Act I	20 7:00 PM - 10:00 PM Clean up rough spots -- OFF BOOK Act I	21 7:00 PM - 10:00 PM Run both acts -- Off Book Act I On Book Act II	22	23
24 7:00 PM - 10:00 PM Work on lines -- Off Book Act II	25 7:00 PM - 10:00 PM ALL CAST MEMBERS -- run through for Valente	26 7:00 PM - 10:00 PM Valente, Mike & Carter blocking -- block roster scn	27 7:00 PM - 10:00 PM ALL CAST -- run through	28 7:00 PM - 10:00 PM Run thru, then work on knife fights & rooster scenes	29	30

October 1995

Sunday	Monday	Tuesday	Wednesday	Thursday	Friday	Saturday
1 7:00 PM - 10:00 PM ALL CAST @ ALL REHEARSALS FROM NOW ON -- run thru	2 7:00 PM - 10:00 PM ALL CAST -- ALL PROPS	3 7:00 PM - 10:00 PM Fix stuff -- run trouble scenes twice	4 7:00 PM - 10:00 PM Run thru	5 7:00 PM - 10:00 PM Run thru	6 7:00 PM - 10:00 PM Last night off -- save date for emergency called rehearsal	7 1:00 PM - 4:00 PM 1 PM tech rehearsal -- Edinburg Banquet
8 6:00 PM - 11:00 PM Dress rehearsal	9 7:00 PM - 10:00 PM UTPA NIGHT	10 7:00 PM - 10:00 PM UTPA Night	11 7:00 PM - 10:00 PM OPENING NIGHT	12 7:00 PM - 10:00 PM Performance	13 7:00 PM - 10:00 PM Performance -- Photo Call @ 10 PM	14 7:00 PM - 10:00 PM Alumni banquet @ 5 PM -- Performance
15 1:00 PM - 4:00 PM Performance -- Strike @ 4 PM	16	17	18	19	20	21

Figure 10.5 Rehearsal calendar from a University of Texas–Pan American show

Developing a Film Shooting Schedule

Scriptwriting software can help with the paperwork of developing a shooting schedule by automatically generating specific forms already filled in and on numbered pages based on the shooting script of the production.

The breakdown sheets will list, scene by scene, each physical location or set, whether the scene is an interior (INT) or exterior (EXT), the time of day the scene takes place, and the required cast, costumes, props, vehicles, stunts, and special effects.

The production board takes the information from the breakdown sheets and translates the data into long, thin strips like the columns on an Excel spreadsheet. These individual strips represent the production scene by scene. All of these strips are then arranged in a board to indicate the scenes to be shot on a specific day of the production. Days are separated by solid black strips and weekends are indicated by double day strips. The schedule, once completed and approved by the director, becomes the guiding document for all personnel, equipment, and location scheduling. The strips are likely to be constantly shifted. The shifting is caused by all the different elements that come into play in shooting a film.

If you are renting a very expensive location, then those scenes are shot as closely together in time as you possibly can because you want to save money by renting the location for as few days as possible. If you have an actor you really want who is available just for a particular week of the shoot, the scenes may have to be arranged to "shoot out" that person. Normally, in any good film schedule, several different and conflicting parameters are at work in determining the shooting schedule. Figure 10.6 is a sample of the original order of shooting from a film that we did. However, circumstances changed as problems developed, and the final shooting schedule looked like Figure 10.7.

Special Considerations

Sometimes, as in, *Let the Eagle Fly* you have a cast that contains a number of people who are new to the "business" and don't know the basic elements of stage decorum. We made up this list of "ten commandments" for them. It may come in handy for you.

Ten Commandments of Production Decorum

1. *Always* have a resume and, for actors, a head shot—one that looks like you. Actors with resumes will be given priority at all auditions and get one extra hour of practicum credit for bringing one to the audition.

2. Be on time for all appointments. If we hold the entire company to start until the last person arrives, we can cause the rehearsals or film shoots to go into overtime. Missing an appointment or being late can mean delays for the entire company or result in not getting your costume on time.

Scene #	1	2	3	4	5	6	7	8	9	10	11	12	13	14	15	16	17
INT/EXT	EXT	EXT	EXT	INT	EXT	INT	INT	IN	IN	INT	INT	EX	INT	INT	EX	EX	EX
Breakdown Page	1	2	3	4	5	6	7	8	9	10	11	12	13	14	15	16	17
Day or Night	D	D	D	D	D	D	D	D	N	N	N	D	D	D	D	D	D
Script Page #	1	1	1	1	5	6	6	8	15	16	18	19	22	23	25	26	29
Location or Studio	L	L	L	L	L	L					L	L	L	L	L	L	L
No. of Pages (1/8)	1/8																
Number of Set Ups																	
Set Name	UNIVERSITY - Est Shot	FACULTY PARKING LOT	STUDENT UNION - Est.	STUDENT UNION-J&M 1st Me	CLASSROOM BUILDING-Est.	CLASSROOM - Intro Lecture	STUDENT UNION - S&T	STUDENT UNION - J&NIL,D&	AMANDA BDRM - 1ST NITE	AMANDA'S KITCHEN-Good N	SAIRY & ERIC'S BEDRM	APT PARKING LOT-Fixing Ca	STUDENT UNION WORKRM	CLASSROOM	CAMPUS	CAMPUS REFLECTION POOL	CAMPUS BENCH
Title: THE THING ABOUT LOVE																	
Director: Jack R. Stanley																	
Producer: Ali Naqvi																	
Asst. Dir. Emily Ruby Ferrio																	
Prod. Mngr.Sara Martinez																	
Script Drafts/Dated: 5- 17 - 2007																	
CHARACTERS (ABV)																	
AMANDA (A)		A			A				A	A			A				
KURTIS (K)				J					K	K							
JAKE (J)								J				J					J
MAGGIE (M)				M	M												M
SAIRY (S)						S	S				S						
ERIC (E)											E						
DEANNA (D)						D	D							D			
HECTOR (H)						H							H				
LILLIE (L)								L									
GREG (G)								G						G			
NELSON (N)								N					N		N	N	N
CASSIE [C]													C		C	C	C
KRICKET (Kr)															Kr		
PERRY (P)															P		
BRAD (B)																	
THEO (T)						T	T						T				
ZOE (Z)														Z			
MOTHER (Mo)																	
FLECK (F)																	
MISS WALKER (W)		W															
EXTRAS (X)	X																
VEHICLE: (1)(2)(3)		1											2				
LIVESTOCK																	
SPECIAL EFFECTS																	

Figure 10.6 Original shooting order for *The Thing About Love*

3. Be quiet unless you are called upon to speak. A distressing amount of chatter at production sessions and rehearsals adds up to noise and distraction. It requires discipline to be quiet—get some.
4. Be courteous. Students can lose scholarships for mouthing off to faculty or being impolite to someone in the company.

	42	43	7	32	45	22	70	13	27	72	44	1	5
Scene #	42	43	7	32	45	22	70	13	27	72	44	1	5
INT/EXT	INT	INT	INT	INT	INT	INT	INT	INT	INT	INT	INT	EXT	EXT
Breakdown Page	42	43	7	32	45	22	70	13	27	72	44	1	5
Day or Night	D	D	D	N	D	D	D	D	D	N	D	D	D
Script Page #	67	67	6	51	67	36	104	22	45	106	67	1	5
Location or Studio	L	L		L	L	L	L	L	L	L	L	L	L
No. of Pages (1/8)													
Number of Set Ups													
(Location)	STUDENT UNION	STUDENT UNION GAME RM	STUDENT UNION - S&T	UNIVERSITY THEATER	CLASSROOM HALLWAY	ANOTHER CLASSROOM	RADIO STUDIO	STUDENT UNION WORKRM	STUDENT UNION - WRKRM	STUDENT CNTR - WRKRM	STUDENT UNION LOUNGE	UNIVERSITY - EST.	CLASSROOM BUILDING- ES
Title: THE THING ABOUT LOVE													
Director: Jack R. Stanley													
Producer: Ali Naqvi													
Asst. Dir. Emily Ruby Ferrio													
Prod. Mngr.Sara Martinez													
Script Drafte/Dated: 5- 17 - 2007													
CHARACTERS (ABV)													
AMANDA (A)													
KURTIS (K)													
JAKE (J)													
MAGGIE (M)	M	M		M	M						M		
SAIRY (S)			S										
ERIC (E)													
DEANNA (D)						D							
HECTOR (H)						H							
LILLIE (L)						L							
GREG (G)													
NELSON (N)							N	N	N	N			
CASSIE [C]							C	C	C	C			
KRICKET (Kr)													
PERRY (P)													
BRAD (B)					B								
THEO (T)				T									
ZOE (Z)													
MOTHER (Mo)													
FLECK (F)													
MISS WALKER (W)					W								
EXTRAS (X)		X			X	X	X					X	
VEHICLE: (1)(2)(3)													
LIVESTOCK													
SPECIAL EFFECTS													

(separator column labeled: Friday - 7-20-07)

Figure 10.7 Final shooting order for *The Thing About Love*

5. Watch your language. There are now children present a great deal of the time in this wing of the building. They may hear these words elsewhere, but they don't need a refresher course here.

6. Learn your lines by the deadline. Those too good to learn their lines on time are too good to get scholarships.

7. The director is the chief executive when he or she is present. In the absence of the director, the stage manager (SM) in the theatre—or the unit or production manager in the film—is the ranking person in the company and *must* be obeyed. If the SM is wrong, the SM takes the blame—but you do as you are told.

8. Quiet backstage and on the set is *absolute*. In our theatre, if you are in the right place the conversations backstage can be louder than the conversation on stage. This rule holds for shoots, rehearsals, and performances.

9. All cell phones and small electronic games (as well as wallets, if you wish) are to be left in the trunk of your car or given to the stage (unit or production) manager by the half hour.

10. No one is indispensable. Anyone can be released from any assignment at any time for due cause. It has happened; it can happen again.

Summary

Obviously, the most important theme in this chapter is the need to have a record of everything and to be as organized as humanly possible. No matter what you do, things will go wrong. Items will get lost. Someone will forget something important. Being organized cannot prevent all catastrophes. Being organized only reduces catastrophes in number and size.

11

What About Rehearsing?

Good directing involves learning certain basic principles. Experienced directing involves learning some quick and easy tricks to make life a little simpler. This chapter will cover a little of both.

Some Basic Principles

Can You Hear Me Now?

Good directing means developing a production that is balanced between visual and aural values. In plainer English, the audience should have no trouble seeing or hearing the production.

Because it is easier to control the visual aspects of the production than the aural, some directors tend to concentrate on all the visual elements: ground plan, movement, settings, and costumes. Pretty soon the audience comes out humming the scenery or the cinematography, because it was too difficult to hear the words.

In Shakespeare's day, people talked about going to hear a play, not to see one as we say today. Even in the more visual media, the audience deserves to hear the dialogue. They paid for both elements, and they should get both. Film and television are visual arts because the camera can see everything, from every position and every angle, and can make us feel with that seeing. Because we are spending far more hours viewing television and film than we do seeing live performances, we directors tend to focus on the visual (a good thing) and forget about the aural (a bad thing). If we are really good, we do both.

Two Challenges

As director, your job is to find a balance between the visual and aural elements that permit the audience to hear without undue effort. True, plays require more audience concentration because they are word-driven. Generally speaking, play audiences and actors need to focus more specifically on the hearing aspects of a production. As director, you must hold the audience's attention by reducing distractions to an absolute minimum.

Film directors can control distractions by using close-ups, editing, looping, and other techniques that the stage directors don't have. Close-ups show the mouth and eyes of the actor in great detail, and we hear well because we are stronger lip readers than we think we are. But as directors, we should not rely on that capability to relieve us of our responsibility to have the script heard and understood the first time.

For the director there are two aspects to this problem—technical and performance. For the stage director, the technical problems of sound are usually (though not always) solved by the designer or architect of the building—it's built so that the audience can hear clearly any performance on the stage from anywhere in the house. The screen director has to pay particular attention to the technical demands of sound well beyond what is normally required for the stage director.

Technical

For the stage director, the technical requirements of sound revolve around making the best use of the performance space. Actors should be coached and prepared to speak loudly and clearly enough to be heard. In a musical, the orchestra should support the singers, not overwhelm them. Sometimes, it is a good idea to invite in someone you know who is not familiar with the play to see a rehearsal shortly before technicals. The guest can make notes on whom or when he or she can't hear. As the director, you may be too familiar with the words to realize they are being overwhelmed by outside forces, such as the orchestra or the background sound—or even, in one theatre in our university, the rain on the roof.

The screen director has more specific challenges technically when it comes to sound.

The biggest difference between a professional and an amateur film or TV production is the sound. Even inexpensive cameras today are capable of capturing acceptable images for the audience. Capturing good sound is a different problem.

With microphones built into many cameras, inexperienced directors often believe that such a microphone will pick up an aural signal equal in quality to that of the visual signal. Such is not the case. Built-in microphones never get professional quality sound. No matter the quality of the production, if the audio sucks, so sucks the whole piece.

To begin with, always plan on using (1) an external microphone—a microphone that can be placed just barely out of the camera shot yet as close to the speaker as possible and (2) someone with a critical ear on headphone listening to the audio as it is recorded. This person must be able to distinguish between background noise and speech or music or anything someone wants to hear, which the human ear filters out (e.g., wind, passing cars or airplanes, intermittent insects, a commercial truck's backing-up beep, or a lawn mower two houses away).

Sound that is acceptable on home movies is not professional and should not be the director's aim. The mere fact that the dialogue can be heard well enough to be recorded and move the needles or LEDs (light-emitting diodes) on the VU meters, an audio mixer, or recorder is far from being professional sound.

Most beginning directors do not have the time, the computer programs, the equipment, or the expertise to loop or replace location-recorded dialogue with clean, lip-synced dialogue and sound effects. Therefore, it is absolutely necessary to get the dialogue recorded properly during the production phase.

Performance

Oral delivery is a major difference between the amateur and the professional actor. Character lives in the voice, not in looks. The mature art of acting is speaking. That is why you see actors (generally young ones) who do very well at one part on screen and never seem to do any other part that well. Yet stage-trained actors frequently can go from role to role over decades of professional work doing each part well.

We should expect actors to have fine voices, excellent articulation, and the intelligence to develop the subtext of the characters they play. Particularly in modern scripts, the subtext of a character may be carried by ideas that are not in the words the character says. You should be able to rely on the actor to understand and interpret that difference.

Directors should be concerned that the actors are able to speak like the specific characters they play. The speech patterns of the actors need to be appropriate to the character as well as be clear and loud enough to be heard. Good actors speak at the proper rate for the character and the situation. Weak actors tend to speed up because of nervousness or inexperience.

We need to be concerned with the speech-decorum aspects of a character. We simply cannot believe an actor playing a highly educated, urbane, and sophisticated gentleman who speaks with a strong South Texas farmer's drawl or a South Texas farmer who speaks like James

Bond. Realistic acting requires the speech decorum that is correct for the character, and it cannot be avoided. Few actors can handle both refined speech and substandard speech effectively. In commercial theatre as well as TV and film, casting directors usually select according to type. We see native lower-class urban- or country-sounding actors usually doing dialect roles and cultivated speakers selected for refined urban characters. How an actor "sounds" can be more important than how he looks.

In the United States, we don't have national standards for speech patterns as some other countries do. Therefore, we tend to assume that the standard American speech is one that does not have any recognizable local dialect. But all of the people in a script are characters, so the actors should be able, with good clarity and projection, to sound like the characters they are playing.

Sound Off

Stage directors have one more problem to worry about. The actors must be able to project. They should be able to be heard without amplification by artificial means. Now, with the technical capabilities of sound amplification within easy reach of any theatre's budget, less and less attention is paid to training actors to project. It has gotten so bad that even television directors are complaining that actors can't project well enough to reach the boom mike effectively.

Stage projection is a very real problem for directors working with young actors. In high schools, directors often need to have students with virtually no voice training project without amplification over a large distance. Speech scientists tell us that only a well-trained voice will consistently project over a distance of fifty-four feet. For this reason, the distance from the front of our university's newest theatre to the back wall is that length.

Yet high school cafetoriums may require someone to project well over twice that distance. The cafetorium is a really criminal example of bad architecture—a monstrosity created to satisfy ignorant school boards. It has a small stage, no backstage space, multiple levels for seating, and hard surfaces, and it opens onto well-trafficked halls with no sound barriers.

Usually because of poor scheduling, bad architecture, and bad training, the actors cannot work effectively. So, on top of everything else, the harassed high school drama teacher must become a vocal coach working in a vocally unsafe environment.

Experienced professional actors should have certain technical capabilities, including clear articulation, correct vowel choice, the knowledge when to use regionalisms and when to avoid them, correct pronunciation, vocal relaxation, vocal quality, adequate volume, a good pitch range, adequate energy, and confidence.

Using Rehearsal Time in the Theatre

Although stage directors are envied by film directors for the amount of rehearsal time they have available, stage directors still contend it is never enough. That may be true, but it is also true that stage directors could learn something from their film colleagues.

If theatre were bread, stage work would be homemade bread and film and television would be bakery bread. Granny used to make bread, but no one could get her recipe. She never wrote anything down, and she measured in miraculous ways that are impossible to duplicate. Ask her how much of an ingredient she used, and she would tell you how many handfuls—more or less—until it looked right. Liquid ingredients were measured by the "glug"—the sound something made as it was poured out of a certain bottle.

Many stage directors are "grannies"—they know what they are doing, and it almost always comes out great. However, they are the despair of their film colleagues because they record so little of it accurately. If a film director didn't keep accurate records—or didn't have people who did it—the darn film would never get edited because no one would be able to find the footage. Actually, that still happens sometimes, in spite of record keeping.

So, we return to the mantra we keep repeating throughout the book—write it down. Student directors in our classes now have developed, with their computers, really good methods of scanning practice scripts, writing down everything, and running off copies for the actors as well as themselves. It's amazing to us how much faster a blocking rehearsal goes when the actor already has it written down. Then the rehearsals are used for adjustments and improvements.

Stage Manager/Assistant Director

In the theatre, your stage manager (SM) is your replacement when you are sick, your record keeper, your Palm Pilot and your notetaker. On TV the job is held by your assistant director (AD). On a film shoot the production manager is as close as anyone to what the SM and AD do for stage and TV. However, in film the director has many assistants, but absolutely no one can step up and replace him or her. Understanding this fact of life, the following is a discussion of the role of the director's primary assistant on stage and for TV.

The SM and AD keep track of everything: your blocking, the blocking changes, the times of the calls, the contact sheets, the rehearsal props and furniture, and the laying out and maintaining the ground plan. Having one SM and more than one assistant can make the production run more efficiently. Basically, their job during rehearsals is to watch everything else so you can keep your eye on the actors. One can take notes for you. Another can prompt actors and watch the blocking to see the actors don't "improve" it without your approval. In that case, the SM and AD watch the script carefully and are ready to say aloud the line the actor needs. The actor simply says "line" and the prompter immediately provides it, so there is a minimum break in the rehearsal flow.

SMs and ADs can run auditions, arrange callbacks, and do anything else that is dignified and responsible. They do not walk the dog—unless the dog is a prop in the show—nor do they get coffee, pick up dry cleaning, or do other personal tasks.

If you could be cloned, then the stage manager is what your clone would be. The SM is not a wife—he or she is second in command and is responsible for everything whenever, for any reason, you are not there. In the professional theatre, once the show has opened, you are unemployed, and the SM and AD rehearse understudies and replacements and generally do your job for the run of the show while you go off and try to find another gig.

Remember that long list of what goes in a stage manager's book for the stage that we wrote down in Chapter 10? The stage manager is responsible for it. Whether or not the SM developed the record, the SM is responsible for the keeping and distribution of all written materials.

On stage the SM calls the show from the production booth and is responsible for seeing that each actor is there and on time for each rehearsal and performance. On stage or screen, the SM and AD are your most valuable allies in keeping the show on track. The SM and AD may call for breaks if you tend to get so involved in rehearsals that you forget to remind yourself that actors have bodily functions. The SM and AD can time scenes to keep them within the proper limits. The SM and AD can be second directors and work with actors or scenes that need extra help. The SM allows you to watch the rehearsal while he or she watches everything else.

Finally, when the stage director has gone off to direct another production, the SM keeps the show intact and on track as it was conceived by the director originally. Sometimes a stage director will come back to visit a production after a few months' absence to discover that the show has been changed considerably by the actors in his or her absence. With a really good SM, this is less likely to happen.

Have a French Scene Chart or Scene Breakdown
The French scene chart or the scene breakdown are two names for one sheet of paper. In either case this sheet tells you whom you need in each separate scene and with exactly what lines of dialogue the scene begins and ends. So if Caliban had to run out for an emergency costume fitting, you still know who among the actors called for that rehearsal are available and what scenes you can run until Caliban gets back.

Give Everyone the Rehearsal Schedule
The rehearsal schedule is your breakdown of the number of hours you need for each step of the stage rehearsal process. Generally, there are eight to ten steps in the process: read throughs, blocking, run throughs, interpretation development, more run throughs, scene-by-scene breakdowns, run throughs, dry techs (without actors) or wet techs (with actors; also called full techs), dress rehearsals, and then sometimes previews.

Chapter 10 contains a suggested thirty-five-period rehearsal process. That number is always an approximation. Longer plays like musicals and Shakespeare require more rehearsal time than many contemporary plays that run ninety minutes or less. We suggest you plan for as many rehearsals as you think you will need. You can always give people a day off if you don't need the time, but it is nearly always impossible to add a day.

Learning Lines
Directors want actors to learn lines as soon as possible. Stage or screen, all directors know very little can be accomplished as long as the actor has a script in hand.

Most stage directors want actors to start memorizing as soon as the scene is blocked. As soon as the scene is supposed to be learned—a date announced to one and all at the beginning of rehearsals—the director should give the cast one rehearsal to stumble through, calling "line" every other word. (Actually, most actors usually do better at this rehearsal if the director is not running it. We don't know why.) Then, if the actor calls "line" every other line at the next rehearsal, set that person up with someone who can run lines with him or her when that actor is not rehearsing to get him or her up to speed.

All actors will blow an occasional line here or there. But when the same actor is holding up a scene, it is totally obvious to everyone and needs to be remedied. The cast doesn't learn lines at rehearsals. Actors memorize their lines on their own time.

We should insert a word of caution here. Actors will sometimes make a big deal out of needing a prompt. This is an avoidance technique. Don't allow an actor to do or say anything but the word "line" in a loud voice. At this point, an AD, in a very loud voice, gives it to them. The AD should not be looking at the play—just at the script so the cue can come fast. Otherwise, the whole scene loses energy and focus as we all try to sit around and figure out who says what to whom.

Some actors want to waste a lot of rehearsal time and energy apologizing for, explaining, or defending the fact that they are not firm on their lines. Do *not* allow it to happen. Actors forget lines in rehearsals—it is part of the acting process. You need to give actors sufficient time to practice their lines, but learning their lines is their homework.

Time Frames

If you break the rehearsal schedule into weeks, you can see where you want to be when you open and how much you should accomplish in each week. Then you can see how much rehearsal time per week you will need.

Week 1. Acquaint the actors with the world of the play and your perspective on it. Many good directors use the first rehearsal for a full read through, where each actor reads aloud his or her lines with no interruptions or asides. Frequently, for a variety of reasons, this is the first opportunity some actors have had to read the entire script. Now you know they are all on the same page—in a fairly literal sense.

At the next rehearsal, you can lay out your view of the script. The designers can be there to help the actors to visualize the world of the script. The cast and key department heads should get to see the costume sketches and the scene design, models, maquettes, and so on. This look will help the actors to see the world of the play in specific terms.

Do table readings—not on your feet or in a theatre but in a comfortable room. Everyone should have plenty of space to write. Long tables are great. Be sure everyone knows what all the words mean and how to pronounce them properly. On longer or more difficult shows, table readings can last the entire week. If the actors are comfortable with the world of the play before they need to start blocking it, the process becomes more efficient.

Then, in the second half of the first week or at the start of the second week, put them on their feet for blocking. Try to get in one stumble-through rehearsal by the end of that week. "Stumble through" or a similar term is slang for going through the whole play just to demonstrate that the blocking looks good and is generally correct. Major mistakes can be corrected, and actors "sorta-kinda" know where they are supposed to be at key points.

Week 2. Some directors don't allow books at this point, but they do allow unlimited prompting. That technique does not work for us. We allow actors to carry books because our rehearsal periods are fairly short. Use this week to do detailed work-throughs, scene by scene. Encourage actors who have limited lines in a scene to go off book for those scenes to help their fellow actors.

Week 3. Put those books, down, actors! Use prompting as necessary. Be sure the prompter is keeping "score" so actors will be made aware of a real trouble spot and not worry about the temporary mind glitches that will occur at this point. Continue working through the play, stopping as often as necessary to work out anything that needs the work. Have a run-through at the end of the week.

Week 4. Based on your notes from the run-through, work through the whole show, giving particular attention to those spots you noticed at the end of last week. By the end of the week, you should be running tech and dress rehearsals.

Week 5. Conduct more dress rehearsals and special scene work where needed before previews and openings take place.

At our university, we have fewer dress and tech rehearsals than most places. If we were properly staffed, we could, would, and should have more of them to guarantee a tighter, smoother opening night show.

Some directors side-coach actors through some rehearsals like line coaches in baseball. Others give notes at the end. If notes are really very long, think about going home, writing them up, and handing or e-mailing them to each actor before the next rehearsal. It gives you and the cast time to think, and no one wants to listen to really long notes from really long-winded directors. Actors tend to "zone out" while a director goes on at great length on a point that is of interest to other actors but not to themselves.

Some college directors talk far too much at the end of a long rehearsal. They seem to think every note session is the occasion for a fifty-minute lecture. The actors are too tired to remember and are worrying about the algebra test tomorrow. The KISS principle for note-giving can also be interpreted as "Keep it short, stupid!" If you have long, elaborate notes for one actor or one group of actors in a scene, deal with them separately, not in a large group setting.

It is always proper to give the note, "Learn your lines!" As you get into week 4, it is even proper to say, "Learn your damn lines," or more correctly, "Damn it, learn your lines!"

220 DIRECTING FOR STAGE AND SCREEN

Using Rehearsal Time in Film and Television
The time frames are totally different in film than they are in television. The SM function in theater is replaced in televsion and film by the AD but also by some other people including (a) the production manager, (b) script person, and (c) continuity.

The fact that there is *truly* never enough rehearsal time in these media is one reason so many shots are taken of each scene. The theory, as far as the media is concerned, is that number of shots, like the number of professionals involved, somehow increases the chances of creating something that can be assembled to look like a polished performance of a well-thought-out story in spite of an almost total lack of rehearsal. Theatre is always short handed and it's often a miracle that the production comes off at all. In electronic media, nine women are trying to have a baby in one month, whereas in theatre, one woman is having trouble just getting pregnant, and yet that's the magic of live theatre.

For TV, rehearsal time allocation depends on the type of production. Obviously, for daily soaps, actors absolutely must be off book and dead cold on their lines as well as be flexible enough to learn new lines on the spot each and every day.

The cast of sitcoms must learn what is equal to a short one-act play each week. They have one day at the table and walking around with scripts, two days in a rehearsal, and then two days on the set. Actors frequently find they have new lines each day, so they may have to relearn dialogue as well as learn it. Taping or filming occurs the second day on the set. They get two days off and, for the sitcom regular, it starts all over again.

Hourly dramatic series and location-filmed sitcoms are shot much like films. All actors—the series regular cast, the featured players of the week, and the under-five-lines players of the day—are expected to arrive on the set at the prescribed time with their lines totally committed to memory, ready to block, film, or tape the assigned scene. These series often work a six-day week. Usually, they end one episode on one day, even early on a given day, and move directly into the next episode that afternoon or the next day. Some series episodes are shooting less than a week before the work is to be aired. Actors need to learn lines quickly, but they have to learn only one day's worth of dialogue at a time, and they don't need to keep it memorized.

A TV movie of the week (MOW) employs the same methodology that hourly dramatic series use. Obviously, being a quick study is mandatory for a screen actor. Film performers work much like the TV MOW and dramatic series actors unless there is a considerable budget and time for rehearsals. Such films do happen, but they are the exception rather than the rule.

Some Tips That Can Help

Directing Is Like Parenting. A good parent does not make idle threats. If you say, "learn your lines by Thursday or I will replace you," then you have to do it. It is the same thing with lateness and absences.

Good parents only give choices with which they can live. Mommy doesn't say, "What do you want for dinner?" or Mommy gets stupid answers like "Apple pie and caramel candy." Mommy says, "Do you want fried chicken or fish sticks?" As a director, don't ask actors what they want to do. Ask "Do you think you should sit or walk on that line?" Then do it—make them fish sticks or let them try walking on that line.

A good parent tries to use everyone's time as efficiently as possible. If there may be a long wait at the dentist's office, Mommy has Billy bring his homework to do while they wait. A good director can often arrange to have an AD working a scene for memorization in another room while the director works with a group of actors in the rehearsal.

But sometimes people are forced to sit around without much to do for reasons that are unavoidable. Encourage them to use that time wisely. They can run lines with a partner or study for a math quiz. One of the busiest actors we know, Brian Warren, never complains about downtime at a rehearsal. But he never has any—he always brings something else to do so that he can make maximum use of the time without being distracted by gossiping and joking around. You will often see him sitting in the house with his course record book and a pile of homework to grade.

Remember to tell people they are doing a good job. Bad parents always remind us when we mess up but never tell us when we did something well. Without using false praise, try to remember to let people know when they have done a good job on something. "Please" and "thanks" are very useful words.

Little Things Mean a Lot. Repetition is the key to successful learning. The word says it all—"rehear-sal," not "reher-sal." So give them enough time to "rehear" the material.

Be early yourself. It gives you time to get set up and to get your thoughts together away from the rest of your world and on to the world of the production.

Listen—sometimes we pay so much attention to what we think we want that we don't always hear what is really happening.

Try to see how other directors work. You can learn a lot about what works for you from watching. The second best technique is to read as much as possible about how other directors work. You will find that other people have techniques that work for them but not for you. You can make selective choices, but first you must have a variety of options to choose from.

The director's tracks on many DVDs have useful information for student directors. But don't be too overwhelmed. Many times we say what we think we did, but it is not necessarily how it really happened. Still, get all the advice you can and pick what works best for you.

Help actors and others have the research tools they need for this production. You and the designers have already done a mountain of research. The actors could start all over, but it helps if you save it for them. For example, dictionaries of Shakespearean pronunciation and the meanings of words in that period are very necessary. Some directors, with the aid of computers, provide annotation for all the vocabulary.

The actors may need to know about life and customs of the time period in which you are setting the production. Arrange a safe place where designers and you can share research materials with the cast. When doing *Fuente Ovejuna*, for instance, we had collected book articles, which were not available online, about life and customs of seventeenth-century Spain. They were all in a notebook, and actors could read the book while not on stage. The actors playing soldiers, for instance, could learn about what life for a Spanish soldier was really like during that period. Doug La Prade, an English professor, had been to Spain and shared photos of the actual place, which is still a sleepy little bump in the road.

Sometimes the strangest things can be helpful. Working with children in an adult production, for instance, we find it useful to have a "kid wrangler" whose job is to stay with the little lovelies, get them to the set on time, keep them from wrecking anything or killing themselves backstage, and so on. One used to bring a thermos of hot chocolate to provide a little lift without too much caffeine during the rehearsal break. Only good behavior merited a mug of it. She also ran lines with them, supervised their homework, and generally made the set more pleasant for the kids and the adults.

Use your technology to the max. You can keep all your production material, including your annotated script, on your laptop with all your notes intact and have the stage manager update that instead of a hard copy of the script—as long as you back up *daily* and religiously. You can generate rehearsal schedules, make changes in lists, look up something on line, e-mail a designer or cast member, have online staff conferences—there are all sorts of ways to use it. Now we can use a laptop at rehearsal, download it to a flash drive at the end of each working day, and make a backup at home. Then, if you do a lot of work on the home computer, you can whip out the flash drive to back up the laptop, which is locked up safely in another location.

How did we ever survive before e-mail? Even cell phones have good uses as well as bad. In this book we use a lot of Ricardo Gutierrez's materials from *Let the Eagle Fly*. As a guest director, he worked on a borrowed computer every night after rehearsal, generating material that he could then share as necessary through e-mail attachments to whomever. Everyone in the cast and crew were e-mail-a-holics; so it was easy to keep in touch. A number of them had cell phones that were also e-mail capable. Since he was commuting weekly from Chicago to South Texas, this made life a little simpler. It also cut down substantially on the long distance charges.

Now that we have such good storyboard programs, students enjoy making storyboards for stage plays as well as for film projects. People who grew up with computers love to play with the "toys," and tasks that used to seem like drudgery when done manually are now fun.

Each time we direct we discover some task that we used to have to do by hand the hard way that can now be done electronically. In developing this book, for example, we sent it to our students online. We were able to imbed 133 illustrations, including streaming video, so students could click on each illustration and open it up to view. As for our production books, they have started looking so good that one can't decide whether to use them or frame them.

Summary

For the director, rehearsing is the most enjoyable, frustrating, interesting, and sometimes tedious part of the creative theatrical process. You never feel you have enough rehearsal, but it is even possible to overrehearse. Rehearsals are where you get to share your creative input with people who think you know what you are doing. Producers and designers may not feel quite so warmly about you, but the cast is convinced you could—and certainly should—solve all their problems, even the ones that have nothing to do with the production.

For us, we would often rather watch the rehearsal or filming of a production than the actual end product. It is a great idea to visit as many other directors in rehearsal as you can. If you like their techniques and think you can use them, do so.

Suggested Reading and Viewing

Reading

Stage
Albright, Hardie. *Stage Direction in Transition*. See chapters 12–15.
Catron, Louis E. *The Director's Vision: Play Direction from Analysis*. See part 4.
Dean, Alexander, and Lawrence Carra. *Fundamentals of Play Directing*. See part 5.
O'Neill, R. H., and N. M. Boretz. *The Director as Artist*. See chapter 9.
Kirk, John W., and Ralph A. Bellas. *The Art of Directing*. See part 4.
Patterson, Jim. *Stage Directing*, See steps 5 and 6.
Vaughan, Stuart, *Directing Plays*. See part 2.

Screen
Armer, Alan A. *Directing Television and Film*.
Bell, Mary Lou, and Phil Ramuno. *The Sitcom Career Book*. See chapters 2–4.
Lukas, Christopher. *Directing for Film and Television*. See chapters 6 and 8.
Proferes, Nicholas T. *Film Directing Fundamentals*. See chapter 7.
Weston, Judith. *Directing Actors*. See chapter 9.

12

That's a Wrap!

Our students have helped us enormously in writing this book, so we asked for their input for the final chapter. What did they want to know that we had not previously covered? These were the topics that most of the students suggested.

1. Where and how do we get started?
2. Where do we get royalties and permissions for using material that is copy protected?
3. What other legal issues should we be concerned about?
4. What about the actor–director relationship? How do we separate the personal from the professional?
5. What are the usual positions in a professional directing situation?
6. What do you do when the unexpected occurs?

Where and How Do We Get Started?

Start where you are. Get as much experience as you can as soon as you can. You can take classes if they are available, work on other people's projects, and learn as much as you can where you are before you think about moving on.

Remember that experience equals mistakes and successes. You want to make as many of your mistakes as possible while you're still below the radar of the professional world. This is exactly what college, community, and summer theatre programs, school film projects, independent projects, and low-budget productions have to offer.

You're not going to direct like anyone else—you don't really want to. You will develop your own style, but you can't do it without putting in the hours. (It's like the old joke that a lot of people want to be writers, but they don't want to do the paperwork.)

Every production you undertake or participate in will teach you something if you will let it. Learning what *not* to do is just as important as discovering what works. Every script, every budget, every cast, and every production limitation will offer you insights into similar circumstances you are bound to encounter once you've begun supporting yourself with your creativity. Don't squander them.

Do you have a plan? If you know where you want to be in ten years, you should be able to figure out where you'll need to be in five years to get to your ten-year goal. Once you have nailed down a five-year destination, work out what's going to be required in three years, then two, then one—and keep focusing until you know what you need to do in six months, next month, next week, tomorrow, and today.

Without a plan you can't expect to end up fulfilling your dreams. It's like leaving on a road trip with no destination. If you end up in Alaska without the proper clothes, you'll spend all your effort and time there just trying to stay alive. If you know that's where you're going, you can pack for the journey, selecting the needed items and the best route before you get in the car. The same is true with your professional career.

Understand that nothing you learn, no experience you acquire, is a waste. Day by day, working at a fast food joint or a law firm, you're dealing with people—your ultimate audience for your directing efforts. What delights people? What moves them? What stirs their greatest fears, their most altruistic passions? What are the common denominators of the human experience? What are the exceptional moments, events, hidden desires, and uncontrollable obsessions? What are the stories people like to hear? What are the qualities of the best storytellers, the best communicators? What kind of person makes the best, the worst, or a mediocre boss? As a director you're always working because you should be always observing and analyzing.

Make it a practice to never stop learning about your field. See every play, every movie, every DVD you can. Know the history of your medium so you don't have to repeat the mistakes of the past.

Read, read, read. Read at least one script a week. Exercise your imagination by bringing words on the page to life in your head as you would if you were to direct this script. Don't read just the easy stuff. Find the difficult to understand, the odd, the obscure, the old, even the ancient, and make them a part of your working knowledge. There will come a time when you'll realize that "everything old is new again." Will you be ready for it?

If you're going to make a living as a director, you need to live where the work is. Theatres, studios, and production companies are not going to reach out to the boondocks to find talent when there is so much available close at hand. Get on the radar of professionals with the means to pay you to do what you have prepared yourself to do. There's nothing wrong with doing church, community, or civic theatre, just as there's nothing wrong with directing public service announcements or your own YouTube or MySpace productions. But don't plan to make a living doing it. These are all free gigs.

You have to set your eyes on cities or parts of the country (or the world) where people get paid to direct if you want to feed your cat, your car, and yourself with your directing income. Of course, that means putting yourself in the big game in the major markets.

If you don't want to do that, you still have other options. One is educational directing (for public or private school systems or colleges or universities). Another is working for the production facility of a fairly large company. The advantages to the education path are steady income, health benefits, and association with an ever-changing but always challenging student body. Many a professional educator in theatre or film is better paid than his or her professional freelance counterpart. But there are downsides here, too.

As an educator you'll never have the audience you may get as a working professional. Your choice of directing material will also be much more restrictive due to budgets, performance space, equipment, casting, and audience as well as the demands and expectations of school boards, administrations, or even legislators.

Either direction, professional or educational, will require you to seek a larger market. In education this may only be temporary because after obtaining sufficient education, you can return to the sticks and have a very happy life working within the limitations of your field.

Many people select working for the media division of a large corporation. While the creative aspect may be limited, you still have the advantages of a steady income, a benefits package, and a life that is reasonably regular.

Don't go to a major city without the means of survival. You still have to eat and sleep until you get that first job. The overnight success stories usually have a back story consisting of several years of "salad days" when the new discovery struggled to eke out an existence while continuing to work on his or her plan to reach victory.

What are you willing to do to stay alive until you are discovered? What kind of day job can you hold down while you attend auditions and workshops or put together your own project? Waiting tables, telephone solicitation, delivery, office temping, even part-time substitute teaching are among the most popular options from which young directors pick. Remember, the big city doesn't need or want you. You are going to have to make yourself indispensable before someone who has succeeded is going to be willing to gamble real money on your success.

You need to have a portfolio of work you have already accomplished. This is where college is so valuable to you. As a student you have access to space, equipment, even talent that will all cost you a considerable outlay of funds to achieve in the big city. A slick, varied, professional looking reel or portfolio will kick down doors that will stay closed to those with no evidence of their level of professionalism.

You also need to be relatively debt-free and have some start-up cash. Apartments are expensive—much more than you'll believe until you start looking. Food is, too. If you are burdened with car payments, house payments, medical bills, educational loans, child support, or alimony, you are starting out with at least one hand tied behind you. It is best to settle as many of your debts as you can and have some kind of nest egg of savings to survive your first year. That's how long it will take you to learn the territory, the buzzwords, and the shortcuts to living in the most competitive markets.

To live in Los Angeles, you need a working vehicle. To live in New York City, a bike, some good walking shoes, and an understanding of the transportation system will serve you much better. In all major cities, living accommodations are much more affordable the farther from the center of the action you are. But the other side of that coin is that you then have to spend more time and money getting from "home" to "work."

Read "the trades"—the trade papers (e.g., *Variety*, *Backstage*, *The Hollywood Reporter*) about six months before you go. This will become a habit once you get to the major markets. Not only will the trades will put you in the know about "who's on first" and who's even in the game, but also these publications are essential tools to professionals at every level.

Timing is everything. You shouldn't start off with a blank slate, but when you see you have exhausted the learning opportunities where you are, it is time to move to a tougher market. You need to move where there is more competition and greater opportunity. Usually it is a step-by-step process rather than a leap from a couple of high school productions to Broadway or Hollywood.

Education is important, but in this industry you don't get a job by waving your diploma. You ought to have the diploma or diplomas, but people who want to hire you need to see what you can do, not just what classes you took. It cuts both ways. Many times an employer will hire the person with the degree and the portfolio over the one with the portfolio and no degree. Employers always want to see the portfolio, degree or no degree.

The competition in the entire field of dramatic production, stage or screen, is fierce, so face the facts. It is what you know, but it is also who you know. People will not trust a major production responsibility to someone they don't know, so you get the jobs by being known or by being recommended by someone who knows you and the person who is thinking of hiring you. Everyone wants to work with their friends— people they trust, those they know they can depend on in a pinch. Make sure you are one of those people—and keep a working Rolodex of business cards with contact names and numbers of those with whom you work. This organized list of contacts will prove to be one of your most valuable resources.

Get a strong resume. Do a good job on all the productions you can. When you apply for a position, the employer will look at your resume and call someone on your list that he or she knows personally. The employer will then ask what you are *really* like. If you did a good job for the person you listed on your resume, you have a much better chance of being hired. If you messed up, forget it.

You can't lie on a resume, but you can eliminate those early botched jobs you did before you figured out how to do things properly. Your reputation may precede you in any case. The word gets around about the idiot who messed up faster than it does about the person who did a great job.

Don't falsify your resume. As soon as you list a phony credit and someone spots it, you are sunk—even if the rest of the resume is true. Most people assume that resumes are full of lies. If your portfolio can back up every credit you have listed, then you can prove you really did the job.

Save something from every job listed on your resume. If you were paid for being in a film, photocopy your pay stub for your portfolio, even if you have nothing else to prove you did it. Your big scene may have been cut from the released version, but you did the work and got paid.

Actors often list credits as "studio." To many, it means you did a scene in an acting or directing class, and the reader just regards the credit as a page filler. If you really did the work in a studio setting, save a copy of the program or footage from the reel for your portfolio.

At our university, each graduate has to present his or her portfolio to a faculty committee to demonstrate a work product for every class taken. Acting II? May I see your marked scripts for your scene work? Editing? Show us your editing reel. Someday, if they become great successes, these people may be pulling out those portfolios for their American Film

Institute retrospective and the Drama League luncheon. Or they may be showing them to the other folks at the nursing home. But they have proof of what they did in any case.

Use connections. Ask around. Who do you know who has connections with someone who can hire you? This is where your Rolodex comes in. If your uncle went to college with a famous actor and you want to be an actor, then the connection is not terribly helpful. Actors are not usually able to find jobs for other actors. If your uncle is a good friend of a producer, see if you can get him to call that person on your behalf. The call won't get you a job, but it may get you an interview.

Don't expect people to lie for you. If you did a bad job for me and I give you a good recommendation, when you mess up on the new job, I have ruined my reputation. No one will trust my recommendation again.

If you can wangle an introduction to someone who is "in the business," make the contact, find out if you can take the person to lunch, and ask for some getting-started advice. That takes the pressure off, and if the producer (or whoever) likes you, he or she may make a suggestion. The producer may know someone looking for a production assistant. Use that contact to make another contact until you find a way into the industry—starting at the bottom.

Your first professional jobs will be far below your capabilities, experience, and training. It is your way of getting a foot in the door and demonstrating that you are truly capable. You can then work up to your next job and so on.

Stick in the area you want to be in. If you are interested in dramatic television production, don't take news jobs—they will only lead to news jobs. Save those jobs for the broadcast journalism majors. Otherwise you will get sidetracked onto a totally different career ladder that you don't want. But if it is in your area, take the job, even though the job you are offered won't be the one you really want.

Generally, most people in our field want to be in one of four different professions—acting, directing, writing, or producing. Yet the industry supports many other positions that will help you to get where you want to go. You can learn a great deal as you understand and appreciate all the various kinds of work that go into a finished production.

Talk to everyone you can. You will get tons of advice, much of which is conflicting. Everyone got to his or her position by a different route. Don't be discouraged. It just means that many roads lead to the same destination. Some of us have to walk; some of us get to fly. But if we keep on going, we can get there. Most other people will have given up somewhere along the road.

Where Do We Get Royalties and Permissions?

Generally, information about royalty and copyright production is listed somewhere on every work product. If no information is listed, then the copy you have is probably pirated. Someone may have copied a script and not copied the copy production information.

No matter how hard it is to find the copyright owner, it is your responsibility to do so. A colleague came across a delightful story that he thought would make a wonderful fantasy film. As he searched for the copyright owner, he wrote an excellent adaptation. He had the script complete before he finally tracked down the copyright holder, who had no interest in the deal. It was a gamble. If the script suited the writer, then the film was ready to go into production. But without the permission, the script won't ever become a film.

Scripts and recorded productions (i.e., films and videos) are usually copyrighted within the copyright laws of the country of origin. In the United States, it's with the Library of Congress. Most countries belong to some or all of the international conventions on copyright—the Berne Copyright Convention, the Universal Copyright Convention, the Trade-Related Intellectual Property (TRIPS) element of the World Trade Agreement, and the WIPO (World Intellectual Property Organization) Copyright Treaty. It is possible to search records for a particular item registered with the U.S. Library of Congress through its Web site (http://www.copyright.gov).

What Other Legal Issues Should We Be Concerned About?

This is the age of litigation. Be sure that you have clearances for what you do from everyone involved. You may do a backyard film for fun, and it gets picked up later for professional distribution. Do you have clearance from everyone who worked on or participated in the production? What about the music? What is your source? Do you have permission to use it?

It is illuminating to sit in on a preproduction meeting for a professional film and listen to how much the lawyers have to say. Does the location scout have the proper permission to shoot at that location? If actual physical changes to the property are required for the film, has permission been granted for that? What about the poster on the wall of the boy's bedroom? If it is a copyrighted poster, then you need to have permission to show it on the wall. If one pop star's lawyers won't allow such use, you have to use another pop star who will gladly give permission.

The actor releases have to include all future use and publicity, even though when you are doing the film there doesn't seem to be a chance on earth it will ever get shown anywhere. Do you have waivers from the crew? All of these waivers should be secured prior to the beginning of production and not after the fact.

What About the Actor-Director Relationship?

For a question like this, there is no general answer. Each case is specific. With that in mind, we can present a few generalizations.

When you start out, you are working with friends. Because you or they can't afford to hire people, you are usually working with people who are friends or colleagues in a different context. Suddenly you have moved from a personal to a professional relationship and one of you has become the boss. When you become a boss, someone may resent it, especially if you have asked him or her to work on your project. We have a few general suggestions that may help the situation.

First, don't ask someone to do something such as act in your project. Ask them to audition. Then the person is competing for the part and expects to be directed and to follow the rules. If you commit to the person in advance, then the person has the power and can dictate the working conditions.

If it is not an audition situation, offer to trade: "I'll do costumes on your project if you do lighting on mine." That way, there is a form of payment involved, and the person working for you knows that in order to get your work on his or her project, he or she has to come through on yours.

Second, don't assume that a good friend is the same as a good colleague. You may find that the people you love the most are not the people you can work with under certain circumstances. Similarly, you may find that a person of whom you are not overly fond on a personal level makes a great colleague. It takes a lot of trial and error to tell the difference, but it is important. If your best friend wants the acting lead, you will feel uncomfortable. You may have to come right out and say "I would feel very uncomfortable directing you, and I would rather have your great friendship than your great acting skills."

It is also true that when a production bombs, fingers start to be pointed. Trying to protect or salvage one's own reputation will cause many to sidestep blame or direct it at others rather than shouldering the responsibility themselves. This is a fact of professional life. As the director you are always responsible and should have as your motto the one former President Harry S. Truman had on his desk in the oval office: "The buck stops here."

As educators we have seen friendships dissolve over directors who were quick to blame their cast for failures that were the director's responsibility. As a director, you will have both hits and misses. Fully accepting the blame, even if it rightly belongs to others, is what directing is all about. If you can't take the blame, don't put yourself in a position where you can take the credit either—don't direct.

As a director you never know when you may want to work with a particular actor in the future. If you torch your relationship over the failure of one project, you may well end up sacrificing future opportunities you can't even imagine at the moment.

And the blame really is yours as the director. If an actor doesn't deliver the performance the production requires, you as the director are responsible for getting the performer to a place where he or she can convey the needed presentation or you should recast the role. If the director isn't willing to recast, then the director is in effect saying, "I accept the performance I've been given." That includes a willingness to take the heat when the production flops.

What Are the Usual Positions in a Professional Directing Situation?

This question is easy to answer. Check out directing books in the medium that interests you. Most books will give you a good picture of the structure for any organization. In real life, expect to find some variations. For instance, stage directors in an academic setting often play very different roles than they do in professional settings. A director in a small high school may be the producer–director–designer. In a professional setting, the director has very specific responsibilities. These responsibilities may vary with the size and location of the professional company.

Remember, too, that a stage director, unlike a screen director, is expected to serve the script first, last, and always. Film directors in particular have the power to demand rewrites of the script and to completely change the concept of the production with little or no regard to the script (which is fine for the director as long as the end product is a success).

Ideally, be it stage or screen, a director should be the focusing creator among collaborating artists, all of whom want the same thing in the end: a satisfying, successful production. This ideal, however, is many times not the working reality of the project. There are directors who relish their power to embarrass and humiliate others above and beyond any creative responsibilities. If this is your style or motivation, you may find yourself hard-pressed for colleagues—unless, in spite of and not because of your approach, you achieve continual success and notoriety. It happens.

There are always people who are willing to work with tyrants for money or rewards no matter what the cost. The ultimate problem is that such directors have no one with whom to share their success because they will treat everyone with the same contempt. Such a miserable existence, even when crowned with awards and mammoth financial compensation, makes for an unfulfilled life. The problem is, by the time these people realize it, it's too late to change.

The bottom line, as we stated in earlier chapters, is that your goal should be to be the kind of director with whom you would want to work.

What Do You Do When the Unexpected Occurs?

Expect the unexpected. As much as possible, have a plan B. If it rains Tuesday, what can we shoot in place of the outdoor scene we have scheduled? If Joe can't come to rehearsals on Wednesday, what scenes can we work on without him? Many events will occur over which you have no control, but plan for as many as you can reasonably expect. It is bound to rain on Tuesday if that is the only day you had put in your schedule for the outdoor shoot.

No one can possibly anticipate all the problems that will occur. When the unexpected happens, try to buy some time. In your panic, the first decision you make is likely to be the wrong one. If you can wait twenty-four hours before making a decision on how to cope with the particular crisis, a pretty good alternative may occur to you. If it is not the greatest solution, it is probably better than the first one that occurred to you.

A good way to start is to seek a simpler solution. Most problems occur because we are planning a tricky, complex operation, usually depending on some hi-tech program or equipment. That is very likely to fail. Think about going back and doing it the old-fashioned way, before the technology existed. Perhaps there is a simpler way out of the mess that will actually end up improving the product.

We often see examples of directors who waste innumerable hours trying for a special effect—a spectacular actor entrance or a really complex crane shot—only to have to go to something simpler. The end result was fine. No one missed the fancy effect. The crew was exhausted from hours of trying to make plan A work, and plan B turned out to work just fine with virtually no extra labor involved.

Also, trust in the creativity of your team. Seek their input. The ultimate decision may be yours, but the options can come from any of those you trust. Remember the words of Reinhold Niebuhr's "Serenity Prayer": "God grant me the serenity to accept the things I cannot change, the courage to change those things I can, and the wisdom to know the difference." In addition, these words from the poem "Desiderata" by Max Ehrmann may help: "Do not distress yourself with imaginings. Many fears are born of fatigue and loneliness."

But, when all else fails, try to remind yourself that crises will always occur, and you can't solve them all. The crisis will be just as bad as before, but at least you will be slightly less stressed about it.

Just Do It!

People often hesitate to get started, knowing all the difficulties they will face. Heck, if it were easy, everyone would do it. If you really want to get into this business, don't let us or anyone else scare you away.

The truth is, you can't imagine all the difficulties you'll face—but that's to your advantage. If you really knew, you would never try it. But your ignorance is more than just bliss, it's a strength. Years from now, you'll look back and laugh at how being naive was, hands down, the best thing that could have happened to you.

Another truth is that there are people with a lot less talent who make it in this business. If they can make it, you can too. You have read this book. Now, go out and work twice as hard as those with less talent.

Glossary

(Artistic)

arc: The semicircular movement of performers or equipment.

boom: A pole or metal extension whose function is to support and move either a microphone or camera above or below a particular position. With a mic, it is used to keep the pickup device close to the talent and yet out of the picture frame; with a camera, a boom (sometimes called a *crane* or *jib*) is used to smoothly make sweeping moves up, down, or across the set. It is also a camera command dictating the up or down movement of the Camera on a crane or camera boom.

Camera: (Camera with a capital "C") The entire device of the Camera including lens, viewfinder, and handles; camera mount; tripod or pedestal; and cables.

camera: (camera with a small "c") The camera body minus any and all attachments such as lens, viewfinder, and cables.

camera cable: The multiwire cable that connects the camera to its CCU. *Note: Never step or walk on camera cables.*

camera mount: The device that attaches the camera head to the pedestal or tripod and allows panning or tilting movements.

carry: A camera command to follow a performer across the set with proper head room and look space.

CCU: Abbreviation for camera control unit. The set of controls that is usually rack-mounted in engineering and connected to the Camera by the camera cables. This is where all adjustments are made to set lens opening, color response of the tubes, and so on.

center: A camera command to move the key person or object to the to center of the picture frame.

center line: An imaginary line drawn down the center of a set, from upstage to downstage, to indicate the id line.

comp: A camera command to compose the camera shot when it is not correct.

cross: Movement of talent from one location to another on the set or location. Generally such movement is in an arc or in a diagonal fashion.

CU: Abbreviation for close-up. An intimate shot of the head or face of a person or a shot that isolates an object for careful examination.

defocus: A camera command to roll focus to a blurred picture.

dolly: (a) A movable platform with wheels (e.g., chair, shopping cart) or a vehicle that will support a Camera and sometimes its operator. (b) A camera command to move a Camera into or out of the set. Much like a zoom except that the visual perspective changes as opposed to the image just enlarging or shrinking.

dynamic: A type of microphone design built around a moving coil and operating much like a loudspeaker in reverse. It uses a single diaphragm, wire coil, or magnet, which converts audio waves into an electrical signal.

downstage: The area on the set that is nearer the audience or camera. Directional commands are always given from the perspective of the actor, not the audience or camera.

down-the-line: A diagonal shot of a group of people or objects.

ECU: Abbreviation for extreme close-up. The most intimate shot possible of a person or object, usually including the eyes and mouth of a person.

edit controller: An electronic device, stand-alone or with a computer and/or video source, used to facilitate editing, either in linear or nonlinear form, with accuracy, speed, and convenience.

Est: Abbreviation for establishing. A wide shot that helps the audience fix in their minds the location of and relationship between objects and people in a scene. This is usually the first or one of the first shots in any scene.

focus: A camera command to correct or adjust the focal point of the camera lens using the focus handle.

focus control: A handle, knob, or switch located on the camera pan handle and connected to the camera lens via a control cable, which is used to adjust the focal point of the lens.

frame up: A camera command that is the same as comp or recomp.

headroom: A camera command to adjust and amount of headroom currently allotted to the person, persons, or objects in focus.

lens: The tube containing the combined ground glass sheets that, together with the f-stop aperture control ring, the focus ring, and servo zoom control rocker switch, make up the image-gathering device of the camera.

lock in: A camera command to adjust pan and tilt locks so the shot will remain stationary.

look space: A camera command to adjust the space between the person's face and the edge of the frame in the direction the person is facing. To allow more space in front of a person than behind him or her.

Med: Abbreviation for medium. A "normal" view of a person from midchest to just above the top of the head.

mic mount: A built-in or attachable mount for a microphone.

OTS: Abbreviation for over the Shoulder. A two-shot from behind one person and focusing on the other.

pan: A camera command describing the horizontal pivoting of the camera head left and right on the camera mount.

pan/tilt drag: A knob or lever on the camera mount that is used to adjust the amount of tension affecting the lateral or horizontal movement of the camera body.

pan handle: One or more rods extending from the camera mount that are used by the camera operator to move the camera body horizontally or vertically.

pan/tilt lock: A knob or lever on the camera mount that is used to either secure the camera head in a fixed position or free it for movement. *Do not confuse this with the pan/tilt drag.*

ped: Abbreviation for "pedestal." The vertical movement of the camera head without tilting. Often used to raise the camera with the talent as he or she stands.

pedestal knobs: Knobs on the camera support device that lock or free the raising or lowering of a studio Camera.

recomp: A camera command to recompose. Same as comp.

roll focus: A camera command to rotate the focus handle or knob to move the picture into or out of focus as the director requires.

set: An existing or constructed place, interior or exterior, where the production is to be executed.

stage left: The area on stage that is to the left of an actor facing an audience or camera.

stage right: The area on stage that is to the right of an actor facing an audience or camera.

talent: Any actor or performer whose image or voice who participates in any stage or screen production.

Teleprompter: Patented name of the device mounted on the front of the camera (usually a studio camera) that allows a script to be projected on a one-way mirror in front of the lens.

tilt: A camera command describing the vertical pivoting of the camera head up and down on the camera mount.

tracking: A camera command describing a dolly-like movement made with talent or objects in motion.

two faces east: A two-shot with both people facing the same direction, usually toward the camera.

two-shot: Two people or objects or one person and one object in the same shot. This may be a "tight" or a "loose" two-shot.

up stage: The area on the set that is farther away from the audience or camera. Directional commands are always given from the perspective of the actor, not the audience or camera.

viewfinder: Either a small mounted TV monitor or eyepiece with which the camera operator sees the image the Camera making.

wide: A shot that includes as much of the set, scene, or location as possible.

zoom control: A knob, button, lever, or switch that is attached to a pan handle and connected to the camera lens via cables and is used to control both the speed and the extent of a zoom.

Bibliography

Stage

Albright, Hardie. *Stage Direction in Transition*. Dickenson, 1972.

Ball, William. *A Sense of Direction: Some Observations on the Art of Directing*. Drama Publishers, 1984.

Catron, Louis E. *The Director's Vision: Play Direction from Analysis*. New York: McGraw-Hill College, 1989.

Dean, Alexander, and Lawrence Carra. *Fundamentals of Play Directing*. 5th ed. Belmont, CA: Wadsworth, 1989.

Giannachi, Gabriella, and Mary Luckhurst, ed. *On Directing*. New York: Palgrave Macmillan, 1999.

Grote, David. *Script Analysis*. Belmont, CA: Wadsworth, 1984.

Hodge, Francis. *Play Directing: Analysis, Communication and Style*. 4th ed. Prentice Hall College Division, 1994.

Kirk, John W., and Ralph A. Bellas. *The Art of Directing*. Belmont, CA: Wadsworth, 1985.

O'Neill, R. H., and N. M. Boretz. *The Director as Artist*. Holt, Rinehart, and Winston, 1987.

Patterson, Jim. *Stage Directing*. Allyn and Bacon, 2003.

Russell, Douglas A. *Theatrical Style*. Dubuque, IA: William C. Brown, 1976.

Shapiro, Mel. *The Director's Companion*. Belmont, CA: Wadsworth, 1997.

Vaughan, Stuart, *Directing Plays: A Working Professional's Method*. Longman, 1992.

Screen

Armer, Alan A. *Directing Television and Film*. Belmont, CA: Wadsworth, 1986.

Bare, Richard L. *The Film Director*. New York: Collier Books, 1973.

Beaver, Frank E., *Dictionary of Film Terms: The Aesthetic Companion to Film Art*. New York: McGraw-Hill, 1983.

Behlmer, Rudy. *Behind the Scenes, The Making of. . . .* Hollywood: Samuel French, 1989.

Bell, Mary Lou, and Phil Ramuno. *The Sitcom Career Book*. New York: Back Stage Books, 2004.

Benedetti, Robert. *From Concept to Screen*. Boston: Allyn and Bacon, 2002.

Block, Bruce. *The Visual Story: Seeing the Structure of Film, TV, and the New Media*. New York: Focal Press, 2001.

Corliss, Richard. *Talking Pictures*. Overlook Hardcover, 1974.

Crittenden, Roger. *The Thames and Hudson Manual of Film Editing*. Thames and Hudson, 1981.

Flower, Joe. *Prince of the Magic Kingdom*. New York, John Wiley & Sons, 1991.

Fussell, Betty Harper. *Mabel*. Limelight Editions, 1992.

Gabler, Neal. *An Empire of Their Own*. New York: Doubleday, 1988.

Gross, Lynne S., & Larry W. Ward. *Electronic Moviemaking*. 4th ed. Belmont, CA: Wadsworth, 1999.

Goldberg, Fred. *Motion Picture Marketing and Distribution*. Boston: Focal Press, 1991.

Hindman, James, Larry Kirkman, and Elizabeth Monk. *TV Acting: A Manual for Camera Performance*. New York: Hastings House, 1979.

Jones, Peter. *The Technique of the Television Cameraman*. 3rd ed. New York: Focal Press, 1972.

Katz, Steven D. *Film Directing Shot by Shot: Visualizing from Concept to Screen*. Studio City, CA: Michael Wiese Productions, 1991.

Kindem, Gorham. *The Moving Image: Production Principles and Practices*. Scott Foresman, 1987.

Kindem, Gorham, and Robert B. Musburber. *Introduction to Media Production from Analog to Digital*. Boston: Focal Press, 2001.

Konigsberg, Ira. *Complete Film Dictionary*. 2nd rev. ed. Penguin Non-Classics, 1998.

Lewis, Colby, and Tom Greer. *The TV Director Interpreter*. Fern Park, FL: Hastings House, 1990.

Lukas, Christopher. *Directing for Film and Television*. Rev. ed. Allworth Press, 2001.

Madsen, Roy Paul. *Working Cinema: Learning from the Masters*. Belmont, CA: Wadsworth, 1990.

Nemy, Phillip. *Get a Reel Job*. Woodland Hills, CA: Angel's Touch Productions, 1999.

Proferes, Nicholas T. *Film Directing Fundamentals: From Script to Stage*. St. Louis: Focal Press, 2001.

Rosenblum, Ralph. and Karen Robert. *When the Shooting Stops*. New York: Da Capo Press, 1988.

Schatz, Thomas. *The Genius of the System*. New York: Pantheon, 1996.

Simon, John. *Ingmar Bergman Directs*. New York: Harcourt, 1974.

Squire, Jason E. *The Movie Business Book*. New York: Simon & Schuster, 2004.

Taub, Eric. *Gaffers, Grips and Best Boys*. New York: St. Martin's Press, 1994.

Tirard, Lurent. *Moviemakers' Master Class: Private Lessons from the Worlds' Foremost Directors*. New York: Faber and Faber, 2002.

Travis, Mark W. *The Director's Journey: The Creative Collaboration between Directors, Writers and Actors*. Los Angeles: Silman-James Press, 1999.

Weston, Judith. *Directing Actors: Creating Memorable Performances for Film and Television*. Studio City, CA: Michael Wiese Productions, 1999.

Wiese, Michael. *Producer to Producer*. Studio City, CA: Michael Wiese Productions, 1993.

Yule, Andrew. *Fast Fade: David Puttman, Columbia Pictures, and the Battle for Hollywood*. Delacorte Press, 1988.

Index

above the line, 220
academic theatre, 28
Academy Flat, 1, 120
actor, 1, 4, 5, 10, 14, 15, 19, 46, 47, 48,
    53, 55, 56, 57, 60, 61, 62, 65, 66,
    67, 68, 69, 80, 81, 82, 83, 84, 85,
    87, 88, 89, 90, 92, 93, 94, 95, 96,
    97, 98, 100, 101, 102, 103, 104,
    105, 106, 107, 108, 109, 110, 112,
    114, 115, 116, 122, 123, 125, 126,
    129, 131, 132, 133, 134, 135, 136,
    137, 153, 154, 155, 156, 159, 160,
    161, 163, 164, 165, 166, 167, 168,
    169, 170, 175, 176, 177, 179, 183,
    185, 189, 190, 191, 201, 204, 206,
    208, 209, 210, 211, 212, 213, 219,
    222, 223, 224, 225, 227, 232, 233,
    234, 235, 236, 237, 239, 240, 242,
    244, 247, 252, 253, 255, 257
acts, 60, 222
adjustments, 60, 201
Adobe Premiere, 186
aesthetic distance, 49
analysis, 13, 45, 47, 60, 70
anamorphic, 120
antagonist, 68
arbitrary symbol, 58
arc, 199
area, 125
arena, 2, 112, 113, 115, 116, 125, 127
art, 2, 19, 47, 48, 49, 123, 127, 155,
    157, 181, 186, 204, 211, 215, 220,
    233
artist, 15, 18, 47, 200
aspect ratio, 116, 118, 119

assistant director (AD), 194, 235, 236,
    239, 241, 242
audience, 1, 5, 17, 18, 47, 48, 49, 51,
    52, 53, 54, 55, 56, 59, 62, 63, 89,
    93, 97, 98, 107, 114, 115, 116, 118,
    120, 123, 124, 125, 129, 131, 132,
    157, 160, 163, 164, 165, 167, 175,
    177, 179, 181, 183, 185, 187, 199,
    201, 208, 209, 211, 212, 213, 231,
    232, 248, 249
audio, 103, 159, 210, 221, 232, 233
audition, 94, 95, 97, 101, 102, 103,
    104, 105, 106, 107, 109, 110, 227,
    254
AutoCad, 204
Avid, 185
axis, 131, 155, 159, 165

balance, 94, 122, 127, 161, 210, 231
Ball, William, 67, 93
beat, 60, 61, 66, 87, 172, 173, 183
below the line, 220
blocking, 5, 15, 61, 84, 95, 113, 114,
    115, 116, 123, 127, 138, 154, 160,
    166, 167, 168, 183, 189, 190, 191,
    192, 194, 197, 200, 201, 202, 204,
    206, 207, 210, 211, 212, 213, 214,
    219, 235, 236, 237, 239
body position, 125
boom, 199
breakdown, 101, 102, 220, 237
breakdown sheets, 227
Broadway, 10, 62, 85, 86, 89, 94, 107,
    114, 116, 177, 179, 250